MW01406274

YES

THE AUTHORISED BIOGRAPHY
DAN HEDGES

SIDGWICK & JACKSON
LONDON

First published in 1981 in Great Britain
by Sidgwick and Jackson Limited.

Copyright © 1981 by Dan Hedges.
The Yes logo is a registered trademark
and is used by permission of
Topographic Music Inc. and Star/Rights Co.

Picture research by Dan Hedges.

Designed by Steve Henderson

Photo Acknowledgements

The author and publishers are grateful to the following for providing and granting permission to reproduce the illustrations on the pages listed: page 6, Atlantic Records; 7, Atlantic Records; 8 (2), Yes Archives; 9, Atlantic Records; 12 top, Atlantic Records; 12 bottom, Yes Archives; 13, Connie Biegler Collection; 14, Connie Biegler Collection; 15, Mr and Mrs Squire; 16, Mr and Mrs Squire; 17, Decca Records; 18, EMI Records; 19, Bill Bruford's private collection; 20-1, EMI Records; 22, Decca Records; 24, Mrs Brockbanks; 25, Mrs Brockbanks; 26, Mrs Brockbanks; 27, Atlantic Records; 28, Atlantic Records; 29, Atlantic Records; 30, Atlantic Records; 31, Atlantic Records; 33, Atlantic Records; 34, Barrie Wentzell; 35, Barrie Wentzell; 36, Barrie Wentzell; 37, Barrie Wentzell; 38-9, Barrie Wentzell; 40, Barrie Wentzell; 41, Atlantic Records; 42, Yes Archives; 43, Steve Howe's private collection; 44-5, EMI Records; 46, Yes Archives; 48, Atlantic Records; 50 (2), Atlantic Records; 51, Atlantic Records; 52, Atlantic Records; 53, Atlantic Records; 54, Atlantic Records; 55, Barry Plummer; 56 top, A&M Records; 56 bottom, Rick Wakeman's private collection; 57, Yes Archives; 58, Atlantic Records; 59, Atlantic Records; 60, Atlantic Records; 61, Atlantic Records; 62-3, Michael Putland; 65, Atlantic Records; 66-7, Yes Archives; 68, Atlantic Records; 69, Atlantic Records; 70, Barrie Wentzell; 71, Island Records; 72, Mrs White; 73, Atlantic Records; 74, Atlantic Records; 75, Barry Plummer; 76, Robert Ellis; 77 top, Roger Dean; 77 bottom, Martyn Dean; 78 top, Roger Dean; 78 bottom, Martyn Dean; 79 (4), Martyn Dean; 80-1, Roger Dean; 82 (3), Martyn Dean; 83 top, Roger Dean; 83 bottom left, Jean Ristoni; 83 bottom right, Martyn Dean; 84 top, Roger Dean; 84 bottom left, Yes Archives; 84 centre right, Yes Archives; 84 bottom right, Lisa Tanner; 86 (2), Atlantic Records; 87, Robert Ellis; 88, Atlantic Records; 89, Atlantic Records; 90, Barry Plummer; 91, Barrie Wentzell; 92-3, Atlantic Records; 94, Yes Archives; 95, RCA Records; 96, René Moraz; 97, Atlantic Records; 98, Atlantic Records; 100, Richard E. Aaron; 101, Atlantic Records; 102, Atlantic Records; 103, Atlantic Records; 105, Robert Ellis; 106, Atlantic Records; 107, Atlantic Records; 109, Yes Archives; 110, Phila Inquirer; 111, Charisma Records; 112, Atlantic Records; 113, Yes Archives; 114, Yes Archives; 115, A&M Records; 116, Yes Archives; 117, Yes Archives; 118, Lisa Tanner; 119, Atlantic Records; 120-1, Lisa Tanner; 122, Barry Plummer; 123, Robert Ellis; 124, Lisa Tanner; 126, Lisa Tanner; 127, A&M Records; 128, Lisa Tanner; 129, Lisa Tanner; 130, Lisa Tanner; 131, Lisa Tanner; 132, Polydor Records; 133, Island Records; 134, Lisa Tanner; 135, Lisa Tanner; 136, Atlantic Records; 137, Lisa Tanner; 138, Atlantic Records; 139, Michael Putland/London Features International; 140, Atlantic Records.

ISBN 0-283-98751-0 (hardback)
ISBN 0-283-98761-8 (softcover)

Photoset by Robcroft Ltd, London WC1
printed in Great Britain
by The Garden City Press,
Letchworth, Hertfordshire
for Sidgwick and Jackson Limited
1 Tavistock Chambers, Bloomsbury Way
London WC1A 2SG

Contents

	Acknowledgements	4
	Author's Note	4
	Introduction	5
	Yes – The Cast	10
1	First Steps and Teen Dreams	11
2	Dues	32
3	'It's okay, I'm with the band'	49
4	America	64
	Colour Section	77
5	Delusions of Grandeur	85
6	Musical Chairs	108
7	Drama	125
	Discography	140
	Index	145

Author's Note

This book was conceived and written over a period of three and a half years – from early 1977 to autumn 1980. Most of it was completed long before the last Yes personnel changes. While the book does, of course, cover these changes, I decided to let the bulk of the text remain the way I originally wrote it and not alter the context or the terms in which the band members and their associates expressed themselves at the time.

D.H.

Acknowledgements

Special thanks to the following people for their time, their tea, and their sympathy while this book was being written: Lee Abrams; Jenny Anderson; Connie Biegler; Mrs Brockbanks; Sandy Campbell; Phil Carson; Roy Clair; Patti Conte; Steve Cook; Roger Dean; Tom Duke; Roy Flynn; Stu Ginsburg; Steve Goldberg; Harvey Goldsmith; Keith Goodwin; Jim Halley; Elliot Hoffman; Jan Howe; Bob Kaus; Karen and Kate at A & M (N.Y. and London); Brian Lane; Nancy Lewis; Gary Lilley (from South Shields); Nigel Luby; Karen Macrine; Colin Miles; René Moraz; Brian Munns; Eddie Offord; Phil Rauls; Sherrie Rubin; Alex Scott; Pennie Smith; Denny Somach; Mr and Mrs Squire; Cheri Squire; Nikki Squire; Michael Tait; Lisa Tanner; Russ Vas Dias; Mrs White; the chaps and chapettes at *Melody Maker, Sounds, N.M.E.* and *Record Mirror*; the Gentlemen of the Road Crew; the boys and girls at the Yes office and, needless to say, the Gentlemen of Yes – Jon Anderson, Chris Squire, Bill Bruford, Tony Kaye, Peter Banks, Steve Howe, Rick Wakeman, Alan White, Patrick Moraz, Trevor Horn, and Geoff Downes.

INTRODUCTION

'I don't think we've gone far enough,' Christopher Squire insists. Then he thinks again. 'No... I don't mean that ... I mean, it could have happened quicker, you know? To get to here. But on the other hand, we *are* still here, and we *are* still relatively sane after all these years, so I wouldn't like to say whether it should be anywhere else, other than where it is now.'

He's greased his way around that one easily enough, though maybe he has a point. To speculate is to tamper with the natural order of things that, for all nobody knows, might be the key to why an English rock band called Yes has made it into the Big Time.

The Stones, The Who, and a few others have clocked up even more mileage. But the period they helped set the pace for was basically that of the sixties, when rock was rougher and rawer, and the majority of its practitioners knew three chords and had yet to reach their twentieth birthday.

Yes were arguably the last of the major bands to emerge from the Marquee era. As such, their influence was more heavily felt during the seventies. Largely through their efforts, technology finally matched step with rock and roll's inbuilt energy – raising the quality and professionalism of recorded music and live stage presentation to a level comparable with any of the performing arts.

Yes music has always been fairly controversial – cold, postured, and mechanical to some; powerful, soaring, and profound to others. Different strokes for different folks. But then the criticism and arguing has come, not only from outside the band's circle, but from within its own ranks. The mortality rate has been high. Chris Squire was the last survivor of the original line-up that he and Jon Anderson put together back in 1968, with everyone else who has cruised through over the years having quit, been kicked out, or otherwise done away with at a rate some found so alarming that one sly rock critic suggested dragging the Thames for the bodies.

Although things look pretty ruthless at times, the primary motivation behind Yes's behaviour – and the changes they've gone through – has always been that obscure animal known as The Music.

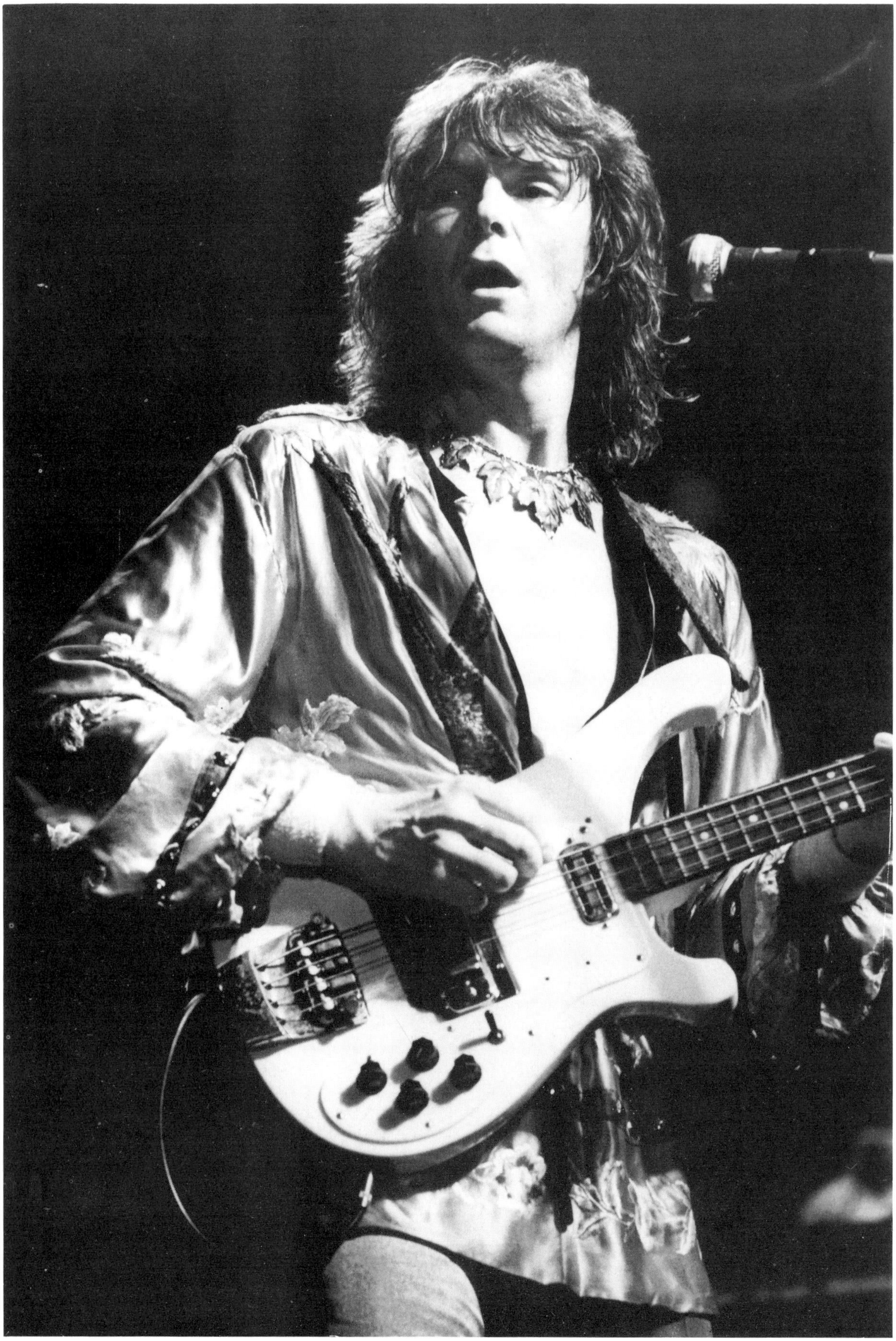

Above: Jon Anderson, 1978
Opposite: Chris Squire, 1977

Personalities, friendships, and patriotic bonds don't seem to come into it a whole lot, because the gentlemen who have played a part in Yes have very little in common *but* their music.

It's caused more than its share of problems. As Steve Howe says, 'In most groups, there are at least three or four people who are basically the same. On the same wavelength, straight across the board. This group is like a box of Licorice All-Sorts, and it gets really insane sometimes. If anything, I think it's made it harder for the band to stay around.'

To the average Fan In The Street, Yes's majestic, multi-coloured music and their often elaborate stage shows have always been the most, if not the only, visible facets of the band.

Yes have always been, if you like, fairly private people. Hollywood starlets, cocaine busts, and drunken brawls on transatlantic flights just aren't their style. They'd rather watch TV.

'Yeah,' Alan White agrees. 'But it's because we're so low-profile that we're as big as we are in an underlying sense, a low-key sense. We've never gone for the big sell out, the Big Sell. We're not known for that, therefore we maintain a steady ascension. Would you rather sell twelve million copies of your first album and not *be* there three years later? Or would you rather sell steadily – back catalogue, current albums – up through the eighties and still be enjoying yourself?'

Yes is a band that's always been off on its own tangent, fairly oblivious to any real need to flow with whatever trends happen to seem big in *Billboard* this week. Maybe that's hurt them in some ways – the fact that they haven't turned to disco riffs, eye make-up, cowboy hats, horn sections, or safety pins – but they maintain a proud sense of dignity about what they do. And they've created a sound, a style, and a school of music, call it what you like, that's stood the test of time, regardless of whatever passing silliness is going on in the rockbiz around them.

As Jon Anderson says, 'I think the band's been influenced most by the people who've come to see us. The people out *there*, in that audience, and we just wanted to please, mystify, and excite that audience. To please is to show them something visually amazing. To mystify is to let them hear something new and make them wonder what's going to happen next. To excite is to generate a high.'

For the most part, that idea has been the driving concept behind Yes from day one. Although the desire to be rich, famous, and meet lots of girls was probably in there somewhere at the outset, the music has won out in the end.

Dan Hedges
October 1980

Above left: Alan White, 1977
Above: Steve Howe, 1976
Opposite: Rick Wakeman, 1977

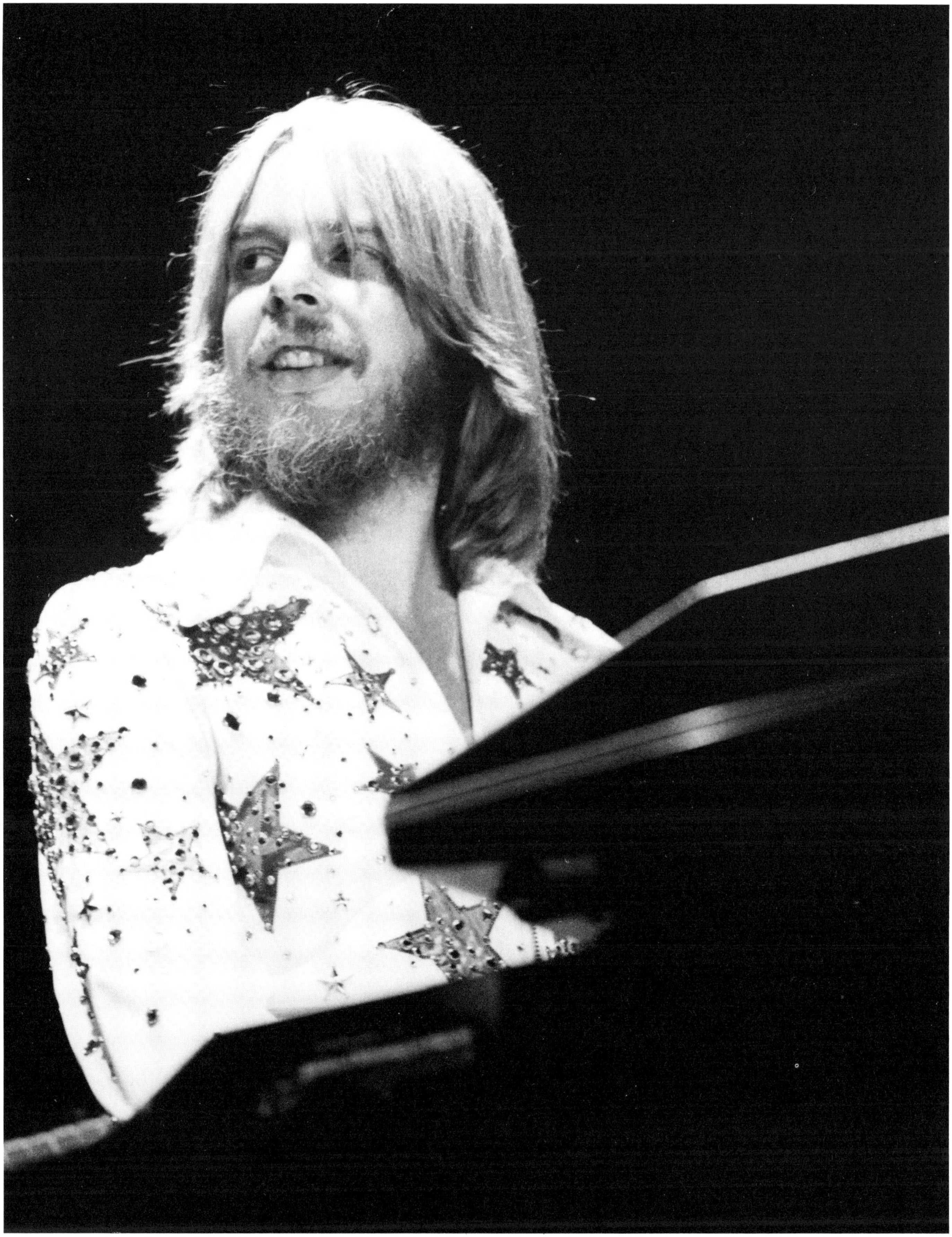

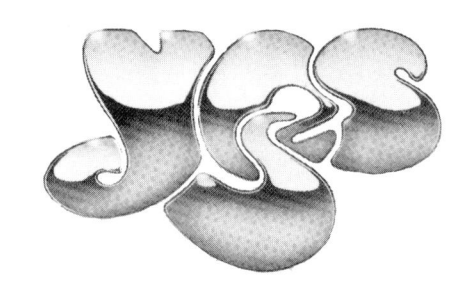

JON ANDERSON
Spring 1968 – Spring 1980

CHRIS SQUIRE
Spring 1968 –

BILL BRUFORD
Spring 1968 – Summer 1972

TONY KAYE
Summer 1968 – Autumn 1971

PETER BANKS
Summer 1968 – Spring 1970

STEVE HOWE
Spring 1970 –

RICK WAKEMAN
Autumn 1971 – Summer 1974
Autumn 1976 – Spring 1980

ALAN WHITE
Summer 1972 –

PATRICK MORAZ
Summer 1974 – Autumn 1976

TREVOR HORN
Spring 1980 –

GEOFF DOWNES
Spring 1980 –

CHAPTER ONE

FIRST STEPS AND TEEN DREAMS

My dream? To be a musician. A real musician.
JON ANDERSON

I was a failure as a Cub Scout.
CHRIS SQUIRE

It's half-time in Texas when Jon Anderson wanders from the shower, hotel towel wrapped around him, to adjust the fine tuning on the colour T.V.

The Dallas Cowboys Cheerleaders are bouncing across the screen – tits, thighs, and all-American energy – and Anderson can't help but pause for a moment of reflection. 'Eeeeeeeeeeee,' he smiles, stretching his Lancashire accent to the limit. 'They'd nowt like that in Accrington when I were a lad.'

He doesn't mention the place very often, but when he does it's usually a passing reference. He was born there on 25 October 1944, and that place and those times – 'the old days' – are the reference points that Jon uses to keep the here and now in some sort of reasonable perspective.

His high, clear voice is one of the most instantly recognizable things about Yes. He's respected for it, but throughout most of his career he's been a prime target for the less Yes-minded corners of the rock press. On the one hand, he's often depicted as the blissed-out, post-psychedelic dreamer. On the other, he's been marked as the tyrant in Yes – 'The Hippie With The Iron Hand' as the *New Musical Express* once dubbed him – a cross between Adolf Hitler, Al Capone, and Attila the Hun, running the band like a protection racket and not averse to breaking a few psychological legs along the way.

Both views are highly exaggerated, though as Keith Goodwin, former Yes publicist and an old friend of Anderson, suggests, 'Whatever Jon does, he does it primarily for Jon, though not in a selfish way. He wants to be liked. He wants his music to be liked. But he's a very stubborn man.'

After more than fifteen years in this business, Anderson's got it fairly well sussed. While he doesn't keep a set of thumbscrews in his back pocket and *isn't* the Innocent he's often said to be, he's perfectly capable of copping a quick daydream while sounding somebody out for 'not being organized'. It's just his way, and if his apparent inner serenity is tempered by a no-nonsense severity, that's where it comes from, the North – Accrington, Lancashire.

'We had coal mines and such like up there, but it was a mill town,' he remembers. 'My mother worked in a cotton mill. *Amazing* sound in there. My

11

father was a salesman, and also a comedian. He used to do the odd show when he was in the army, and he was a dancer too. Him and my mother used to dance together. They won titles and a couple of cups, you know, so there was obviously a little bit of showmanship ingrained in me.'

Mill towns in the north of England tend to be pretty grim, dead-end places, where kids leave school at fourteen to spend the rest of their lives clocking in and out at the factory gates.

The Andersons lived on the edge of town, and Jon worked at a near-by farm – first at weekends and during the summer holidays from St John's Catholic School, and later full time. 'We lived about a hundred yards from the country,' he explains. 'We were right near the hillsides which led out on to the moors. Until I was about seventeen, I was there on and off. Milking the cows, delivering the milk, collecting the eggs, looking after the chickens. Farm business.

'It was a good upbringing in terms of knowing and appreciating the values of life, in terms of what you put in you got out. Everybody's different. Some people don't want to work, and some people don't need to work on that kind of level, but I always thought that I *should* be working. You learn a lot more about life, and there was always a *group* of people working together – the farmer, his wife, my brother, and me. We used to sing a lot together. Everly Brothers while we milked the cows, while we were haymaking.'

The buzz began to fade, however, and though he was physically too small, he daydreamed of becoming a professional

Above: Jon Anderson in Munich, *circa* 1967
Opposite above: Yes, spring 1969. Left to right: Chris Squire, Tony Kaye, Peter Banks, Bill Bruford
Opposite below: Jon Anderson (lower left) with the Warriors, 1965. 'I wanted to see the world'

soccer player, 'who were the rock stars of that time, in the sense that being a footballer was the only way to get out of town. You'd be in a group, a team, and that team travelled the country. So the appeal of being in a football club was (a) because I liked football, and (b) because it was a travelling experience. It was escape. I didn't want to get tied down. A lot of my friends at school were married by the time they turned eighteen, and I said to myself that I wouldn't get married for a long time. I'd try to find out a little more about life first. See what's going on.'

Anderson found work as a lorry driver, delivering bricks to exotic ports of call like Manchester and Liverpool, forty miles away. 'Up to that time, to travel ten miles to Bolton or Blackburn was an event,' he says. 'You talked about it for two days before you went and a couple of days after.'

It was during a trip through Liverpool that a passing street scene later proved to be something of a vision of the future. 'I saw all these people coming out of this club called the Cavern,' he remembers. 'I wondered what was going on, because it excited me – the fact that *they* were excited. I didn't know what they'd been hearing down there, though, as it turned out, the Beatles and the Merseybeat thing was just starting out at that time. That's what all those people were excited about, and I suppose that made a pretty strong impression on me.'

Back home, Jon's brother Tony had already taken the plunge by forming a group called the Warriors. Their forte was mainly Top Forty – Everly Brothers' tunes, with things like 'Twist And Shout' thrown in for a touch of raunch. When their singer left, Jon stepped up to share the vocal chores with Tony. When his brother later quit to get married, Anderson stayed on as the Warriors (David Foster, Brian Chapman, and Ian Wallace) took to the German club circuit, where they stayed for a solid year and a half.

'I used to copy other people's voices,' Jon says. 'I did a great Paul McCartney on "I'm Down", though somebody said I sounded more like Cilla Black. I did everything, though. I'd go pick everybody up. I'd drive the van. I'd help load the gear. I was the odd-jobman, because in those days the singer wasn't regarded as a musician. I helped organize songs, but I generally did a lot of the extra work nobody else wanted to do.'

The U.S. Army is everywhere in West Germany. Since jukeboxes and bands catered to the tastes of the G.I.s who drank in the clubs and strip joints the Warriors played in, Jon picked up on the music of Joe Tex, Sam and Dave, Otis Redding, and Wilson Pickett, and began writing songs himself. Decca had released a solitary Warriors single in 1965 ('Don't Make Me Blue'/'You Came Along'), but 'like all bands back then, you either made it on your first single, or forget it. But I wanted to be a success at what I was doing, and I was always happy when old friends told me what a good group it was, even though we weren't making any money. It was nice to be able to turn around and say, "I said I'd do it, and I'm going to damn well keep on trying my best until I *really* make it."'

By 1967, laziness was creeping in.

Anderson quit in disgust, realizing that five years of hard slogging had amounted to nothing. 'I went through my changes for about a month,' he says, 'until I finally woke up one day in the English Gardens in Munich. I was sitting there on the grass, contemplating why I was so upset, when it suddenly came to me that *nothing mattered*. Everything will take care of itself. Look after yourself, and things will be all right.'

Jon returned to the apartment he was crashing in to find that his mother had forwarded a telegram from a Bolton band called the Party, who were also in Germany and looking for a singer. Jon joined. 'They thought I was a great singer, and I'd never been treated like that before,' he says. 'I felt I had a lot to say, and they listened and followed instructions. That's when I realized I had a talent for getting people together and formulating a direction. We were playing the worst clubs in Germany, but were getting a great reaction just re-arranging the hits. Doing our own soul versions.'

It didn't last. Ripped off once too many by shady promoters, the group fell to pieces. Left out in the cold again, Anderson decided that he'd finally had enough, and packed his suitcase.

'I remember I was standing on the platform at Waterloo Station,' he says. 'I'd just arrived back in London after all that time, and in those days I had a tenor saxophone. I couldn't play it, but it made me feel a little closer to being a musician.

'I was just a singer in a band, and now I didn't even have a band. When I had my saxophone with me, even though I only blew three notes a night, I felt a little more like a musician. Only a non-musician could appreciate that.

'But I felt so happy when I got to Waterloo Station. I was so glad to be back in England, back on the old turf, that I just stood there on the platform with all these people rushing by, and played "God Save The Queen".'

It's the middle of the night and this hotel is shut down tight – cold and empty like the city morgue. That surreal, four a.m. nothingness hangs over the silent corridors like a mist, and it's so dead you can hear the guy in the next room dreaming.

Chris Squire appears on the far side of the deserted lobby, night-wandering again and looking vaguely lost, with a fizzy glass of Perrier for company.

'Oh . . . hello . . . ,' he says, scanning the joint. 'Where *is* everybody?'

The fact that everyone else crashes out before sunrise always seems to amaze him. Chris operates on Squire Time and these unhurried, solitary strolls through sleeping hotels are a tradition – though he never really seems to be on his way to or from anywhere.

'Aloof?' Chris says over breakfast at one in the afternoon, wondering whether the word is an accurate way to sum up the Squire Persona. He shakes his head. He's wearing shades. 'Well . . . I'd like to think that I'm a member of the most aloof *band* in the world.'

Maybe so, though if Yes are the world's

Above: On the German club circuit the Warriors' audiences were largely made up of American soldiers
Opposite: Chris Squire, aged 6, on the beach at Clacton-on-Sea

most remote band, then Squire (or at least the Public Squire) is their most eminently distant member. Although his bass playing can swoop, dive, rumble, roar, break windows, drive the neighbours crazy, give Ben Hur a run for his money, and cop a few speeding tickets along the way, Chris himself calmly saunters through life at a less intense pace than most.

Whereas Anderson can be a bit trigger-happy without worrying about the consequences, Squire is more cautious and analytical. He thinks carefully before he answers, rarely uses twenty words where three will do, can keep a straight face while passing himself off as Jon Anderson to a stoned-out fan, and has an extraordinary talent for switching off the circus around him and drifting off to who-knows-where.

The rolling lawns and woodland surrounding the big house in Surrey where he lives with his wife Nikki and daughters Carmen, Chandrika, and Camille suit him down to the ground – though once a year, when someone pushes him a little too far and he blows a fuse, the entire room will step back ten paces. Most of the time, though, the whole building could collapse and he wouldn't even twitch.

Squire was born on 4 March 1948, and was destined to spend his first sixteen years or so in the Wembley/Kingsbury area of North London, where his father drives a cab, 'and my mother is a professional housewife-cum-mother'.

Music came into the picture fairly early. Through a schoolfriend, Andrew Jackman, who lived round the corner, Chris hooked up with the choir at nearby St Andrew's Church. 'My father had a few records by Lena Horne and Ella Fitzgerald,' he remembers, 'and I used to really like those, funnily enough. But my main interest was church music, and the choir was fortunate to have Barry Rose as its choirmaster, who's probably the best in England.'

Squire was a failure as a Cub Scout, but singing was one area where he felt in control. Under Barry Rose's guidance, the choir supposedly became the finest in Britain. 'It was considered better than St Paul's Cathedral Choir while I was in it and while Barry was choirmaster,' he says. 'Barry actually had a large influence on me in terms of the skill and the amount of effort he used to put into that choir. He made me realize that working at it was *the* way to become best at something. The whole standard of it was so high. I suppose the actual understanding of, and spiritual feeling towards, music that I got from that is something that's stayed with me, although it was church music we were dealing with.'

Chris shelved the singing after entering public school (Haberdashers' Aske's) at fourteen, but likes to think that he was 'a little bit influential in what happened at school, music-wise. Barry Rose was held very much in awe among people in music circles, and the teachers were always asking me, having been one of his pupils, about the best way to do this Christmas carol or that song.'

The sixties were well under way, and though rock and roll had been around for a few years, most of it left him cold. 'I had no ambition about what I wanted to do,' he explains. 'I had no thoughts of being a dentist, a lawyer, or even a singer once I left school. In fact, I was quite an anti-system sort of person. Therefore, music was something personal to me that I didn't even consider as an occupation until the emergence of the Beatles – the whole Northern Beat Boom that happened when I was about sixteen. That was the catalyst, which I suppose interested me as a developing teenager, and also because it was something I could apply my love of music to.'

15

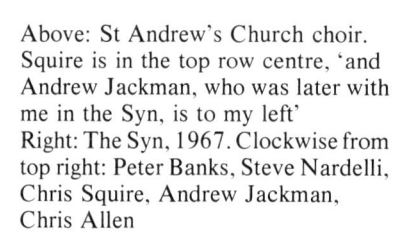

Above: St Andrew's Church choir. Squire is in the top row centre, 'and Andrew Jackman, who was later with me in the Syn, is to my left'
Right: The Syn, 1967. Clockwise from top right: Peter Banks, Steve Nardelli, Chris Squire, Andrew Jackman, Chris Allen

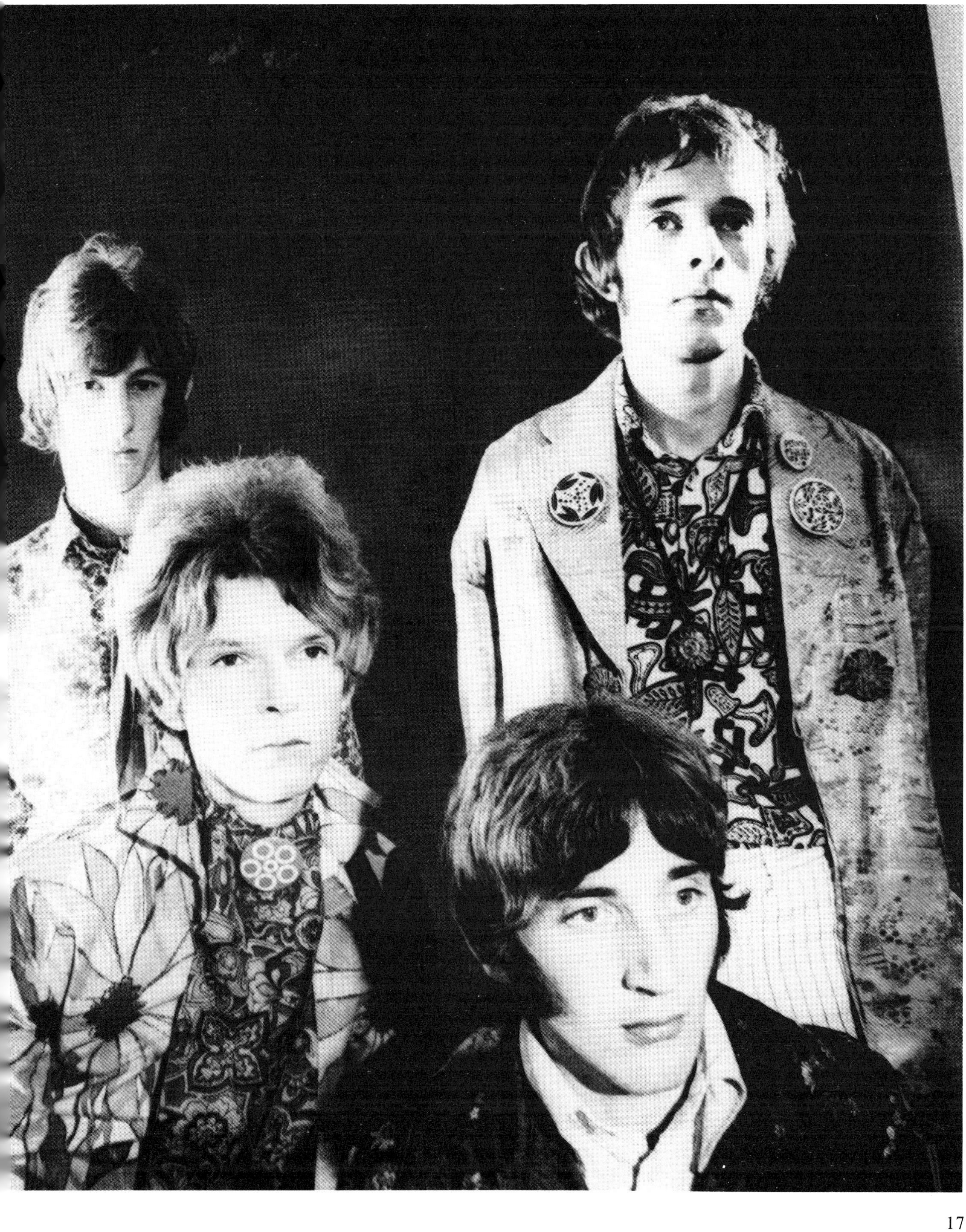

Inspired by Paul McCartney, his associates, and a guitar-playing schoolmate, Squire took up the bass, 'basically because I was tall and had big hands. I really did put some effort into learning how to play it right from the beginning – the whole art of what it was all about – even though I really knew nothing about guitars before that.'

With the sudden rock explosion, the outlying residential areas of London rapidly developed their own individual scenes. Tiny, makeshift clubs sprouted up overnight in church halls, school basements, and any other place big enough to accommodate a handful of neighbourhood groups and a few dozen spotty kids, half out of their heads on purple hearts.

While the Harrow/Wembley/Kingsbury area was something of a mod stronghold, its streets weren't necessarily the safest place to be. 'Yeah, Wembley was a bit of a rough place, especially if you were a bit more mod inclined, which I was. You had to be pretty careful around there, though I was influenced a lot by friends at school who lived in the Hampstead/Finchley Road area. There were a lot more beatniks and pre-hippie hippies up there.'

Most of the local groups modelled themselves on the Yardbirds or the Stones, and Squire's earliest forays into show business predictably ran along those lines. In 1965, playing his new Futurama bass, he made his first public appearance at a youth club called the Graveyard (in St Andrew's Church Hall) with a ragged, Friday night group called The Selfs.

Chris's old schoolmate and fellow choir member Andrew Jackman was in the group, though after a few nebulous changes the Selfs evolved into the Syn: Squire, Jackman, vocalist Steve Nardelli, guitarist John Painter, and an Icelandic drummer named Gunnar Hakanarssen. Their style was an English garage version of Tamla Motown, featuring tunes like Martha and the Vandellas' 'Dancing In The Street' and the Four Tops' 'I'll Be There'.

With his school years behind him, Squire sold guitars at Boosey and Hawkes' music shop by day, where he took advantage of the employee discount and bought the Rickenbacker bass that would later become his trademark. Within a few months, John Painter took a walk, a new guy by the name of Peter Banks stepped in to replace him, the group became something of a hot item around North London, got themselves an agent, and slowly gathered the momentum that everyone involved was convinced would take the country by storm.

The Syn soon dumped the Tamla Motown bit, however, and jumped on the psychedelic bandwagon – not the most inspired move, Chris admits, 'but that's what was happening. Our singer had quite a knack for coming up with a song and adapting the times to his lyrics ... or was it his lyrics to the times? Anyway, he was quite flexible.'

With a stage act that dived head-first into mock-destructo theatrics à la Move, the Syn became moderately popular around London and in several far-flung corners of the country. They landed a regular weekly spot at London's Marquee (then *the* most important showcase for up and coming groups in Britain), signed with Deram and cut two singles ('Grounded'/'Created by Clive' and 'Flowerman'/ '24 Hour Technicolour Dream'). Neither sold more than a handful of copies outside the group's immediate families.

'But I'm not sure that we weren't destined for some kind of success in France,' Squire remembers. 'We were always going over to Paris to do stupid TV shows. We could have made it, there was no doubt about that, though we lost our drummer and the guy we replaced him with [Chris Allen] wasn't as good.'

After two years of trying, the Syn fell apart. Chris spent a fairly large slice of the next twelve months drawing inspiration from the work of the Who's John Entwistle and the Byrds' Chris Hillman, practising his bass, and staring at walls. 'It wasn't the high point of my life, really,' he says. 'I was quite despondent. I'd been through quite a bit by then – "tasted the success of it" – and I tasted quite a bit of failure too. But I was determined to keep at it, if only from the point of view that I still couldn't find anything else that I particularly wanted to do.

Above: Bill Bruford, aged 8
Opposite: Jon Anderson, alias Hans Christian, late 1967

'I did have a Final LSD Experience around that time. I mean, it was the last time I ever took it, having ended up in St Stephen's Hospital in Fulham for a couple of days not knowing who I was, or what I was, or who anybody else was. I still did some sitting about after that, but I was . . . straighter! Obviously, I had a certain amount of reassembling to do, though I didn't do too much hanging out during that period. I didn't have a lot of friends.'

A loner?

'To a certain degree, yeah.'

The first 'constructive' thing Squire got into after his acid incident was Mabel Greer's Toyshop – another psychedelic group run by the Syn's Peter Banks and a second guitarist named Clive Bailey – though the group were barely managing to hold together.

'Mabel Greer's Toyshop did some pretty avant-garde stuff,' he remembers. 'But we also did some Doors and Moby Grape and Byrds material. I can remember doing "So You Want To Be A Rock 'n' Roll Star", and we probably did "Eight Miles High" at some point. I know we did "Light My Fire", but then who didn't? With interminably long guitar solos.'

For Squire, it was a vague period. His playing was rapidly improving, but little else was happening on the surface. The Toyshop, as it stood, wasn't going to make him a legend in his own time – though he admits that in the end he didn't really care one way or the other.

'It was better than doing nothing,' he shrugs.

Ask anybody. There's no good reason in the world why a place like La Chasse should even exist. Make a sharp right as you're kicked out of the Marquee at closing time, wobble up Wardour Street, keep an eye peeled to the right, and you've found it – provided you haven't missed the drab doorway completely, or been stopped by the cops on the way.

It's up the creaky stairs, a hard knock at the door, and if you've got some reason for being there (it's Members Only), you're in. Inside, it's like a shoe box, or the dumpy living room of a particularly uninspiring London flat. After the first ten people, it's standing room only. Dark. Cramped. Thick with cigarette smoke and the low rumble of the clientele over the crappy stereo. It's people making promises, people making deals, people bullshitting each other stiff about albums that never quite seem to get recorded, and coast-to-coast American tours that never quite seem to get off the ground. There's a couch or two if you're early enough, and a drink at the tiny bar will set you back the equivalent of a small bank loan.

For whatever mysterious reason, La Chasse attracts people like flies. La Chasse itself is a legend, and as legend has it, La Chasse is where Yes were born.

In May 1968, Chris Squire was a semi-regular customer at the club, while Jon Anderson (back from Germany only a few short months) was working there and at the Marquee, collecting empty glasses and dragging crates of Heineken up from the basement.

In the months since his return to England, Jon had got involved in one or two dead-end capers in an effort to establish connections on the London scene. He'd been living in a basement flat where an upstairs neighbour (who happened to be a record producer) needed someone to sing on a couple of demos for E.M.I. Anderson had agreed, done his bit, then promptly split for Holland to join a band he'd met in London called Les Cruches, 'but then I got a phone call from England,' he says. 'They told me they were going to release two of those tracks as a single. Come back.'

He did, and the single – a heavily orchestrated cover version of the Association's 'Never My Love' – came out under the pseudonym of Hans Christian. The *New Musical Express* liked it, impressed by its 'explosive crescendo with fanfare trumpets, cascading strings, spirited chanting, and rattling tambourine', summing it up as 'an authoritative performance by Hans'. Unfortunately, that single and a follow-up vanished without a whimper. Drifting into another late psychedelic group called the Gun (led by Paul and Adrian Gurvitz), Jon rehearsed 'for about six weeks and did two gigs. One was at the U.F.O. in Covent Garden; the other was with the Who at the Marquee, and we went down very well.'

Anderson and the two brothers didn't hit it off personality-wise, however. He was a free agent again within two months, killing time, making barely enough to live on, and occasionally sleeping on the couches up at La Chasse.

As Chris Squire remembers it, Jack Barrie (who ran both La Chasse and the Marquee) made the formal introductions. 'Jack was always very ... *forward* towards me, and I think he said, "Oh yeah, Jon here is a singer, he's just made a single, and if you're thinking of getting a group together you should talk to ... 'ere, come over 'ere. 'Ere Jon, this is Chris, and he plays ...". I think it was a bit like that, because he was *very* friendly. Old Jack! It's difficult though. I remember sitting there, and I probably wouldn't even remember doing that if people hadn't reminded me about it so many times.'

Although they came from radically

different backgrounds, Chris and Jon found that, musically at least, they shared some of the same interests – Simon and Garfunkel and the Fifth Dimension for a start. Mabel Greer's Toyshop was, as Squire puts it, 'very flakey, but still a going concern'. Anderson, with no fixed plans, not surprisingly got in on the act.

'Mabel Greer's Toyshop were playing at Highgate in North London, supporting the group which had been called the Action, but were then called . . . something else,' Chris recalls. 'I remember Jon turning up there when we were setting up. At the time it was me, Peter, Clive, and this drummer, and Jon actually got up that night and sang a couple of songs in the set. One of them might have been "I See You".'

(Peter Banks says that he didn't have the faintest idea who 'this little guy' was. 'He used to sit in after that, but I never really got to know him. No one introduced him. He just came along.')

As Anderson says, 'I was willing to go into a big band . . . anything. I just wanted regular work, but as it happened, nothing had come up for a few months, so I just carried on helping out at the clubs and hanging out at the Speakeasy. I met nearly everybody in the business in the process, though nobody knew what I was up to, or that I could even sing.'

Within a few weeks, Peter Banks bailed out from boredom, leaving Chris, Clive Bailey, and 'the drummer' to carry on with a handful of widely scattered gigs. Jon Anderson unofficially climbed up to sing when the mood struck him, though, as Squire says, 'It wasn't a very long period of time we're talking about. Maybe a month.'

That drummer was becoming a problem, with a flair for rocketing through the first number at full throttle, only to collapse from exhaustion by the end of the second. Deciding it was time for a change, Chris and Jon checked out the musicians' classified of *Melody Maker* where, among a couple of dozen others, a nineteen-year-old drummer named Bill had placed an ad.

Deep down inside, Bill Bruford's a jazzer. In his Joe College sweatshirts and dirty tennis shoes, he might look like he's en route to Advanced Economics II. But the spectral beret is there if you look hard enough, along with the shades, the sandals, and the paperback copy of Kerouac's *On The Road*. Be Bop for breakfast. Blue notes for lunch. If Bill had been around ten years earlier, it would have been blue lightbulbs, espresso machines, and pony-tailed/poetry-spouting girlfriends for sure, but he was born too late (17 May 1950), in the wrong place, and missed the call.

He's the vet's son from Sevenoaks, Kent, and lived life in reasonable comfort during the early years. Nice home, good schools, the whole bit – with the automatic pilot set for university and the highway to success beyond.

That was the family's view anyway, though Bill had doubts. He applied to several universities in late 1967 without really thinking he'd got into any of them, or particularly caring whether he did or not. In the interim period he had the better part of a year to kill. Faced with a similar situation, most of his ex-classmates either slept the time away or bombed across Europe in clapped-out Volkswagens, getting thrown into Dutch canals and bailed out of Spanish jails. Bill, however, played the drums.

'I didn't think the university thing would work out,' Bill says. 'On the assumption that it wouldn't, I thought, "I know what I'll do. I'll be a musician" – or at least for the nine months until September, which was when I'd actually start at university.'

The family weren't thrilled. 'Well, I was the regular middle-class lad, and being a musician was next to heresy,' he says. 'I'd be throwing a big expensive education away. I'd been to a public school, so my father was beginning to twitch, thinking that his son might turn into a musician. And we *all* know what happens to musicians after two or three years . . . .'

Slumped inside a public toilet with a needle in the arm.

'*Exactly*. Dear oh dear!'

Bruford went ahead and became a musician on 1 January 1968. 'I always do everything on 1 January,' he explains. 'I started ringing up advertisements, and on 16 January I auditioned for Savoy Brown at some pub in Battersea. It was one of those terrible things with thirty drummers and thirty drum kits.'

He says that they settled for another man, 'but in my own inimitable style, I hung around until the end and told them they had the wrong guy. They'd be much better off if they had me. So I talked my way into it, and off we went in a blue Transit, which was *bliss*! I'd never been

The Federals in early 1965. Tony Kaye is second on the left. 'I was a very restless person. Always wanted to explore. New countries. New experiences. I was on the road for a long time'

north of London, and to go to *Leicester* on my first gig . . . I was on the road! I couldn't wait to grovel on the floor of a Transit van. It was everything I'd fantasized about in my room at Tunbridge School.'

That was where Bruford had learned to play drums, while under the influence of older kids who listened to Art Blakey and the Jazz Messengers and formed jazz quartets while the Beatles passed them by. As far as Bill as concerned, jazz was precisely where it was at, though he was open to suggestions.

'When I was fifteen, I'd seen Ginger Baker, Graham Bond, and Jack Bruce wasted on heroin and all that stuff,' he recalls. 'I thought, "Ah! Well this is also jazz." It had that jazz spirit, but it was also very hard rock. They were exciting. I'd never seen such a bunch of animals in my life.

'So it didn't strike me at all odd that I'd joined a rock band. There was a crossover happening. But jazz always struck me as very high standard, very difficult, so I didn't think I'd be able to get a job as a jazzer for awhile. I figured I'd just sling it around with an R&B band for a spell, which was dead simple.'

It was so simple that after three local gigs, Bruford was asked to leave. Far from considering himself a failure, 'I had a notch on my gun now. Credentials. I was "ex-Savoy Brown".'

He joined a full-blown psychedelic band, Paper Blitz, just as the Acid Era was beginning to fizzle out – another blue Transit van job, with two gigs a week if they were lucky. Most of the time they weren't.

Four months later, Bill spotted an ad in a record store. Somebody needed a drummer for a club residency in Rome. 'Ah! the Big Time,' Bill laughs. 'It was a complete washout, with a one-way air ticket. Ended up at the Piper Club, which is a grotty dance place, for five or

22

six weeks. It was dismal, we were grim, and I finally decided that I'd had enough of it. I had to hitch back from Rome with my drum kit.'

Back in England, he placed the ad in *Melody Maker*: 'Name Drummer Seeks Work, etc., etc.' 'I was up in my North London flat, busy taking messages from the Pakistanis on the next floor who'd never answer the poxy phone correctly and always forgot who called.'

Somehow or other, Jon Anderson got through.

At their first meeting, virtually the only thing that impressed Bill Bruford about Anderson, Squire, and Clive Bailey was their car. 'They had an orange Mini with black-out windows which was *very* impressive,' Bruford says. 'I thought maybe I'd struck some pop stars or something.'

Bill had cunningly thrown a few coats of black paint over his bargain-basement Olympic drum kit to make it look like a Premier. The Toyshop were probably more impressed with the drums than with Bruford, but the four played a lightning gig that same June evening, at Rachel McMillan College in Deptford, South-East London. As Squire recalls, 'We were still calling ourselves Mabel Greer's Toyshop, and we played "Midnight Hour" twice.'

'Probably three times,' Bill adds. 'They threw in a bit of harmony, and I was most impressed.' Bruford mentions that Anderson struck him as something of a hustler, eager to get something going fast but anxious to do it properly and well, having decided to throw his lot in with the Toyshop full time. 'He didn't even give me an evening to think about it,' Bill says. 'It was "Do you want to join or don't you want to join? Don't waste my time. Yes or no. In or out."'

Jon doesn't deny that he was pushy. 'The main thing I didn't want to happen again was for anybody who came along to be anything less than serious about it,' he explains. 'If you want to come, you've got to work, and if you work, you just might get somewhere. I had contacts, I knew people, so the rest was up to us and whether we could entertain an audience.'

At the time, Bruford had a couple of soul bands up his sleeve who were offering hard cash – £30 a week, which wasn't to be sneezed at. At first glance, however, Mabel Greer's Toyshop obviously had an extra point or two in their favour.

'They looked as though they knew a few people,' Bill says. 'They knew the guy who *owned* the Marquee, John Gee. I wasn't quite sure what I'd hit, and I'm sure they didn't know what they'd hit with me, but I said yeah.'

In terms of manpower, the Toyshop were still understaffed. The line-up of one guitar, bass, drums, and vocals was weedy at best, and it was down to getting a second guitarist or, preferably, an organ player. As it happened, Squire knew of one named Tony Kaye, who was mouldering away in a Chelsea basement, a stone's throw away from World's End.

Evening is slowly settling over L.A. In Tony Kaye's apartment just off the Sunset Strip, you can't see the sunset because the terrace faces the wrong way. Although it's early October, there's a warm breeze blowing, the sangria is flowing, and the Dodgers are getting the crap knocked out of them on Kaye's ancient black and white TV.

'I played baseball for the first time about three weeks ago,' he's saying. 'It's so s-l-o-w! It's so boring! Nobody hits anything. Nobody does anything. You just stand around in the hot sun getting baked to a crisp. Crazy Americans.'

It's another home run for the Phillies, and Tony moans sympathetically and refills his glass. It's been over three years since he moved over here and eight years since he and Yes parted company, though the passage of time hasn't dented the image one iota. He still carries that classic aura of The English Rock Musician – impeccably dressed in casual black, with streaked hair and that unmistakably grey London pallor that seeps through even the deepest California suntan.

Born Anthony John Selridge in Leicester on 11 January 1946, the kid had his course steered towards Great Things right from the start. There'd been a grandfather who'd played jazz sax and emigrated to America, and a grandmother who dabbled as a classical pianist, which led to piano lessons for young Tony from the age of three.

His tastes were inclined towards classical music, though an elder brother who was into Elvis later pointed him in the direction of rock and roll, talking Tony into playing tea-chest bass in a teenaged skiffle group.

By the age of fifteen, Kaye was already

Jimmy Winston and his Reflections, later known as Winston's Fumbs

playing four nights a week with the fifteen-piece Danny Rogers Orchestra around his home town, and though his interests veered towards more 'contemporary' music, his path was leading to the Royal College of Music. He passed the entrance exam, turned up for lectures, then took a good look around him.

'When I was seventeen or eighteen, I discovered that I wasn't quite the calibre to make it as a classical pianist,' he explains. 'There's only a handful who do. The only course open to the rest is either playing their second instrument in an orchestra – which was clarinet for me – or teaching. So I backed out and went to art school – Leicester Art College – which was the sixties thing to do if you weren't good at anything else and didn't want to work.'

By this time, he'd ditched respectable music completely in favour of rock and roll, joining Johnny Taylor's Star Combo (a group that would later evolve into Family). It led to the late nights and skipped classes that got him kicked out of art school in record time.

Kaye worked with a string of fly-by-night groups after that, cruising around France and Sweden for a year or so, until his reappearance in London and an ad in *Melody Maker* dropped him into a show-band called the Federals, who promptly set off on a European tour backing Roy Orbison.

'That was my first really professional gig,' Tony remembers. 'We backed Roy for three months, and the band was a lot older than I was. It was showband – kind of that Freddie and the Dreamers-type slapstick thing. We had a little trumpet player, and a tall bass player who slapped him around . . . .'

Tony stayed with the Federals for over two years, touring England and Europe, putting out the occasional single for E.M.I., and appearing on TV programmes like *Ready, Steady, Go!*

As legend has it, Kaye himself became something of a Teen Idol in the Iron Curtain countries. Big In Bulgaria, as they say.

He'd been listening to other keyboard players like jazzer Jimmy Smith, though the first person to make him sit up and take notice was undoubtedly Graham Bond. '*This* is what I wanted to sound like,' Tony explains. 'He had that enormous Hammond sound. Up until then, I'd been playing piano and a Vox Continental à la Dave Clark Five.'

Psychedelia was at its peak when Kaye split for Scotland to rehearse with a group called the Yellow Passion Loaf, 'a Floyd-type thing,' he says. 'I passed through that stage very quickly, though we played the Speakeasy, Blaise's, and all the other clubs. The Covent Garden underground thing was happening at the time, but I never got into it – the kaftans, beads, and bells. I couldn't make that somehow. In fact, I used to steal kaftans from a store in Kings Road and sell them to tourists in Hyde Park.'

When the Small Faces' original keyboard man, Jimmy Winston, formed his own outfit, Tony joined him. For the next two years, Jimmy Winston and his Reflections (soon rechristened Winston's Fumbs) recorded forgettable singles like 'Sorry She's Mine', drank up a storm, and generally lived the so-called Swinging Sixties to the hilt. 'The bucks were flying,' Kaye recalls. 'London was fan-

Above: Peter Banks (né Brockbanks)
Opposite: Peter Banks (centre) aged 10 with his father on washboard and the proverbial kid from down the road on bass

tastic in those days. Everyone was going down the Scotch of St James. Everyone was hanging out together.'

After a short stint with Bittersweet, he joined an unnamed blues band, which lasted all of two weeks. 'I guess I didn't have the blues,' he says sadly. 'I always reconciled it with the fact that I'd had all this classical training. I was trying to think music instead of seeing it.'

Unfortunately, Kaye was also flat broke – 'an extremely poor person' – living in a sparsely furnished hole in a row of spectacularly crumbling dumps in Chelsea's Lot's Road. For lack of anything else to do, he'd been hanging out at the Marquee and La Chasse, where he'd met Chris Squire during the closing hours of the Syn.

One night, very late, Squire came down and pounded on Tony's front door. 'He came into my little dungeon with Jon,' Kaye says. 'It was a room about *this* big, I was asleep in bed, and there was my Vox Continental in the corner. They said, "You wanna join our group?" and I said, "Yeah. Sure."'

'Then I went back to sleep.'

'Clive Bailey?' says Chris Squire, puffing calmly on a Dunhill. 'He was around for a while. A couple of days at least.'

As the original guitarist in Mabel Greer's Toyshop, Bailey had co-authored 'Beyond and Before' with Squire. As part of the Toyshop's repertoire, it was recorded, though never released, under the aegis of producer/'talent scout' Mike Leander, and the song would later resurface on the début Yes album.

'Clive was around when Jon and I wrote "Sweetness" too,' Chris remembers. 'He had ideas of being a concert promoter. Perhaps he thought that's where the money was, so he left and started promoting gigs in Kingston, where he lived.'

Meanwhile, Peter Banks had been biding his time since leaving the Toyshop with yet another Marquee group called Neat Change – one of the first skinhead conglomerates, and a bunch of tough customers to boot. As Peter remembers it, he didn't stay very long, simply because he refused to cut his hair.

Chris Squire invited Peter down to hear his new band. 'I asked him what it was called, and Chris said, "Well . . . we're going to call ourselves Yes,"' Banks says. 'I said, "That's *nice*" because I'd had this idea of calling the Syn Yes years before. That was my idea.'

They were rehearsing in a basement beneath the Lucky Horseshoe Café in Shaftesbury Avenue, Banks innocently turned up according to plan, and by the next day the new Yes were finally complete: Anderson, Squire, Bruford, Kaye, and Banks.

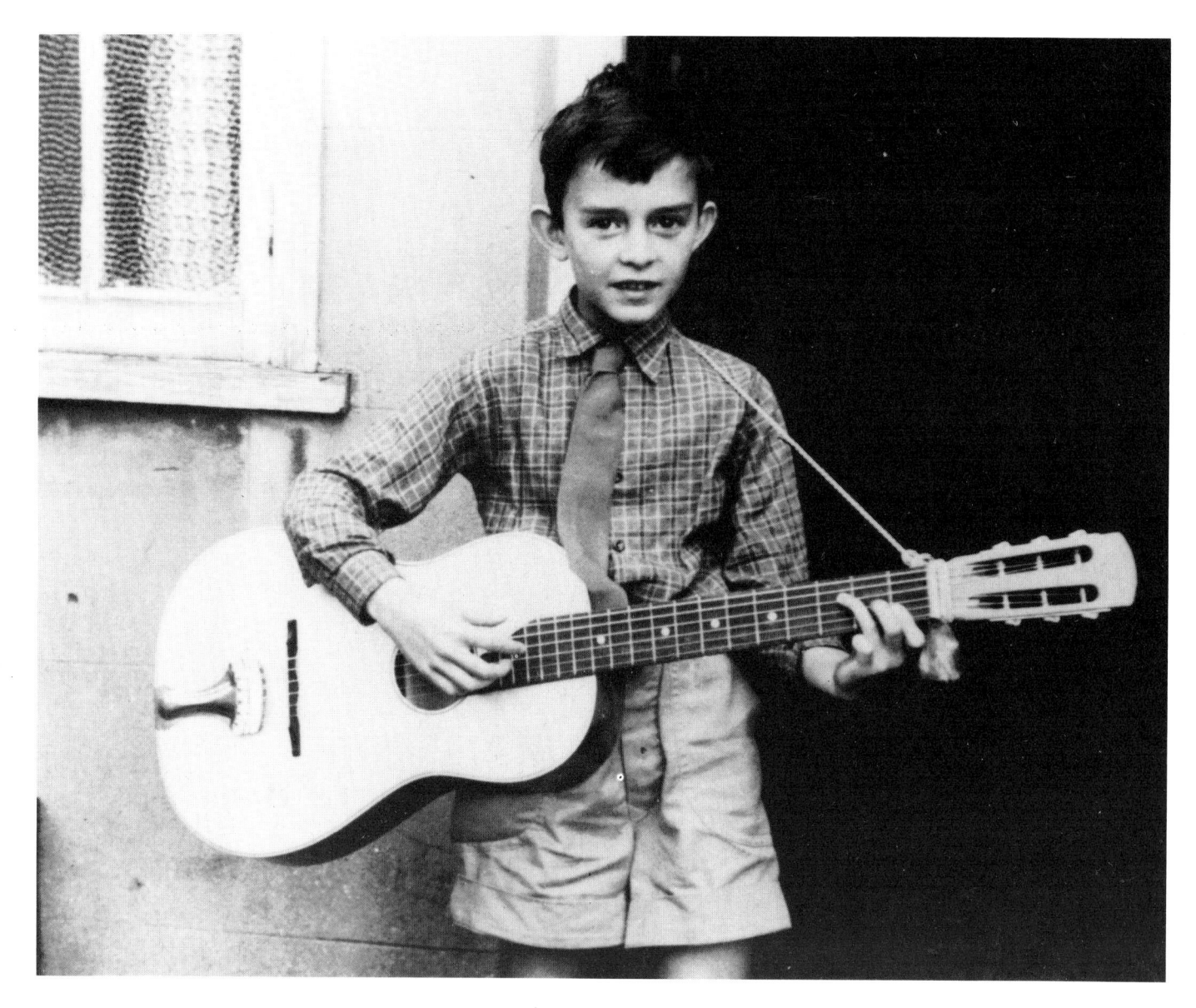

Jon borrowed £300 from a Northern mill-owner named John Roberts, and began doling it out to the group at £5 a week per man, just to keep things going. He was out hustling for gigs as well, though with no live reputation they took work when and where they could get it.

So on 4 August 1968, three days after Banks joined, the group made their début as Yes at the East Mersey Youth Camp, out in the wilds of Essex. The following night, Yes dragged their gear through the door of the Marquee club for the first of many times.

A very serious Peter Banks is leaning out the front door of his West Hollywood apartment, having a civilized confrontation with his landlord in the hallway. The landlord's accusing him of keeping a dog, which 'ain't allowed in the terms of the lease', and since it 'ain't allowed', that'll be another twenty-five bucks on this month's rent. Or else.

Peter politely assures him that the dog isn't here anymore, it was only visiting, it left three days ago, and won't be coming back. The landlord grunts suspiciously. Poodles in the piano? A saluki in the shower? A borzoi or two under the bed? He grumbles something that could only be a threat and goes away. Peter shuts the door and locks it more than once. 'If he's going to go through all that trouble of coming up here to bother me, maybe I ought to get a dog,' he says philosophically.

Yes are over nine years in Peter Banks' past, and while he claims that the past doesn't particularly interest him any more, reminders are all around. The framed sleeves of *Yes*, *Time And A*

Above: The first guitar
Opposite: 18 May 1969. Chris Squire on stage at the Camden Festival, Parliament Hill, London

Syn were playing all this Tamla Motown material.

'I thought, "Hey, great," because nobody else was doing that stuff at the time apart from the Action, who were famous and played the Marquee. So it was as easy as that. It was very simple. "You wanna join?" "Yeah." "Okay, you're in."'

As Squire's already mentioned, the Syn phased out the Tamla Motown angle and plugged into psychedelia. 'Lo and behold, everybody's taking acid,' Peter says. 'I think Chris was probably the first guy who turned me on to that. There's me with my rum and cokes, then all of a sudden the next week everybody's taking drugs. I went head-first into all of that – wearing bells, going to the U.F.O. and the Round House. It was lots of fun.

At the Marquee the Syn began staging strobe-lit, flower-power rock operas 'which were probably diabolical', wearing different-coloured gangster suits while acting out the role of the hoodlum of their choice. 'Chris was Legs Diamond, actually,' Banks recalls. 'It was all very silly, though that band was going for about two years, which was a long time in those days – considering we probably spent half of it waiting around for Chris.'

By late 1967, the Syn were a memory, the Toyshop were born, and Anderson started turning up – the wheels beginning to turn in his head. Banks left, then came back for a second helping.

'Everybody on that whole London scene was very naive in those days,' Peter says. 'Everybody was in it for the fun, but nobody could really materialize anything beyond that. You just went from gig to gig. You'd see somebody in one group, and then you'd see him playing with somebody else the following week. It wasn't business, more like a recreation – though you called yourself a musician.'

In the summer of 1968, as Yes played a handful of crummy gigs and slowly hammered their act together beneath the Lucky Horseshoe, a fire broke out in the Speakeasy, closing the place down and effectively putting half the poseurs in town out of action.

In those days the London club scene was still very much alive. Some of the places opened one week and were out of business by the next, but the scotch-and-coke community spirit that first reared its head with the Beatles was still going

Word, the (later) Flash albums, and his own solo L.P. displayed in a neat row by the front door. The poster from a Yes gig in Norway that hangs near the fireplace. The old diaries and tapes from live gigs that he's carted all the way over from England.

Born in Barnet, North London, on 7 July 1947, Banks (*né* Brockbanks) had played guitar since secondary school, though his musical career didn't get under way until he'd been bounced out of art college at seventeen.

With fingers snapping to Martha and the Vandellas, the Beatles, and the newly-emerging Who, he threw his lot in with a series of weekend blues and R&B groups (like the Devil's Disciples) working their way round the youth clubs in the area. 'The whole band would get £5 to split between them,' he recalls. 'Maybe you'd be able to buy yourself a couple of rum and cokes, but that was it.'

In time, he linked up with Chris Squire's Syn. 'The Syn had been going for about six months,' Banks says. 'I knew their drummer, and I ran into him one day when I was wandering down Denmark Street. That's where everybody used to hang out in those days, in the little coffee-bar called the Giaconda. A lot of people would sit around in there, hour after hour, day after day for weeks, pretending they were in the music business.

'Anyway, the Syn's guitarist was just leaving and the drummer said, "Wanna join?" So I went to see Squire and the rest of them play in this terrible little club in Swiss Cottage, North-West London. There were about ten people there, most of them probably worked there, and the

27

full steam – fuelled by psychedelics, but stronger than ever.

As Chris Squire says, 'There was this whole "We're all in this together" vibe.' Whether or not everyone actually was, people were hanging out, Cream and Hendrix were the main men, new groups were mushrooming out of the floorboards overnight, record companies were slowly emerging from the Middle Ages, and everyone who thought they were anyone was down at the clubs. Dressed to kill. Blasted to the gills. Out-posing each other as if their very lives depended on it.

So the sudden demise of a prime-time hangout like the Speakeasy was a tragic blow, though that segment of the scene quickly regrouped at Blaise's – another trendy, if marginally more exclusive, establishment ten minutes across town. Live music was invariably the order of the evening in most places, though some of the more successful joints competed with one another over the booking of American acts – always guaranteed crowd-pullers, no matter how obscure.

In keeping with the times, Blaise's hired Sly and the Family Stone for the evening of 15 September 1968 – a Sunday. Although the Woodstock Festival and the appearance of big money were still a year away, Sylvester Stewart had already cultivated the peculiar habit that would drive more than one promoter to the wall in years to come. Sly didn't turn up.

A mildly panic-stricken Roy Flynn, who had managed the Speakeasy and was temporarily handling affairs at Blaise's, was obviously in a spot. When a friend, Tony Stratton-Smith (then manager of the Nice), mentioned a new group he'd heard of who sounded as if they might be worthwhile, Flynn didn't wait around for a second opinion. He went down to a glorified crash pad in South Kensington where Yes – half asleep, unheard, and sight unseen – were hastily offered the gig.

As legend has it, Yes blew the ceiling off the place, the walls caved in, thousands fainted in the crush to get in, and a Whole New Age of rock music began on that very night. As Bill Bruford remembers it, the group's impact wasn't on quite such a nuclear scale. 'It seemed to go well, but I don't really think there were a lot of people *in* the club that night,' he laughs. 'These legendary stories sound great years later, even though on the night you probably played to two drunks and a couple of waitresses. It wasn't that bad, but it wasn't Standing Room Only. It was a rotten, boring night at Blaise's. As usual.'

Jon Anderson takes a less cynical view of the evening, reasoning that Yes had only been together for three months. The rush was enough. 'It was a surprise, and it was good because most of the people who were there had never seen me perform,' he says. 'It was quite a nice feeling to smile down at your . . . associates, as if to say, "Here I am doing my thing. Bet you didn't know I could sing." '

If nothing else, the gig got them a manager in the shape of Roy Flynn, who was on drinking terms with more people in the business than Jon. Yes didn't yet have an agent, but through their joint efforts the gigs began to trickle in.

Musically, it was still early days. No clear direction had been mapped out, though Squire and Anderson were consciously taking cues and pointers from the already well established acts of the day. 'There were certain things we liked about the Nice,' Jon says. 'There were certain things we enjoyed about the Fifth Dimension, and Vanilla Fudge, and even the Beach Boys. We adapted their styles.'

Or as Squire explains, 'I think Jon and I actually did share very similar ideas, which is possibly the reason why it did work from the beginning. There was no doubt about the kind of music we were aiming to make. Jon and I decided that we liked the idea of strong vocals, strong instrumentals – there wasn't much we disagreed on really, in terms of what would make Yes music a strong, powerful thing.'

Unfortunately, there was a slight snag.

Above: Bill Bruford – 'The Nice weren't our rivals. But they were the Big Time, and we wanted to be somewhere near that'
Opposite: Jon Anderson – 'I realized there was a gap, a need for a group like Yes'

Bill Bruford had been accepted by Leeds University, and his nine months of living life to the hilt was finally running out on him. 'I was crucified for a couple of weeks just thinking about it,' Bruford says, but in the end he chose higher education. 'I thought university was a slightly better bet than Yes at that point.'

Bill split for Leeds to study economics, and Yes found themselves a new drummer named Tony O'Riley, whose main claim to fame was that he'd played with the Cougars, who'd toured with the Beatles once upon a time. Tony, as it turned out, was also fairly unreliable and spent most of his spare time in pubs.

Michael Tait, destined to become a Yes employee, remembers the period clearly. In the early autumn of 1968, he'd resurfaced in London after a six-month solo odyssey across America. An Australian with a background in engineering, he'd been in with the Speakeasy crowd before the place burned, so it was only natural that he homed in on Blaise's to link up with his old cronies.

Roy Flynn was telling anyone who'd listen about his hot new discovery, so Tait made a point of checking Yes out. He notes that they were obviously improving because 'people were sitting there spellbound that night. Nobody had heard anything like it, and we're talking about people who were used to hearing incredible musicians. Jimi Hendrix would be down there jamming some nights, and all these well-known people were hanging around.'

Anderson and Squire were beginning to write songs together but were fairly insecure about using any of them, so their sets relied on heavily Yesified renditions of other people's greatest hits – 'Eleanor Rigby', Traffic's 'Mr Fantasy', the odd Move tune, as well as all the old Toyshop standards like the Byrds' 'I See You' – not to mention Leonard Bernstein's 'Something's Coming' from *West Side Story*.

'I think we may have done an Association song,' Chris Squire says. ' "Along Comes Mary"? I don't know, but we liked them a lot. We might have done "You Keep Me Hanging On", but that was Vanilla Fudge's big Supremes' cover, so I don't know if we would have been that obvious. Knowing Yes, we probably found another Supremes song that we could do the same sort of job on. We probably did "Eight Miles High" at some point too.'

Yes weren't a copy band in the strictest sense. The influences they were absorbing were only evident in the most subliminal way, and their grandiose versions of the songs bore little resemblance to the originals. As Chris adds, 'We failed as imitators, but in the process came up with something of our own. I mean, we definitely did songs by the Fifth Dimension – "Paper Cup", "Carpet Man", and things like that – but they were very similar in feel to much later things like "Your Move"/"I've Seen All Good People". We still have a lot of that flavour – the Association feel, too. That's always been in Yes. It's even with us now, I think.

'But we never tried to imitate anything. We'd hear something we liked, and then do a hotter version of the same thing. Playing small clubs made us very aware

29

of how necessary it is to make sure it drives home.'

A month after Blaise's, Yes embarked on their first British 'tour' – in reality a series of scattered gigs supporting a varying line-up of the Small Faces, the Who, Joe Cocker, Family, and the Crazy World of Arthur Brown.

Since Anderson, the ex-lorry driver, didn't want the responsibility (and nobody else in Yes could drive without hitting something), Michael Tait was recruited to pilot their new van.

Yes played a gig on their own at Leeds University, where Tait (destined to become the technical whiz kid behind the group's stage shows) stood around watching them set up their three microphones, three amps, and ramshackle drum kit because 'I knew absolutely nothing about that sort of thing.'

A dance band playing in another part of the University that same evening drew hundreds. Yes pulled about twenty. Among them, pints in hand, were Bill Bruford and a couple of his friends. 'I'd been there for about six weeks,' Bill recalls. 'I'd said to all my new-found mates, "Come and have a look at this band, they're really good. I used to play with them." But they were dismal. The rest of the group were all right, but the drummer was at least a beat behind everybody else. I was absolutely crippled with embarrassment.'

Bruford went backstage to say hello, where Anderson and Squire 'turned on this sad story about how they had this Albert Hall gig with Cream lined up, and they were in a fix because they didn't want to do it with that drummer. Before I knew it, they'd talked me into it. I thought, "Oh well, I'll do that gig, then come back to University."'

The next thing Yes knew, they were on stage at the Albert Hall, opening the bill for Cream's farewell concert through the manoeuvring of Roy Flynn. It was actually their second appearance there (they'd done a benefit for Czech refugees a few weeks earlier), and they were politely received by the Cream crowd. More significantly, they attracted the attention of the British music press, who were sufficiently motivated to begin spouting things like 'You just try and label them', while predicting Great Things for the future.

In retrospect, Chris Squire is a bit sceptical of the timing. 'Who knows whether we were ready for all that?' he says. 'It happened, and what we eventually got out of all of it was that "Yes Are The Greatest Thing Since Sliced Bread" sort of thing. One or two people said good things about us, but of course it didn't continue because we hadn't really had enough time, and experience, and reality to back it up.'

It was ludicrous, Yes playing the Albert Hall, because they were barely toeing the line at poverty level. Roy Flynn had them on a tiny weekly wage, and any extra income went towards travel and equipment expenses.

Although Peter Banks lived at home with his parents, the rest of Yes lived in Drayton Gardens, South Kensington, sharing a crumbling wreck of a house with a group called Sleepy (which featured Boz Burrell and Ian Wallace).

To everyone's disappointment, Bill packed his bags and headed back north to his books. Michael Tait, the only one with a car, drove him. 'On the way up, we talked about the whole thing,' Tait says. 'Bill was moaning, "What am I going to do?" In the end, I told him he had no choice. When you've got a choice between being a musician and being anything else, there *is* no choice. He said, "Yeah. I guess that's what I really want to do."'

So Bruford returned, Yes were officially in business, and the long slog of one-nighters up and down the motorways really began: colleges, pubs, and dreary thirties dance halls masquerading as teenage hangouts, all of which made the odd T.V. appearance (on I.T.V.'s *Magpie*), the occasional prestige gig (the Albert Hall again with Janis Joplin), or even a perfectly boring night at Blaise's

Above: Tony Kaye at the Camden Festival
Opposite: Peter Banks – 'Tony and I used to hang out a bit more together than the rest of the band. We'd be the two who'd go out raving after a gig'

or the reopened Speakeasy seem like heaven.

To help push Yes to the record companies, Roy Flynn financed several demo tapes. Supposedly, the Beatles' Apple Corps showed vague interest, to the point where Yes were allowed to do a tape at their studio where, as Peter Banks recollects, 'Peter Asher was supposed to be producing us, and he sat there reading a newspaper the whole time.'

Gigs were on twenty-four-hour standby, nothing was ever arranged, and as Bill Bruford says, 'We were always short of petrol money, always short of leads, and cables, and guitar strings.'

The grind wasn't exactly paying off. Away from central London, reaction was mixed and at times non-existent. 'We did terrible little gigs,' Bruford recalls. 'Bracknell Sports Centre? It was a joke. They were miserable places. We busied our way through the arrangements and got out of there as fast as we could.

'There wasn't any blinding light – *This Is The Future Of Rock And Roll* – or anything like that by any means. It was a long dither. Jon was the leader. I was pretty strong-willed and wanted to play drums a certain way, but he'd start singing drum licks to me. There was a bit of friction, but it was all good stuff. Jon wanted to get somewhere in a hurry, but he wasn't quite sure where. He just knew he could be better at something than anyone else around. Everybody else was piddling around, but Jon knew he could crack it.'

Still caught up in the psychedelic dream, and delving into more esoteric books and outlooks, Jon struggled to put his ideas across so that they could be understood by the group.

'I never understood what the hell he was talking about,' Tony Kaye laughs. 'I couldn't understand him – what I thought was a Northern mentality, with a Northern accent.... The difference between the London sophistication of Chris and the way Jon was ... it was just incredible.

'But Jon *knew* what he was doing. I guess it was a lesson in patience for everyone, just in trying to figure out what he was going on about. He'd read so many things and had so many crazy ideas going through his head.'

If Anderson was trying to prod Yes along faster than some of them wanted to go, it's only because he felt there was no other way to get there. As he says, 'The funny thing is, as it started to gain momentum, I just let it go. But I'd push everybody in a manner which, hopefully, I became respected for. Nothing gets done unless you get down to it, sweat it out. We had problems with all sorts of people. Agents. The first agent we went to said we'd never make it unless we changed our style. That was the kind of thing we were up against.'

All they could do was load up the van again and again, get lost a lot, grace the inside of every fish-and-chip shop south of Hadrian's Wall, and generally bide their time. They had publicity pix taken. They became Wednesday night regulars at the Marquee. Roy Flynn was in the midst of doing a deal with Atlantic Records. But as Peter Banks says, 'If it hadn't been for the Marquee and the Speakeasy, we would have starved.'

CHAPTER TWO

DUES

I remember how crazy-erratic Bill was, and how spaced-out Jon was in the beginning, in the naive way he thought about things.
TONY KAYE

We needed strings, we needed French horns, we needed ... sounds.
JON ANDERSON

On 3 July 1969, as Atlantic Records were preparing to release the group's first album in Britain, Yes were hired to entertain at a ritzy garden party thrown by a certain Prince Lowenstein at his flash Holland Park pad.

The champagne bubbled in the warm summer evening. Jewels sparkled like distant galaxies around the necks of beautiful women. Monkey-suited waiters stood at attention behind mile-long buffet tables as film actresses, famous authors, politicians, and heiresses nibbled on pâté and caviar – the small talk breezing around horses, racing cars, country estates, and what a simply *soopah* little gathering it was, darling. Peter Sellers was there, along with Princess Margaret. As Chris Squire recollects, so were half the London Metropolitan Police.

'It was quite a hot little get-together,' he grins. 'All you had to do was take a deep breath, and all these cops had turned up. Neighbours kept calling them because of the noise, but they couldn't come in and *do* anything because all these important people were there, so the cops were standing around out in the street all night.'

Peter Banks admits that Yes probably didn't make many new fans that night. 'We played and died a complete death,' he says. 'After the first number there was absolute silence. We did three or four more and were asked to leave. It was in a big tent in this back garden and *nobody* was amused. They were all boogalooing around, and the last thing they wanted to hear was us.

'So Tony and I grabbed two bottles of champagne and went down to the end of the garden at five o'clock in the morning. We were already pretty well out to lunch, but we wandered into a clump of rhododendrons, drank them both, and passed out.'

It was still a case of rotten gigs galore. The fact that Yes were on the eve of becoming Recording Artistes made no difference at all. The album sessions themselves had been sandwiched in, a day here, a day there, in between gigs at Madame Tussaud's and one-day sprints to Germany.

For a first shot, *Yes* worked pretty well – not destined to put everyone behind the wheel of a Lamborghini, but well spoken of by the British rock press,

Yes, 1969: Kaye, Bruford, Anderson, Squire, and Banks

which in the anti-commercial atmosphere of the late sixties, was worth far more than a gold record on the office wall.

The Yes on *Yes* were bright, sunny, and almost naive – teetering on the fence between pop and progressive. The interplay was often untidy around the edges, and the seams showed traces of model-airplane glue, but apart from the lumbering sledgehammer and concrete overcoat job they gave 'Beyond And Before', Yes came across as a group to watch.

They were obviously reaching for Greater Things, particularly in the case of that blazing Bruford/Squire rhythm section during the pre-Armageddon intro to 'Survival' or the snappy, morse-code gymnastics of 'Looking Around'.

The three-part vocal harmonies (though occasionally echoing traces of the Association) were *Yes* harmonies. While a big deal was made even then over the classical influences supposedly running rampant through their music, you'd need a fine-tooth comb to find them. If the classical thing was there, it was purely subliminal and solely in the structuring – the push towards a Grand Approach that dynamited tracks like the anti-war 'Harold Land' and 'Survival' into motion with brash, busy overtures that only died down to a low rumble when the vocals came in, then flared up again full blast the moment Anderson stepped back to take a breather.

Yes were out to make a point, even if they had to half beat the material to a pulp in the process. But it was a noticeable jazz undercurrent, rather than a classical flavour, that really set them apart – particularly in the work of Bruford and Banks.

'Bill and I used to sit up late some nights listening to his albums,' Peter remembers. 'He *was* a jazzer, a hundred per cent. In fact, the first day I saw him, he had a pair of plimsolls on his feet with JAZZ written across each toe, and I HATE MOON – meaning Keith Moon – on the sides. I don't have the foggiest idea of how the jazz thing got into my guitar playing though. I never paid much attention to jazz guitarists. It just appeared somehow.'

The music was ambitious, but counter-balanced as well by Anderson's simple love songs – soft, ethereal, acoustic 12-string/piano things like 'Yesterday and Today' or 'Sweetness' (co-authored with Squire and Clive Bailey), with its choirboy aaaaaaahhhhhhhhs and double-take lyrics:

> She brings the sunshine to a rainy afternoon
> She puts the sweetness in, stirs it with a spoon

If Anderson's contributions were a bit too blissed out at times, they had a weird charm nonetheless. As he says, 'There's nobody whose work I've seen and said, "I'd like to do that". I liked so many lyricists at that time. Obviously the Beatles were a big influence, and Jimmy Webb appealed to me too. *The Magic Garden*. Slightly surreal. Into fantasy.'

MacArthur Park is melting in the dark, etc.?

'Yeah, but though I was basically the only guy who could get my ideas down, I didn't take too much notice. I wrote them, I sang them, but I didn't go around saying, "Hey, I'm a poet."'

Yes were still squeamish about placing all their chips on original tunes, and they homed in on Lennon and McCartney's 'Every Little Thing' with a vengeance. Despite a neo – Vanilla Fudge/knuckle-sandwich intro (with Banks itching to veer off into a raga riff), the track was magnificent – an innocuous Beatles' tune blown up to near-Wagnerian proportions, with a snippet of 'Day Tripper' for a side order.

It wasn't *quite* as good as 'I See You', however – a Roger McGuinn/David Crosby tune lifted from the Byrds' *Fifth Dimension* and rebuilt into a piledriving extravaganza that still sounds surprisingly good a decade later. It cooked, it took off, with Bruford and Banks jazzing it up during a long instrumental duet – not outdoing the Byrds' version, but turning it into something new and just as valid.

Peter Banks writes off those sessions as a near-total disaster. 'We spent two days trying to figure out how to make a Hammond organ work,' he remembers. 'The engineer didn't know what he was doing either, and we were all fumbling around in the dark.'

Atlantic Records' boss Ahmet Ertegun would sail in to hear the tapes, only to find that the band hadn't put anything down. To make things worse, producer Paul Clay wasn't used to working with rock groups, particularly one that required a slightly more inventive approach to recording than the average British blues band. 'I don't really think he knew who

Above: Chris Squire and Bill Bruford in Switzerland, November 1969
Opposite: 'There's the guy who just plays what he's told to on his instrument, the guy who writes something for his own instrument, and at the top the guy who writes everything for everybody's instrument. The Grand Composer. Jon Anderson has always believed, rightly or wrongly, that the composer is the main man' – Bill Bruford

we were,' Chris Squire says. 'Atlantic were distributed by Polydor, and he was a Polydor house producer, or something. A traditional producer of those times with a dog and a pipe. Come to think of it, he looked like Michael Caine.

'He and this engineer, Gerald, would sit there and we'd say, "A bit more of this, a little less of that, let's hear it sounding a bit like something else." It was play-acting in a way. We had disagreements about how things should be mixed, which was all a bit silly because we didn't actually know what we were talking about.'

Yes weren't happy with the end result, and as Peter Banks recalls, 'Each track we listened to, we made excuses for. 'Well, this part's not too good, but the *next* bit's great."'

Squire doesn't have many kind words for the album either. 'We went in there trying to make something monumental, though of course we didn't succeed,' he says. 'The album ended up not sounding the way we thought it could. It was a bit of a disappointment, because I'd imagined it sounding grander and much more together.'

Still, the critics were impressed, with the N.M.E. noting that 'the boys put a lot of light and shade into their music, and can belt it out or keep it smoochy quiet and jazz-like.'

In *Melody Maker*, jazz drummer and guest critic Buddy Rich gave *Yes* five stars 'for choice of material, conception, arrangement, and professionalism in performance.'

When the album was released in the States later in the year, *Cashbox* said it was 'not only one of the finest and most brilliant albums of the year, but may signal in its unusual blend of folk and jazz styles, coupled with powerful and poetic lyrics, a new direction for the contemporary sound. Yes are going to be giants.'

With people in high places dubbing them Britain's Brightest Hope and The Band of 1969, the workload increased to the point where Yes were playing somewhere nearly every night of the week, with a solitary note of stability provided by those regular Wednesday evening appearances at the Marquee.

'Chris was always late,' Michael Tait remembers. 'Peter Banks was always taking mandies, Bill was always on time and eager, "Let's go, let's go", Tony Kaye always had a girl with him, and Jon was always looking around the corner. Always hoping. Wanting this and wanting that. He still is.

'They used to throw bottles at us in Germany all the time. They hated us. Promoters were ripping everybody off so we had to demand the money first. We didn't get paid in some places, and we even did a gig in Italy where no one came because no one knew that the gig was on.'

There were still plenty of on-stage teething problems – the running battle between Squire and Banks to see who could play louder and the free-form soloing during numbers like 'I See You' which was rapidly getting out of hand. At least half of Yes's sets, Bill Bruford explains, 'must have been taken up, not with the arrangements which were supposed to be our *tour de force*, but with these tedious solos.

'There was a terrible solo Chris did over a Young Rascals tune – maybe it was 'Good Loving' – and these things would go on for twenty minutes. It was the same with the guitar solo. The rest of us would leave the stage and Peter would go on, and on, and on. I don't remember if there was a drum solo at that point, but if there was, I'm sure it must have been equally as boring.'

Mr Banks admits that there were nights when he became 'extremely indulgent. I had a thing about never playing the same thing twice in a solo, and some nights it was great, some nights it was really terrible. I'd go on for five, ten, fifteen minutes, and I can imagine what everybody must have been thinking: "Jesus

35

Christ, when's he going to stop?" You take more risks on stage and I was exploring things, though sometimes at cost to the band.'

All this didn't go down without a certain degree of off-stage criticism and arguing. 'If we'd had some aborted European tour and lost five gigs, we'd be a bit edgy when we got home,' Banks says. 'We'd be rehearsing, and Jon would come in with twenty songs. We'd say, "Hold on, let's sift through." He'd always put his songs down on tape, which was great, but he knew about three chords. It wasn't so much arguments as non-communication, though there was a lot of bickering. Chris and Bill were always at each other. Bill would want to speed things up, Chris would want to slow things down, and they'd go on, and on....'

The fact that critics liked the album did wonders for group morale, though that had its inevitable drawbacks. 'We were very arrogant, but we'd do some gigs and die a death,' Banks remembers. 'The scene in those days was a lot smaller, and it was very much word-of-mouth. We'd do gigs in London and there'd be ecstatic applause, then we'd go play Bradford and there'd be no reaction at all. Dead silence. I think we got a little complacent in London, because we began to think we were a little better than we actually were.'

There was also a question of the group's 'image' – London hip and vaguely post-psychedelic, with a preoccupied aloofness that was almost impossible to crack. 'We had a certain coolness to those around us,' Bill Bruford reflects. 'Maybe we turned people off who could have helped us. But then, in those days you were looking for anything that was different from the next band. If we had a certain degree of aloofness or coldness, an intensity that some people may have thought was heavy, then that might have been a good thing.'

Atlantic Records were keeping a low profile. In those days record companies weren't into pumping outrageous amounts of cash into new groups or subsidizing tours, and the fairly undemanding deal that manager Roy Flynn had made on Yes's behalf wasn't likely to change things. The first Yes single released in the U.K., 'Sweetness'/'Something's Coming', sold a grand total of 500 copies, and Bill Bruford wasn't too sure what Atlantic's angle on the group actually was, 'except that down at the

Above: Chris Squire, 'possibly in Geneva, but then, possibly not'
Opposite: Bill Bruford and Tony Kaye

Speakeasy at one o'clock in the morning, they were making ludicrous claims for how big we'd be in America.'

For the moment, they were too busy trying to break in England, and though Jon Anderson set aside enough time to marry Jenny Baker on 22 December 1969, there was already another album in the works.

With strings attached.

Bill Bruford isn't 100 per cent sure where the initial idea to use an orchestra on *Time And A Word* came from, 'but it was probably Jon'. Squire doesn't really remember, but he thought it had possibilities. Anderson says that it came during a conversation between Squire, producer Tony Colton, and himself. Tony Kaye was 'pretty into it, sure'. Peter Banks thought it was a lousy idea from the start.

'We didn't want a large orchestra,' Anderson explains. 'But we wanted, and needed, some additional . . . sounds.'

It was probably inevitable, but a weird move all the same. Just when Yes were beginning to earn a respectably hot reputation as tight, intricate, and totally self-contained, in rolls a busload of music college graduates – violins poised, trumpets at the ready – for what Bill Bruford observes 'seemed to be the *de rigueur* type of thing. Everybody was using orchestras – the Nice, Deep Purple, the Moody Blues – and we were under the influence of other bands at the time.'

If Yes were taking that particular cue from elsewhere, it was probably more out of frustration over the first album than with any real hankering to be fashionable. As Jon says, 'We didn't want to stick to the rock sound that we had, mainly because we hadn't achieved a definite sound aura, which certain other bands I knew had.'

A fullness? A presence?

'Yeah. Tony and Peter weren't working as one aural sound. They weren't interweaving. Tony was over here doing his thing, and Peter was over there. It worked well enough, but the songs we were doing at the time seemed to cry out for a bigger feel. We thought about using mellotrons or whatever, but eventually said, 'Let's try and put it over with a small orchestra. A string section and brass.'''

It nearly worked too. Despite a fairly sterile production job and an odd stereo mix, *Time And A Word* showed that those long months of gruelling roadwork hadn't been in vain. The overall emphasis this time was more progressive than pop, and though Yes still seemed to be trying too hard (those murderous, demolition-job solos were still out in force), the second album was a marked improvement on the first.

Once again, Yes turned to a non-original tune (the first of two) for a showpiece. Ritchie Havens' 'No Opportunity Necessary, No Experience Needed' opened the first side in a whirlwind of Cinemascopic, Big Country strings – courtesy of arranger Tony Cox – that could have been embarrassing, if it hadn't been for Squire's steaming 78 rpm, speedfreak bass work and the hint of that elusive grandeur that Yes so badly wanted to capture on tape.

In contrast, Stephen Stills' 'Everydays' was stark, dark, and skeletal – a hazy, shimmering, nocturnal piece that, barring the misplaced blast of soloing in the middle, had a distinctly dream-like atmosphere.

'We still didn't believe much in our own songs at the time,' Anderson says. 'We didn't think they could end the show. Make that show happen. If we played a song everyone knew, it would make the audience a bit more energized.

I guess we were playing it safe, and we carried that over to our albums.'

But the other six tracks were originals. The driving 'Sweet Dreams' was hypnotic and circular, almost a drone. 'The Prophet' featured Kaye's heavy-duty Hammond intro, sky-over-Montana strings à la Aaron Copland, a brief scrap of melody that Squire would one day refashion into 'the fish' (on *Fragile*), and an adventurous, if slightly disjointed, attempt at dividing the music into 'movements' by gluing together a series of individual musical fragments.

If the sunny, string-quartet-and-piano meanderings of Anderson's 'Clear Days' were a bit too saccharine for comfort ('I once knew a sweet young girl . . . .'), the gruff, lumbering 'Astral Traveller' and the low-key locomotive pace of 'Then' balanced the scales. And if an album needs at least one singalong track, at least one anthem, then the title tune was it.

Jon Anderson's name appeared under all the original songs – either alone, or in collaboration with Chris Squire or ex-Warriors bassist David Foster. As Jon says, 'At the time, I was relying on anyone who just wanted to sit down and try writing with me.'

But, as Bill Bruford recalls, Anderson rarely presented a finished song to the group. 'I think the feeling was that Jon got the ball rolling on tunes, rather than "writing" them,' he explains. 'He'd come along with something that was usually pretty simple, even awful, but because the other musicians couldn't stand it, they'd be forced to come up with something else.

'I'm not being facetious. I think that's generally how it worked. Jon had a guitar, but no facility to play any chords. So he'd just scrub it with one finger up across the strings – Chris will bear me out on this – and sing something. Everybody would go, "How about this chord Jon?" and we'd show him where to put his fingers.

'But he was an active person, an organizer, and he had a sense of melody, no doubt about that. But some of his chords were terrible. On the other hand, it was always on the basis where, if you don't like it, you're entitled to come up with something better, and if we all think it's better we'll accept that. But if you can't think of anything better, shut up. That's the way Yes was run.'

His lyrics were slowly changing scope and subject-matter as well, veering away from you-and-me love themes, and beginning to tackle Greater Themes – Life, Oneness, and the Future – the early stages of that mystical and somewhat oblique track that would eventually place him in the critical firing line.

While Tony Kaye's Hammond work was, to coin a term, 'spirited', the limitations of the instrument were obvious – a Hammond always sounded like a Hammond – which gave a certain sameness to the Yes sound. More conspicuously, however, Peter Banks' guitar work was a mere shadow of its former self. Whether it was due to his belief that producer Colton didn't like him, or to Chris Squire's suspicion that Banks resented the orchestra copping the lead lines that should have been rightfully his, Peter's active participation was minimal. Most of the contributions he did make were buried so far back in the mix that they didn't particularly matter.

On the flip side, the Squire/Bruford alliance was firing away like an artillery line, exploring shapes and patterns that were beyond the scope of most rock rhythm sections of the day – though as Bill admits, 'Some of the things were overworked and sounded really awkward, and silly, and childish, and over-busy. But it didn't seem odd to us at all that a rhythm section should try to be weird.'

Chris remembers Tony Colton mixing 'No Opportunity . . . ' while listening to it through headphones, rather than the studio monitors, 'which was a funny thing to have done. This was the first time Eddie Offord was engineering for us, and Tony Colton kept saying, "Turn the bass up!" because he had this crappy set of cans on that didn't reproduce the bass. In the end, that song probably had the loudest bass guitar of any record that's ever been made. So sheer accident, you see, contributed to My Personal Success!'

By the time they'd finished, Yes weren't much happier with *Time And A Word* than they'd been with *Yes*. 'It was the same problem all over again,' Chris explains. 'I'd imagined it sounding much grander somehow, but we didn't quite get there. I mean, "Dear Father", which was recorded during those sessions but didn't appear on that album, is very much that sort of song. It has that classical, 1812 Overture thing about it, but that feel didn't come through in the studio.'

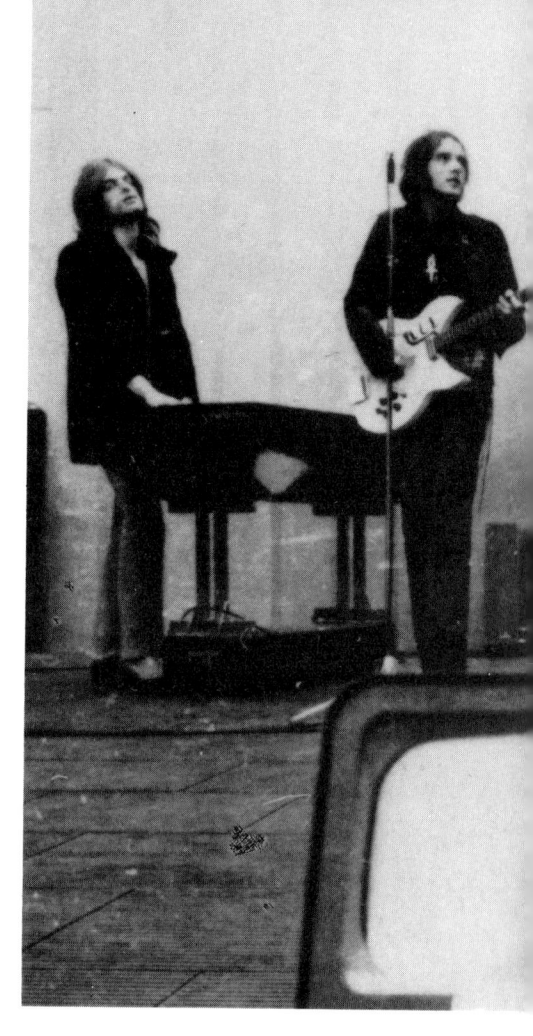

Yes on Swiss television, November 1969. 'We did it outdoors and we were freezing our cobblers off' – Peter Banks

Inevitably, the use of strings and brass was bound to cause problems when it came to reproducing the stuff on stage, though an optimistic Yes played two gigs at London's Queen Elizabeth Hall in March 1970, backed by a twenty-piece orchestra, again led by Tony Cox.

Under-rehearsed and poorly equipped in the P.A. department, the experiment was, in Anderson's view, 'a total shambles. We realized that orchestral musicians are a different breed from rock musicians. Things have changed, but at the time I didn't think we were dealing with very professional people. I always thought the orchestra should get off on the music, but they obviously didn't care too much about it. That's not a put-down, that's the way it was, but it made me think that maybe there *was* a future in trying to evoke those orchestral sounds – though not necessarily with an orchestra.'

Like its predecessor, *Time And A Word* didn't exactly set cash-registers on fire. Reviews were mixed this time – the strings were a touchy area – and though the album made a brief appearance in the British charts at number 39, it disappeared without a trace a week later. In America, few even knew the album existed.

Naturally, Yes realized they could only go so far in Britain and still survive, but while vague talk of American tours was constantly batted around, it was nothing but hot air. As Banks says, 'America was a long way away. It was like going to Mars in those days. Well, great, but how much does the spaceship cost?'

Even after nearly two years together, the underlying feeling within Yes was that they still weren't ready to branch out. 'We had to get a bit more experience and do a bit more work,' Jon Anderson admits. 'It was kind of a paranoid number.'

Atlantic Records didn't have an official U.K. office at that stage. All the shots were being called from New York, where nobody was particularly going out of their way to help Yes to that next plateau. Phil Carson, then the company's British label manager and possibly the only guy around who grasped what Yes were all about, agrees that there was a noticeable lack of enthusiasm in the corporate hallways. 'I was the only Atlantic person actually *in* England at the time, so if I hadn't been into it, Yes would have been in a lot of trouble,' he says. 'Ahmet Ertegun was into them, because he signed the group, but on a working level . . .

'The first album got that great review in *Cashbox* when it went out in America, but it didn't sell. The American record business being what it is, everyone figured this was just another English group that wasn't going to happen because that first album hadn't charted in England either. Even after a year, I don't think that first album had sold more than 7,000 copies.'

While Yes were slowly developing what you might call a 'cult following', a sales figure of 7,000 was cutting things a bit fine. *Time And A Word* fared better – but only just – and the group's second single 'Sweet Dreams'/'Dear Father' sold even fewer copies than the first one had.

Doubt was beginning to creep in. For one thing, there were management problems.

'By that time, we'd done a tour with the Nice and seen that they were getting a hundred quid a week,' Bill Bruford says. 'We looked to our manager and said, 'How come it isn't happening?''

From all indications, Roy Flynn didn't know *how* to push Yes up to the next rung on the ladder, though as Peter Banks sees it, Flynn's 'intentions were great. He loved the band. Into it a hundred per cent. I've never seen a manager work so hard as he did in the beginning. He lost his job at the Speakeasy, he put his heart and soul into Yes, but he didn't have enough weight behind him to handle the record company and all.'

So discontent was beginning to disrupt the flow, despite Jon Anderson's outwardly optimistic hopes for the future. 'Jon seemed to instigate most things, even if it was shifting the wages from cash into cheque or buying new microphone leads,' Bill Bruford says. 'He instigated most of it, and did most of the arguing and shouting.

'He made himself quite ill trying to keep things from falling apart, and I remember seeing him sick to death at the Speakeasy. He was nervous, pushing all the time, and very unrelaxed. We were a *very* unrelaxed group. We were looking toward success, and everybody was telling us that we should be great by now. There was a feeling we hadn't done something that we should have done, and we weren't quite sure how to get to

39

the next step. It may have been that we got bogged down with an orchestra. It may have been that the manager wasn't pulling his weight....'

It might have also been because Peter Banks (who'd already considered leaving) was becoming increasingly remote, which, in Anderson and Squire's eyes, was disruptive to the flow.

There was more than likely a combination of ingredients at the root of Yes's discontent, but the initial reaction was to start making changes. As Bruford puts it, 'Around that time, heads began to roll', and Peter's was the first to go.

'The reason I was asked to leave was something I never really figured out at the time,' Peter Banks says. 'It was all very "You did this." "No I didn't." "Yes you did." "No I didn't." It was never reasoned out.'

If you try to pin Yes down to facts, you'll more often than not get five different versions of the same story. Peter's sudden exit is no exception, though everyone concerned points out that he'd been slowly fading into the wallpaper since before the *Time And A Word* sessions. There was that lack of active input, and Banks' admitted distaste for studio work only added fuel to the fire.

'Peter had a unique way of playing guitar that I liked very much, but he couldn't, for some reason, fit in after a while,' Jon Anderson says. 'It got to the point where he didn't converse with anybody, and we had to drag him to rehearsals because he was too busy buying clothes.'

Anderson's always explained it that way, and maintains his stand that cutting Banks loose was essential to the group's survival. As Bruford explains, 'Jon's a very stiff taskmaster. If he feels you're not pulling your weight, he'll point the finger. Anybody who doesn't say that much at rehearsals, or fight him back on his own terms isn't pulling his weight, and he's got to go.'

So, from the looks of it, a conflict in aesthetic outlook sparked off the sudden change, which Banks admits was 'a very dramatic moment in my life. I didn't really know *why*. We'd been going through so many changes, and there was that thing with Roy Flynn. For whatever reason, I'd ended up sticking up for him, and I remember saying, "If he goes, I go." God knows why I said it, because I knew nothing about the business, but Roy was a friend.'

Above: Yes, early 1970, after completing *Time And A Word*
Opposite: Reeling from the onslaught of fame and fortune – Tony Kaye in Europe, 1969

Peter says that there were also arguments over basic group policy, and the fact that Yes were playing the same material night after night, with no time set aside to work on anything new. In essence, it was Catch 22. 'Jon wanted to take four months off to get some new stuff together, but I said, "If we do that, how are we going to eat?"'

'So when it happened, it was a big shock,' Peter goes on. 'Bill said, "I think it would be better for you if you leave", and I went, "Oh . . . okay." This was in the dressing room after a gig at Luton Technical College. Tony didn't know anything about it, and Bill had been told about it that night.

'Then they said, "Well, listen, if you want to say you *left*, fine." At the same time, I thought, "Yeah, it's the best thing for my career". So that's what appeared in the papers: Banks Quits Yes Over Musical Differences.

'But I'd been working on something for two years, and it was worse than a divorce. Living with these guys constantly for that long, everything you do is geared to that one thing, then suddenly it's all over. It was like, *Jesus Christ, what do I do now?*'

The Memphis fly sitting on the salt shaker is presumably a vegetarian. He's washing his face, pausing every now and then to take a gander at Steve Howe.

It's Yes's first day off in a week. Everyone's scattered out on the town, cruising for burgers – though in Howe's case it's an Avocado Special, washed down with a tall glass of carrot juice, with a mile-high banana split (all natural ingredients) for the *coup de grâce*. The guy waiting on the roomful of empty tables hovers helpfully, inquiring every ten seconds whether 'Y'all want anythin' else?' but Mr Howe is content for the moment.

'Steve's not difficult to work for,' says his equipment manager, Claude Johnson-Taylor, 'but he's fussy, and he's getting worse. If he had millions of pounds, he'd be a recluse like Howard Hughes.'

As it is, Howe goes out of his way to be barely visible when he's not on stage. He lives quietly with his wife Jan and sons Dylan and Virgil in a nice but in no way ostentatious houseful of rare guitars on the edge of Hampstead Heath.

He frequents classical guitar recitals, checks the label carefully before eating anything new, runs up outrageous long-distance phone bills when he's away on tour, reads books like *An Introduction to Medical Radiesthesia and Radionics* on airplanes, drives a Bristol rather than a flashier Rolls-Royce, and spends most of his off-the-road hours hidden away in a small upstairs room, playing solo guitar pieces to his tape deck. Music that may never be heard by anyone else.

Steve Howe's not even in the running in the Great British Eccentric stakes, though he did once mention that he wouldn't mind being buried with his Gibson 175, and, as Claude says, he's fussy – particularly on tour.

If the food stinks, Steve will be the first to point it out. If the next hotel turns out to be a toilet with room service, you'll hear him clearly from the other end of the corridor. Although chaos amuses him for the first twenty seconds, he's got a precise image of the way things *should* be – on tour, in the studio, and on a day-to-day level. Neat, orderly, and done the right way.

If Jon Anderson is concerned with where it's all going the day after tomorrow, Steve Howe is concerned with where it's at right now. The Howe Standards have probably rubbed off on just about everyone in the Yes camp, and they're a contributing factor as to why the organization, compared with that of some other bands, is the well-run thing that it is.

Where his fastidious streak comes from is anybody's guess, though it's more than likely something that was bred into him during his early years in Holloway, North London, where he was born on 8 April 1947.

'I couldn't stand sitting in a classroom day in and day out,' he says, thinking back to what he views as a 'pretty boring childhood', where music became an essential safety valve, if not an obsession pretty early on. As a child, Howe was plagued with nightmares, and found that listening to Chet Atkins' *Teensville*, played softly on his kiddie record-player, was the only thing that could lull him to sleep.

The experts in Child Psychology can figure that one out, but it meant that Steve's everyday life was linked to guitar music, if not dependent on it, almost from the beginning. It was Chuck Berry, Buddy Holly, and Ricky Nelson's guitarist at that time, James Burton, who really steered Steve in the direction of the guitar, even though the image of the guitarist initially had more appeal than the art of playing the guitar itself.

His father furnished the cash for a cheap acoustic, and it escalated from there. 'There was nothing else that I was particularly interested in doing,' Howe says. 'The idea of playing a flashy guitar and standing up in front of an audience seemed a bit more exciting than anything

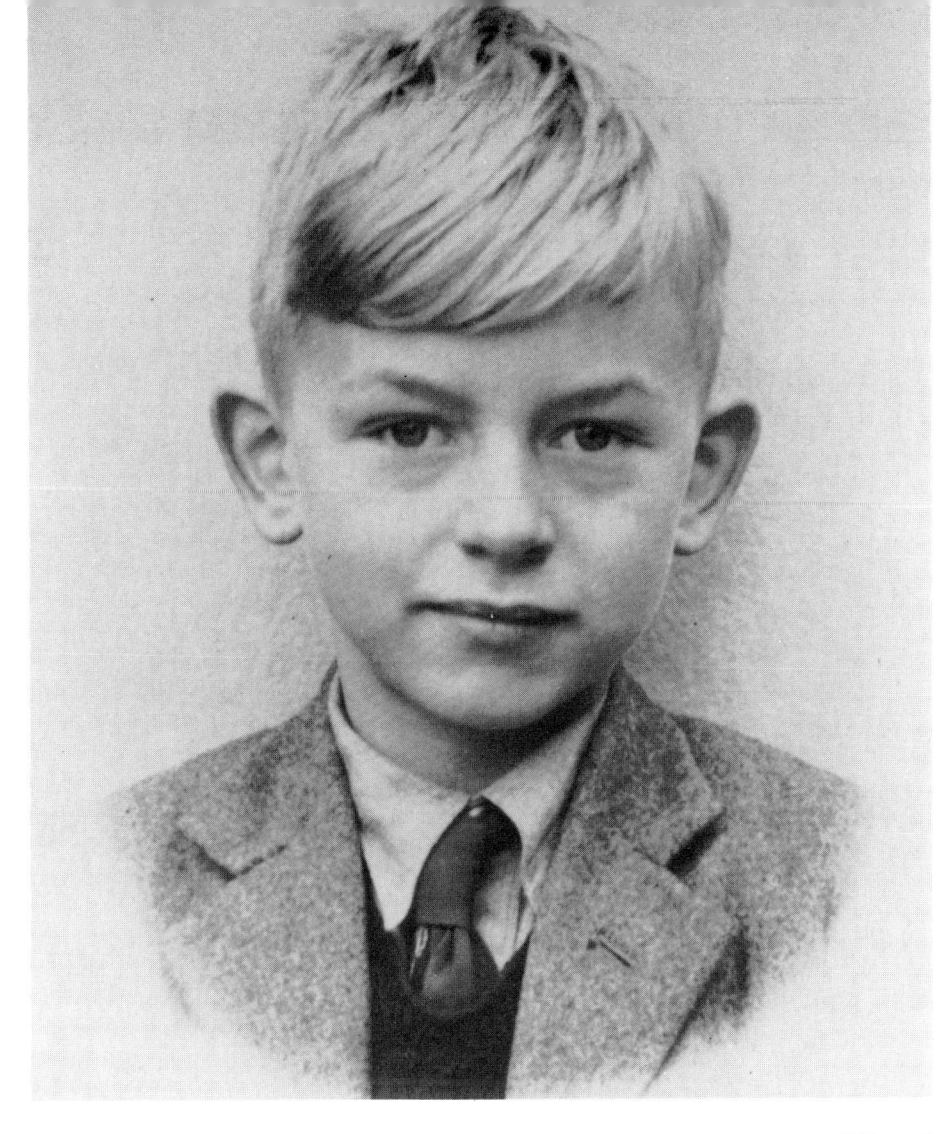

Above: Steve Howe – 'I hated school back then. My mind was always out the window'
Opposite: 'We were big in places like Sunderland. But if there was any Grand Vision, I never heard anything about it, and I was in the band' – Peter Banks

else in my life at the time. When I actually started learning how to play it, I found the whole process was abstract enough to keep my attention for more than three minutes.'

He'd already scoped-out his parents' collection of 78s – Les Paul and Mary Ford, Bill Haley and the Comets, and Tennessee Ernie Ford – and inevitably added the Shadows and Duane Eddy to his list of influences, along with Chet Atkins, who remains his guitar hero to this day. Steve's brother Phil played clarinet and turned him on to the jazz greats like Barney Kessel, Charlie Christian, Django Reinhardt, Tal Farlow, and so on.

Howe made his first appearance in front of an audience just round the corner from his school – the Barnsbury School For Boys – annexe. 'I was asked to play with this little group at a youth club in Eden Grove,' he says. 'They might have been playing together for a couple of years, so I went along with my Antoria guitar and played with this rhythm guitarist, a drummer, and a bass player in front of maybe fifty people. The drummer was a freckle-faced Scottish guy called Jock, and the bass player was called Bones. He was sort of . . . corpse-like, and we played things like "The Frightened City".'

Even by youth-club standards, the performance was diabolical, with some disagreement over whether they were actually all playing the same song. 'It was a bit of a joke,' Steve remembers. 'As far as I was concerned, I played every note right and they played it all wrong – though how it really was, I'll never know.'

By his mid teens, the Beatles Era was well under way. Howe was hanging out/looking cool in the Denmark Street/Covent Garden area of London. He'd already had a go at a respectable career as an apprentice to a piano-making firm, and later as a cleaning boy, but found he wasn't cut out for either.

As a freelance musician his appearances were sporadic – playing with a no-name group at the Prison Club next door to Pentonville Prison, or filling in for people like Albert Lee of Chris Farlowe and the Thunderbirds when they couldn't make the gig, cranking out twelve-bar blues.

By 1964 he'd joined the Syndicats (Kevin Driscoll, Tom Ladd, and Johnny Melton) – blatant Chuck Berry fanatics who lurched around late-night London with 'The Chuck Berry Appreciation Society' painted on the side of their van. Managed by Driscoll's mother, they were once fired from a regular spot at a London club for playing fourteen Berry tunes in a single night. The Syndicats cut a quick handful of moderately successful singles (including 'Maybellene' and 'Howlin' With My Baby') with producer Joe Meek of Tornados fame, before Steve decided it was 'all too amateurish' and left on his seventeenth birthday.

He joined Keith West, Junior Wood, Ken Lawrence, and Boots in the In Crowd, an English soul band and the Syndicats' arch-rivals, who played raunchy clubs but also entertained at 'all these high-class deb balls. The guests would turn up in penguin suits and low-cut evening gowns, and spend half the night getting drunk and trying to drag each other off into dark corners. The In Crowd were kind of into raving and drinking, though. They were into all-nighters. They were a bit more adult and arrogant than the Syndicats really, and I think I saw the seedier side of life.'

In time, the In Crowd discovered acid, got themselves a new drummer named Twink (of Pink Fairies fame) and evolved into Tomorrow, building themselves a substantial following on the U.F.O./Round House circuit on a virtually equal footing with Syd Barrett's Pink Floyd.

Two singles, 'My White Bicycle' and 'Revolution', were released by E.M.I. in 1967, and the former rose to the middle regions of the British charts. *Tomorrow*, the album, followed in the new year, and it was during this period that the group branched out into other areas, appearing in a White Horse whisky ad, and featuring in a Swinging Sixties Lynne Redgrave/Rita Tushingham film called *Smashing Time*, where Howe's Big Moment consisted of standing still long enough to get a custard pie smashed into his face.

'I was doing sessions here and there too,' he says. 'It was pretty forgettable stuff for the most part. Like I'd played on this song called "Tar And Cement", which was a take-off on "Concrete And Clay". I played lead and Big Jim Sullivan played rhythm. I also went to Germany to do this thing with Alan Price called *Greatest Rock Songs* – me and four other guitarists.'

He was listening to virtually anything he could get his hands on – from the Beatles to the Byrds, from Vivaldi to Segovia – subconsciously absorbing elements of their music into his own playing. But if Howe had any notion that he'd finished paying his dues, the worst was yet to come. Tomorrow broke up, largely due to singer Keith West's fleeting solo success, and in late 1968 Steve joined Dave Atkins, Clive Maldoon, and Bobby Clark in Bodast. A group who Atlantic's Phil Carson claims 'everybody wanted to sign', Bodast nonetheless spent most of their two-year lifespan living in misery in a near-derelict Chelsea hovel, not far from where Yes were going through their own growing pains.

Sustained by a small retainer from Deep Purple's managers, the group landed a contract with MGM and cut an album, only to see the record company fold a few weeks before its scheduled release. The unreleased tapes are still sitting in Steve's upstairs room.

Although Bodast was a sinking ship, they plodded around the circuit, getting as far as the support spot for Chuck Berry and the Who at the Albert Hall, the day the Stones played their Brian Jones memorial gig in Hyde Park. Steve had been turning down offers from other groups in hopes that things would improve. He eventually agreed to join Ashton, Gardner, and Dyke, who were backing Pat Arnold ('The First Cut Is The Deepest') on the Delaney and Bonnie/Eric Clapton European tour.

By the time he returned to England in early 1970, Bodast had been given the financial axe by their managers (who were convinced they were junkies) and Steve decided it was time to say goodbye.

'I was sick and tired of struggling, and I wanted to play with musicians who really knew about their instruments,' he says. 'I was determined more than ever to get myself into a group who was actually out playing. I wasn't interested in a studio group, because that's what Bodast were all about. I felt that it was a loser of a direction to go in – to try and record a good album, then hope it's going to start your career off with the group. I wanted to get out of the responsibility of running a group when there was really nothing to run. No gigs. No finances.'

During the final days of Bodast, Steve had auditioned for Vincent Crane's heavy-duty Atomic Rooster, but found the idea of playing with them too ludicrous to take seriously. He'd also joined the Nice for all of one day, replacing David O'List. 'I heard music that, in some ways, I later found in Yes,' Steve says.

Neither the Nice caper nor a subsequent audition for Jethro Tull worked out, however, due to differences in outlook. So with Bodast behind him, Steve Howe was 'available. I sat around for a couple of weeks. I think I even went down to the Speakeasy one night, thinking I might come across a few people there, but nothing happened. Probably nobody knew I was available. I could have advertised, but I didn't want to do anything that would ... cheapen my name! I felt confident that I was a good guitarist, and I suppose I felt a bit snooty – that I was going to wait until the right group asked *me*.

'Then one Sunday, I remember I was just sitting there on the floor in my flat in Lots Road, looking out the window, and the phone rang. I climbed to the top of the stairs, and it was Chris Squire.'

As the story goes, Bill Bruford was wary of Steve Howe on their first meeting – the general impression being that Mr Howe, who was probably wearing shades at the

Tomorrow: John 'Junior' Wood, Keith West, Twink, and Steve Howe

time, was something of a creep and a dope-smoking hippie.

Chris Squire laughs. 'Well, *I* didn't think that, because I'd seen Steve at the U.F.O. with Tomorrow . . . and I was a bit of a creep and a dope-smoking hippie myself. I'd always had an incredible amount of respect for Steve's playing, even though I didn't know him. He was very impressive, though I could see he needed some direction in how to *use* his proficiency on the guitar. I had a feeling that Yes could provide that.'

Nobody in Yes had ever actually met Howe. Although rumour had King Crimson's Robert Fripp tagged for the job, and the group had vaguely considered offering the open guitar spot to one or two others (notably Bernie Holland), Squire was convinced that Steve was their man.

Jon Anderson wasn't inclined to disagree, since he'd watched Howe a couple of months earlier during a Bodast gig at the Speakeasy. 'I kind of stood near him while he was on stage, and I couldn't believe that one man could play so many notes in the space of five minutes,' Anderson says. 'They were all *good* notes too. He wasn't messing about. He was playing some hot stuff.'

Steve vaguely remembered Squire as being 'somebody', but apart from spotting the occasional review, knew nothing about Yes or their music. The group were rehearsing in Roy Flynn's Putney basement by this stage, Steve turned up to audition, and as Anderson says, 'He sat down, played some music to us, and it was spontaneous and unanimous. We wanted him to be in Yes.'

Howe was a bit more hesitant. 'I was desperate, but I felt I deserved something good at the same time,' he says. 'Yes was the first thing that came up, though I sensed that there was something in their music that I liked a lot. It stemmed from Bill and Chris really having their position under control.

'Jon said he wanted to do "Eight Days A Week", and I told him I could understand doing other people's music . . . but, uh . . . the group does its *own* material, doesn't it? That was the most important thing to me. I couldn't envisage doing other people's material unless we had a great repertoire of our own.

'But it was nice,' Steve adds. 'We did manage to tune into each other a bit more than just the surface things – "How many gigs have you got lined up" and all – though I'm sure Bill must have asked me if I wore tight trousers. I didn't feel an immediate sureness, but it was the best thing I'd been offered. I didn't think, "Well, they're successful so I'll join", because they weren't.'

Chris Squire picked up on Steve's apprehension right away, and says it wasn't easy getting Howe to commit himself. 'He wasn't very keen on making positive moves, because he'd had a few experiences with people who'd promised him this and that.'

So there was a bit of arm-twisting involved?

'Yeah, I think that would be one way of putting it.'

In the late spring of 1970, Anderson, Squire, Kaye, Bruford, and Howe shipped themselves off to Devon to get their act together, briefly staying at a cottage called Church Hill, before moving on for a full two months' work at Langley Farm a few miles away.

'Up until then, we hadn't really expected much from each other,' Steve Howe remembers. 'We met, we played, we left, we led our own lives. It was never a case of "See you down at the pub later tonight." But Devon was very much inspired by that whole Dylan/the Band/Woodstock thing, with the idea that it might be easier to get our music together in the country. Like 'Perpetual Change" was definitely a product of the country, though we had the basics for most of our ideas before we got there. In fact, Jon wrote the words to "Perpetual Change" at Church Hill. There was a mist that came into the valley, and it's in that song.'

The problem was that the rest of Yes still saw a lot of mileage left in their old material, and much of the soon-to-be-released *Time And A Word* had never been performed live at all. 'They'd thrown in "Then", or something,' Steve says, 'stuff they already knew. I'd play it, but they'd say, "It doesn't sound right." But of *course* it didn't sound right. Peter had played it originally, and I wasn't Peter Banks.

'But the idea of coming in and playing the full repertoire of what was, to me, a different group really bored me. Being an Aries, I like being there when something's created.'

Howe realized that when it came to formulating material, everyone *was* expected to contribute heavily to the final product. 'I was writing songs, writing guitar pieces, and I saw that I could add something of my own,' he says. 'We all took care of our own areas, and I liked that. Of course, we sometimes got to the point of chaos, the point where nobody knew what they were doing, but then everybody helped each other.'

The addition of Howe helped shove the rest of the group into line. As Jon Anderson says, 'I think all of us started to play and sing a little bit better because we actually had somebody who could take care of his end. Peter Banks was always kind of a sideman, whereas Steve was into interacting with everyone.'

When they weren't fiddling around with a Ouija board or watching the night sky, Yes concentrated on carving out new material: 'Yours Is No Disgrace', 'Starship Trooper', 'I've Seen All Good People', and an epic version of Paul Simon's 'America'.

'We talked about the arrangements for a very long time,' Howe says. 'Arguing. Debating. Experimenting. Arguing. Maybe two more rounds of experimenting, and then a bit more arguing. But when we finally got around to playing it, the energy was unbelievable.'

Mr and Mrs Dartnall, who owned the place and lived a cottage or two down the road, would call in from time to time.

'They let us do the wildest things when we rehearsed,' Steve remembers. 'Chris would test his bass gear for hours and Bill would practise until two or three in the morning, but they didn't mind the noise.'

But Yes still weren't cutting it in the eyes of all concerned. Bill Bruford remembers getting the test pressing for *Time And A Word*, along with a copy of the then-new King Crimson album, *In The Wake Of Poseidon*. 'I thought, "These fucking guys have got it down",' he says. 'I'd seen them a couple of times and I was riveted to the back of the room. They seemed to have all the grace and poise that we didn't. We seemed awkward and angular. They seemed mature, though I'm sure it was a fallacy. I'm sure I was completely wrong.

'But Yes were turning into very much a vocal group with pretty-ish arrangements, whereas King Crimson were much more of an instrumental group. A playing group, with far dirtier minor key arrangements. I've said this before actually, but

Above: Leytonstone, 1970. Steve's first gig with Yes
Following page: Chris Squire, Bill Bruford, Tony Kaye, Jon Anderson, and Steve Howe: Yes 1970

to me, Yes was a major key group, and King Crimson were a minor key group. We always did things in major keys – a sunny, harmony band.'

Even Bruford didn't know he was listening to the writing on the wall. The rift between Yes and manager Roy Flynn had been steadily widening, partially over Peter Banks' departure, but primarily because the group felt trapped in the erratic, small-time gig circuit. In Devon the situation finally exploded when (presumably to recoup his investment) Flynn announced that he was going to keep the advance they'd just received from Atlantic Records – money Yes needed for new equipment and to offset the financial impact of two months off the road.

Nowadays Roy Flynn is reticent about discussing the situation.

'Oh, things were really great at the beginning,' he says. 'Really great. It's just that they started attracting a following, and people started whispering in their ears, you know. It all changed then. They changed, and it wasn't that they were *that* young. They'd been around, they'd been into other things.'

At the time, Yes were on a weekly wage of £20 per man. 'It stopped two weeks after I joined,' Steve Howe says. 'We didn't get any money for a couple of months, and I was living on share bonds. Cashing them in. We even owed money to the people who rented us the farmhouse. I'm sure Chris wouldn't want this to be advertised, but he gave them a cheque once and it bounced. They were more than decent about it, but it was rough. We were basically living on nothing.'

To make matters worse, there was serious trouble brewing on the record company front. Jon Anderson says that the powers-that-be 'weren't going to let us do a third album. Atlantic Records. That was the rumour at the time. So we were flat broke, we owed a lot of money to people, we had no manager, our record company was getting ready to drop us, and the only way we could keep going was by doing gigs.'

Michael Tait was away in Australia. An urgent phone call from the group brought him back to Britain, though he made a brief stopover in the States to drum up support, not knowing that Yes's future was in the balance. 'I went to Atlantic,' he says. 'I told them, "I'm Michael Tait, I'm with Yes, da-da, da-da, da-da" and they said, "What's Yes?"

'I reminded them. "Ah, Yes," they said. "They're that English group on our label, aren't they? Well, very nice. Call in again sometime." I said, "Look, I just came to say that we're alive and we're happening, believe me." They said, "Yes ... uh ... they'll be all right. See you later." Nobody wanted to know, and American agents all thought Yes was a folk act.'

So in the midst of searching for a permanent manager, Tait scraped together enough college and club gigs to keep everyone from starving.

Steve remembers his first gig with the group at a tiny college near Leytonstone. 'After spending months rehearsing, we walked out in front of this group of kids,' he says. 'Yes were still very amateurish, and of course I was too. Chris and I had turned up with a tuning fork, but when we went on stage, we weren't in tune with Tony Kaye at all – which had kind of a disastrous effect on our performance.'

There was no doubt about the music in anyone's mind, but the cash and non-management situation was getting sticky. Tait was still out there tracking down the right man, when a drop-out accountant named Brian Lane unexpectedly strolled into the picture.

'I suppose we believed that even if he wasn't honest, he could do something for us,' Steve Howe says regarding Brian Lane. 'It's a joke really, and he gets very upset when somebody accuses him of being dishonest. But then it's very hard to trust somebody who looks like Brian!'

Lane could pass for an extra in a Clint Eastwood flick – a cattle rustler or a gunslinger – though it's hard to say whether you could spot him as a rock manager if you didn't already know that he *is* one. There's no cigar in evidence. He saves the sharp suit for weddings and bar mitzvahs, as he wanders around the Yes office in a track suit and preoccupied haze, looking like he hasn't slept in a year.

But like all successful managers, Brian's got that slightly devious glint in his eye, a conniving aura that's always angling for a better deal, a heftier percentage, or a discount on the hotel bill. No legs get busted, though Lane could probably talk the shirt off your back and still charge his percentage for the service. And there's something to be said for a man who once went up to the late Groucho Marx on an L.A. street and said, 'I'd like to get your autograph before you die' (to which Groucho replied, 'Better now than later.').

He started out as an accountant, moving into the fringes of the music business during the late sixties, though his managerial experience prior to meeting Yes had been limited to co-managing singer Anita Harris.

In the autumn of 1970, as Yes were wondering where their next meal was coming from, Lane was working for Hemdale (actor David Hemmings' production company) handling another singer named Jack Wild, and serving as an executive producer of sorts on a series of haphazard recording projects for something called Mum and Dad Music, in an attempt to produce an English version of Tamla Motown. He'd also written a song or two.

Yes's entrance into the picture was purely accidental. Brian recalls that he was having his hair cut one day, 'and I was looking for a band to do some session work. This guy named Colin, who was washing my hair, said, "I've got a friend called Chris Squire, and he's got a band called Yes." He said that they were very good, that they'd just sacked their manager, and that they might do the job.'

Yes played the Marquee that night and Brian was in the crowd checking them out. 'The place was choc-a-bloc, wall-to-wall,' he remembers. 'I thought, "My God, this band must make at least 300 quid a night." I did a quick calculation of how much a manager would make out of that and . . . .'

Bruford, Howe, and Squire were offered the session backing a singer called Jonathan Swift, and the pay was £12 each. 'We did the backing track, and they turned the tape over and used it backwards,' Steve Howe says. 'We didn't care. We needed that money.'

When Lane eventually offered to handle Yes, Tait was sent down to investigate. 'Hemdale had a very plush operation,' he says. 'It was all very flashy, but they seemed very nice, spouting figures out to you.'

Compared to some of the characters Tait had been running into, Lane seemed a good bet, and Hemdale had the wherewithal Yes desperately needed to stay afloat. The group deliberated, then agreed, and Brian Lane became Yes's manager. Hemdale provided money, contacts, push, and prestige.

CHAPTER THREE

'IT'S OKAY, I'M WITH THE BAND'

Actually, I always got their names mixed up in the beginning. Couldn't remember who was who.
　　　　　　　RICK WAKEMAN

By the autumn of 1970, Phil Carson had been promoted to European General Manager of Atlantic Records, working under Neshui Ertegun, the man in charge of the company's operations outside of America.

Time And A Word would be a slightly bigger seller than *Yes*. But what little impact the group had was still almost entirely confined to Britain, and Carson admits that Atlantic were seriously considering giving them the axe. The big problem was in America, where as Phil says, 'the second album didn't look like it was going to do any better than the first'.

In the eyes of a company based in the States, Yes seemed to be dead weight who were as good as out of the race – though as Carson continues, 'They *had* started making inroads into Belgium and Switzerland. There was very little interest from America, but Neshui saw that there was European potential. So after talking about the situation for an hour over the phone, we decided to carry on with the group.'

With Brian Lane handling the contractual business, Yes were given the green light to start their next album – the first with the new line-up of Anderson, Squire, Kaye, Bruford, and Howe. 'By recording that album, we got our second wind,' Jon says in retrospect. 'On the first two, we were trying to sort it all out. The third album was the first that meant anything to us in terms of longevity, and that's why we called it *The Yes Album*.'

It's clear that the album marked the emergence of a recognizable Yes style – that wide-screen sonic approach that would prove to be the pivotal point of their music from 1970 onwards. With *The Yes Album*, Yes made the transition from group to *band*. From quaint progressive pop and progressive pop-with-strings, to a style verging on the orchestral – elaborate, multi-layered, and even visual – moving closer to that grandeur and 'bigger feel' Squire and Anderson had unsuccessfully aimed for on *Yes* and *Time And A Word*.

In part, its success was due to Eddie Offord, who'd engineered the second album and been asked back to serve as co-producer with Yes (although, as legend has it, Anderson originally had a pipe-dream of getting Paul McCartney).

Offord had got into engineering through the back door at eighteen, landing a job as all-around Boy Friday at Advision Studios to fill in the gaps between physics classes at university. Over the years, he'd worked his way up from tape operator, to assistant engineer, to engineer – chalking up his first hit single with Julie Driscoll/Brian Auger and the Trinity's 'This Wheel's On Fire' in 1968. Sessions with everyone from Roy Wood to Shirley Bassey followed until Yes, impressed with his work on an otherwise disappointing *Time And A Word*, asked if they could use him again.

But it was no accident, and probably a good indication of Atlantic's continued scepticism regarding the band, that ace house engineer/producer Tom Dowd flew over from America to sit in on the sessions in a more-or-less 'advisory' capacity. Although his actual participation was minimal, Phil Carson credits him with helping to spread the word about Yes back in the States.

Significantly, the album's focus was no longer pieces – taking the initial idea behind 'I See You' and 'No Opportunity . . .' even further. The heavily instrumental mini-epics like 'Yours Is No Disgrace' (clocking in at 9:38) and 'Starship Trooper' (at 9:23), allowed each musician to step out individually, providing an expanded framework for a series of mood changes and climaxes – packed to the rafters with whirlwind solos, neck-twisting tempo changes, layer on layer of shimmering voices, with a helping of Moog for good measure.

It still wasn't 'classical' (Yes were definitely a rock band), but classically *inspired* in the way that individual song fragments were arranged into sweeping movements (e.g. 'Starship Trooper: Life Seeker – Disillusion – Wurm'). Yes weren't too proud to cop a quick riff from somewhere else. With 'Yours Is No Disgrace', Bill Bruford notes that 'the opening riff is a straight rip-off from a cowboy movie. Quite a few of our ideas were lifted from the classics and T.V. shows because Jon is a T.V. addict. If the idea fit, he'd lift it.'

A rhythmically and melodically flashier guitarist, Howe was absolutely wired compared to the low-key, jazzier Peter Banks. He barnstormed a path through *The Yes Album* in such a way that the band seemed to make an extra effort to stretch out, just to keep up with him. He proved throughout 'Yours Is No Disgrace', 'All Good People', and 'Wurm' that he was perfectly capable of cutting just

Above: Tony Kaye – 'We still weren't widely accepted, you know. A lot of people put us down'
Opposite above: *The Yes Album* – Jon Anderson at Advision Studios, autumn 1970
Opposite below: 'Having Steve Howe was a big plus – that somebody with that kind of talent would actually join our band, feel at home, have a lot to say, and express what he had to say' – Jon Anderson

about anyone else in the running.

Then again, his scope extended beyond the realm of the average rock guitarist. 'Your Move' featured a sparkling Portuguese 12-string. Another Anderson song, 'A Venture' (albeit a bit of a filler), glided easy with Howe's mellow, jazzier picking style that echoed traces of Barney Kessel, while a hotshot acoustic ragtime piece called 'Clap' (and *not* 'The Clap') was recorded live at the Lyceum – a celebration tune to mark the birth of Steve's son Dylan.

Lyrically, Jon Anderson's contributions were becoming abstract, hinging more on the way the words sounded than on putting across a unified idea. As Tony Kaye comments, 'Anderson uses words like notes'.

As Jon explains, 'Sometimes I'd just use a series of tantalizingly-sounding words, but sometimes I'd get deeper into meaning and statement. Like in "Starship Trooper", there's a line that says, "Loneliness is a power that we possess to give or take away forever". That's kind of a one-liner, a statement that I like to do now and again. I don't think it's far from the truth if you think about it.

'On the other hand, "Cause it's time, it's time in time with your time" from "Your Move" is a very danceable lyric. It doesn't actually *mean* that much.... But it varies, you know? I've had incredible conversations and get letters from people telling me what they think my words are all about. Who knows? Maybe they're right.'

During the early months of 1971, things *appeared* to be looking up for Yes. In those days, BBC-TV's long-running *Top Of The Pops* included a segment called 'The Album Spot'. Atlantic's Phil Carson, perceiving Yes as the Ultimate Album Band (*The Yes Album*, thanks to all that touring, was number 6 in the British charts) tried to get them on the programme, but to no avail.

Once Yes supporter and *Melody Maker* writer Chris Welch got hold of the news, however, the headline on the music paper's next issue blared IT'S NO TO YES.

The piece sparked off a small avalanche of angry letters and phone calls to the BBC, *TOTP* was forced to relent, and Yes got the chance to perform before millions on their home turf.

Exactly how much impact the programme had on album sales is impossible to gauge, but *The Yes Album* (shortly to be released in America) went to the top spot in the British charts. Gigs were rolling in, bringing in as much as £2,000 a week, work had already started on material for a fourth album, and Yes looked as if they might (after failing in 1969 and 1970) legitimately lay claim to being Britain's Brightest Hope.

Behind the scenes, however, the picture wasn't quite so rosy. 'We were headlining in England, getting the inevitable three or four hundred quid per show, but it would cost us six hundred quid to get there,' Bill Bruford remembers.

'We were permanently in debt, signing away extra percentages to Hemdale in return for these tiny bits of money, just to keep going. We were in off the street, with our bums still sore from all those years of riding around in Transit vans. There was this thick beige carpet in the boardroom. Film stars to and fro. It was us versus Big Business, and we hadn't a clue what we were doing.'

'At the time, I didn't have any money,' Brian Lane says. 'I was working for Hemdale for a flat salary. They financed the operation and their methods of doing business with people certainly weren't *my* way of doing things. They were concerned with making money. Showing an immediate profit. True, they *were* businessmen, but it was a very short-term attitude.'

Meanwhile, Yes continued to haul themselves around the Continent. They'd done a European bus tour with Iron Butterfly and Focus a few months earlier, setting off a mild furore by demanding that English ticket prices be lowered at the gigs. Selling off their publishing rights, they scrounged up the cash to buy the flash P.A. system the Butterfly were using – a system that Michael Tait says 'made Yes sound better than anyone in Europe. It made us sound like the records and really punch through. It was very important to our development. Without it, who knows what would have happened?'

It's no exaggeration to say that America wasn't exactly begging for Yes in 1971. Although *The Yes Album* was out in the States by March, nobody was bending over backwards to extend invitations. Feelers had been put out, and one agent had made an offer, but as Michael Tait says, 'The band would have almost been paying *him* to get on the tour.'

Deciding that the time might be right, Brian Lane flew to New York for a stint of door-to-door selling, and explains that to get to America in those days, 'You had to go to an agent – Premier Talent or A.T.I. – with your tail between your legs and beg.'

When Lane went to the States, *The Yes Album* had just won the *Sounds* poll, and the band had done well in the individual Best Musician categories for the first time. 'I took that poll, reviews, all these bits and pieces,' Brian says. 'I had my sales kit ready, and the time happened to be right. Maybe twelve months before, the time wouldn't have been right. America was ready for a band like that.' Frank Barsalona of Premier Talent agreed to take Yes onto a six week Jethro Tull tour.

So on 24 June 1971, Yes found themselves on stage in Edmonton, Alberta – the first stop on a trek that would head south from Canada, wander down along the West Coast, then swing out across America.

On the average, Yes made $800 per gig, with expenses offset by the $10,000 they'd received from Atlantic, to be deducted from future royalties. With

Opposite: *The Yes Album* – Chris Squire at Advision Studios, autumn 1970
Above: 'We met Big Business here. Big Business had decided we could *be* something' – Bill Bruford

Lane and Tait angling for discounts, Yes roared around in two rented station wagons and stayed in the most economical motels. Michael Tait was working small miracles with whatever crude lighting was available, and for forty-nine shows Yes were on stage for an average of twenty minutes – barely enough time to race through two numbers.

'To be honest, we didn't reach that many people playing to a Jethro Tull audience, but I personally didn't care about that at all,' Steve Howe says. 'Some people said, "Well, you can't have it like you have it back home," but I couldn't relate to that. Success *hadn't* reached us, and we were still paying our dues.'

The battle wasn't totally uphill. In places like New York and Philadelphia, Yes went down extremely well, were offered immediate return engagements in several cities, and as their former publicist Keith Goodwin says, 'You knew the next time back, there'd be a few more people coming by word-of-mouth.'

In the States, radio airplay has always been the crucial factor that determines whether a new act makes it or dies a slow, anonymous death. Although Yes had managed to get themselves onto a fairly prestigious tour, the radio stations took a bit of prodding. Yes music wasn't the most instantly accessible stuff around, and as Phil Rauls, a Tennessean who was then a promo man for Atlantic, explains, 'Disc jockeys liked to put their needles down on a song that was familiar.'

At the time of the first two albums, 'Every Little Thing' and 'Everydays' had had a substantial amount of airplay in the South. 'Those were the only two I could get arrested with,' Rauls says. 'Every record company was unloading umpteen albums by English rock groups, so the market was quite flooded.'

On the road in America that first time, the band were pressed into service to give *The Yes Album* an extra push. 'They were extremely co-operative in going to the radio stations and merchandizing their product,' Rauls remembers. 'They were into being visible: "Hey, I'm Tony Kaye"; "Hey, I'm Bill Bruford"; "Hey, I'm Steve Howe, we're playing in the city tonight, so come out and see us." Three o'clock in the afternoon, two-thirty in the morning. They were always available. We were piling into those station wagons and making the rounds.'

It paid off too. Down in Dallas, *The Yes Album* was suddenly getting regular radio airplay. As Rauls remembers, 'Ahmet Ertegun called and said, 'They're breaking in Dallas! They're breaking in Dallas!' Two or three salesmen and two or three promotion men went in, and it spread from there: Houston, San Antonio, Shreveport, New Orleans, Memphis . . .

While the entire Western Hemisphere still wasn't quite going berserk over Yes, Atlantic woke up and released a single, 'Your Move', on 29 July. It quickly squeezed into *Billboard*'s Hot 100 at a respectable number 99.

In early August, a more worldly Yes arrived back in London, their net profit from nearly two months of touring clocking up to the princely sum of $71.66. Not bad, considering more established bands were returning from the States heavily in the red.

Steve Howe had met his future wife, Jan, by this point. After a short break, Yes were back on the British circuit though things were still unsettled beneath the surface. During the months following *The Yes Album*, a rift had opened up between Tony Kaye and the rest of the band. Although Michael Tait observes that Anderson and Squire were pissed off because Kaye 'only played with one hand. One hand in the air, the other on the keyboard', the ill will was slightly more involved than that. It was down to versatility, and as Anderson explains, 'When the time came where we said, "Let's try the moog and the mellotron," Tony didn't really want to. You can dig that for six months, but then you realize that it's holding you back.'

Chris Squire agrees, but doesn't feel that Kaye 'had *limitations*. To a large degree, he just didn't see any future in moogs, mellotrons, and all. But who's to say whether or not he was, in fact, right? He did sometimes have a ... random approach to playing on stage, but not enough to really remove him, so let's just say that it was a difference in outlook. It was becoming more and more apparent that a change was necessary, if only to get us to that next plateau.'

Kaye himself doesn't quite go along with the theory that he was resistant to change. 'Well, I *did* play moog on *The Yes Album*, didn't I?' he says. 'And I *have* played all those instruments since then, haven't I?'

Another theory is that Kaye just didn't fit in personality-wise. It might not have been totally untrue, though Squire claims that 'It never bothered me personally, but then I didn't share a room with him when we were on tour. Jon was the one who had *that* honour!'

Tony, as everyone admits, liked to have a good time. 'When we went to America, I just wanted to get out and experience things,' Kaye says, 'experience being on the road in a huge, strange place

Above: The Album Spot. Yes on the B.B.C.'s *Top of the Pops*, shortly after the release of *The Yes Album*
Opposite: Tony Kaye's final gig with Yes was at Crystal Palace, London, in September 1971

I didn't know. I was young, and English, and I didn't have a lady back home like the others so, yeah, I didn't see anything wrong with going out and enjoying myself.'

In the late summer Yes played an outdoor gig at Crystal Palace in South London, and with things still left up in the air went into rehearsals for a fourth album.

Several months earlier, the front page of *Melody Maker* had been festooned with a large photo of a young guy with long blond hair. The headline read TOMORROW'S SUPERSTAR? and the accompanying blurb described him as possibly the greatest thing since sliced bread, the Coming of Christ, and the Creation Of The Universe itself. At the time, he was playing keyboards with a band called the Strawbs – ex-folkies gone electric – and his name was Wakeman. Richard C. Wakeman.

By the time Rick Wakeman gets to Phoenix, the colour's slowly returning to his face, though he still lowers himself into a seat near the stage v-e-r-y g-e-n-t-l-y, and praises Divine Providence for small miracles.

'Cor, I didn't have half a hard time last night,' he winces, looking like death. 'I ate three bleedin' plates of refried beans the night before last and the bloody things went through me like a Ferrari. I thought I was going to have to take a bucket on stage with me. I was in *agony*, and Jon kept laughing all during the show. I mean, "Even Siberia goes through the motion" ain't funny when you've spent the whole bloody day sitting in the kahsi.'

Wakeman always gets the last laugh, even when he's the target of his own joke. When he's in good form, he's worth his own TV show – a master of the double-take, the direct insult, and the not-so-masked innuendo of the kind that's been dubbed Schoolboy Humour by some, but leaves 'em laughing almost every time.

As a musician, however, the contrast is clear. Wakeman takes his work pretty seriously, and there's a conspicuous absence of lightning one-liners when half the keyboards break down during the first number, or the mellotron goes out of tune in the heat, or when he's spent an hour overdubbing a mini-moog part and it still sounds awful.

At various points during his career, that sometimes reckless drive to do things on a bigger and better scale than everyone else has both won him critical acclaim and nearly been the ruin of him. That's another example of the contrast in Wakeman's life, and how he's been able to make spectacularly disastrous moves on one level that were simultaneously personal triumphs on another.

Rick was born in Northolt, West London, 18 May 1949, the son of a typical English mum and a builder's clerk father, who once played piano in an army regimental dance band. 'My earliest memory of the piano was probably from when I was about four years old,' Wakeman remembers. 'I saw my dad playing, and of course I wanted to play piano like daddy.'

Rick started on the instrument at the age of seven, trooping over to the neighbourhood music teacher (a certain Mrs Symes) for a weekly course of study that would eventually span thirteen years.

By the age of ten, however, Wakeman was already in the public eye after winning the Southall Music Festival – one of those child prodigy competitions where budding virtuosos are dragged out in front of a school gym full of proud parents, to show that all the money spent on lessons hadn't gone down the drain. Through his pre-teen interpretations of the greats – Bach, Beethoven, Mozart, Haydn, and the boys – he chalked up thirty victories at similar events all over London within three years. 'You name it, and I probably won it,' he says.

In between entering competitions and going to school, he moonlighted as a member of the Boys' Brigade, later staking out a claim on the piano over at the local youth club. At fourteen he joined his first group – a gang of five schoolkids called the Atlantic Blues. With a repertoire predictably based around the chart hits of the day, the Blues rehearsed at a nearby Civil Defence Hall, eventually landing twelve months' worth of weekly gigs at the Neasden Club For The Mentally Handicapped, where Wakeman crashed away on the ivories and sang on tunes like 'Hi-Heel Sneakers'.

Later, on hearing that a local grammar school was offering £40 for a group to play at its annual dance, Rick volunteered the services of Curdled Milk – a band that didn't actually exist, but for £40 Wakeman wasn't going to squabble over technical details. By recruiting kids from around the area (including members of a Salvation Army rock group who also played at that club for the mentally handicapped) Wakeman got the gig and the cash, and his part-time career as a semi-pro musician slowly lifted off the ground.

The weekly piano lessons continued, along with the flow of awards he was still winning at competitions throughout South-East England. In the end he won a hundred certificates and twenty medals and cups.

Rick's cousin, Alan, blew sax and clarinet in a tuxedo-and-Brylcreem dance band called the Concords (later the Concord Quintet), who offered Wakeman £5 a week to join them for their twice-weekly appearances at the Brent Social

Above: Strawbs. Rick Wakeman was only marginally aware of Yes at the time, though the two bands would eventually share a concert bill in Hull
Left: Mr Wakeman
Opposite: '... very glamorous, very hip'

56

Club, up in the Chris Squire territory of Wembley. Rick accepted, and immersed himself in the standard wedding and bar mitzvah repertoire until falling grades at school forced him back down to reality.

Wakeman's sights were set on the Royal College Of Music, but he had to pass the necessary A Level exams before they'd even consider him. Cramming did the trick, and he was in.

Like Tony Kaye, Rick soon realized that he was outgunned by quite a few of his fellow students. As he says, 'All I'd ever wanted to be was a concert pianist, and when I was accepted at the Royal College I was convinced I was the greatest after having won all those awards over the years. Once I started, though, I was brought back down to earth *very* quickly.'

Deflated, he signed up for the teachers' course, as his interest in a classical career began to slip beneath the waves. He began dividing his time between hanging out at the local pubs and at a music shop in South Ealing called the Musical Bargain Centre.

One of the shop's owners, Dave Simms, ran a dance band on the side. Wakeman joined for a short spell playing neighbourhood social clubs, and Simms eventually introduced him to a bass player named Chas Cronk.

Cronk was doing sessions, and managed to line up a few for Rick. Significantly, that led to Wakeman crossing paths with Denny Cordell and Tony Visconti (then two of the most important producers on the scene), and from that point onwards the sessions came rolling in by the truckload. He was content for a while, explaining that even when he was playing a written piece of music, 'They let me add little things which made me different than everybody else. Compared to the classics, there was a lot more freedom in rock music.'

Over the course of four years, Wakeman claims to have played on 2,000 sessions – working for and with the likes of David Bowie, Edison Lighthouse, the Brotherhood of Man, White Plains, T. Rex, Cilla Black, Mary Hopkins, Elton John, Ralph McTell, the Fortunes, Al Stewart, Cat Stevens, Dana, Magna Carta, Black Sabbath, and John Williams – to name but a handful. He also played on a string of British T.V. themes like *The Avengers*, *Simon King*, and *Ask Aspel*.

He rates the mellotron break on Bowie's 'Space Oddity' as his favourite piece of

57

work from that period, and his solo piano on Cat Stevens' 'Morning Has Broken' was of a standard he rarely got the opportunity to use on the average run-of-the-mill session. 'Ninety-nine times out of a hundred, it's automatic,' he explains. 'Like reading a book. You just do it. It helps your technique, and it keeps you going, and it brings in the shekels. It's all useful, but it can stop you from thinking for yourself and forming a musical mind of your own. I didn't realize that until much later.'

Wakeman became a familiar face on the session circuit. He had a workload that often spanned four sessions a day, working eighteen or more hours at a time, and the Royal College was gradually getting swept under the studio carpet.

The faculty weren't amused when Rick started skipping whole blocks of lectures, but he claims they couldn't technically throw him out since he'd kept his grades at an acceptable level. In time, they laid down the law. With no real regrets and little to show for his brush with higher education, Wakeman left the Royal College behind.

He started appearing on Mrs Symes' piano-stool for weekly lessons once again, and donned a monogrammed jacket with the Ronnie Smith Band. With Ashley Holt on vocals, the band alternated between tangos and Top Forty at the Top Rank Ballroom in Watford. Wakeman mastered the act of dodging bar-stools and bottles while perfecting his technique on the Hammond – injecting a touch of showmanship by rocking it back and forth à la Keith Emerson, or raking the keys with an old paint roller.

He was eventually ordered to leave, returned for £24 a week, then was kicked out again for clowning. He promptly joined an Ilford, North-East London, pub band called Spinning Wheel who were pulling a cool £40 a week per man.

A bit earlier on, Rick had done a handful of sessions for Dave Cousins' group, the Strawbs, the result of which surfaced on their early 1970 album, *Dragonfly*. When Wakeman dropped Cousins a line to thank him for including his name on the sleeve, Dave invited him around for a couple of pints.

Like session work, Spinning Wheel gigs were lucrative, but weren't particularly riveting on the creative side. Cousins had vague ideas of expanding the Strawbs' line-up and asked Wakeman to join. He accepted, and married girlfriend Roz Woolford that same week. 'There was no mystery about it,' Rick says. 'I just wanted to get out on the road and start playing. I was beginning to get fed up with studio work.'

But though the Strawbs were, as mentioned earlier, basically a folk act turned electric (with Elizabethan overtones), the somewhat anti-folk Wakeman felt at home with the booze-and-darts lifestyle of the group.

While they were barely making ends meet when Rick signed up, by the time they (Cousins, Wakeman, Tony Hooper, John Ford, and Richard Hudson) played the Queen Elizabeth Hall in July 1970, the critics were picking up on them in force – zeroing in on Wakeman, particularly during his flash classical jazz Keystone Kops piano solo, 'Temperament Of Mind'.

Above: Jon Anderson, 'The Organizer', during the *Fragile* sessions at Advision, September 1971
Opposite: 'Rick came in when we were still rehearsing "Heart Of The Sunrise" in this little rehearsal studio in Shepherd's Market,' Chris Squire says. 'That marked the first real appearance of the mellotron and the moog – *adding* the flavour of those instruments to a piece we'd basically already worked out'

The Times called him 'a different sort of hero', *Melody Maker* told its readers to 'watch out for Rick Wakeman', while the *International Times* went so far as to call him 'a genius'. By the time a live album from that gig hit the shops under the title of *Just A Collection Of Antiques And Curios*, the Wakeman Visage had already appeared on that *Melody Maker* front page. Rick with the Strawbs were on their way up the access ramp to the Big Time.

By the time Wakeman went into the studio with the Strawbs to record *From The Witchwood*, he was well on his way to becoming an ex-Strawb. Part of the trouble centred on his mild aversion to folk music (despite the fact that it was gassed up with electricity), though he was also beginning to branch out as a composer. He'd written and performed two numbers, 'Coat Of Many Colours' and 'Whirlwind', for the Liz Taylor/Michael Caine flick *Zee And Co.*, and was starting to dabble in songwriting.

Dave Cousins wasn't overly impressed with any of Rick's tunes, and since the Strawbs were Cousins' band, those songs didn't get aired in the end.

'We'd just reached stagnation point, I think.' Rick says. 'We'd gone as far as we could go with that particular combination of people. Our social life with each other became more important than the music, and I felt that if I left, it would be the best for all concerned. I was too bogged down with my own ideas. I don't want to sound egotistical, but I suppose the Strawbs just weren't enough of a musical challenge any more. Because of the way the band was run, I knew there was no place for those ideas.'

Over in the Yes camp, the band were going through the motions of rehearsing for another album – originally planned as a double set, with one studio and one live disc featuring unrecorded stage numbers like Squire's 'It's Love' and Paul Simon's 'America'.

Although Tony Kaye was largely unaware that the scenery was being shifted around behind him, his number was definitely up. But as Bill Bruford remembers it, 'There was definitely this vibe of "Well, half a minute. Before we kick him out, who can we replace him with that's better? That guy in the Strawbs will do. He's good. He was on the front page of *Melody Maker* a while back".'

Intrigued by the size of that headline, Chris Squire got Wakeman's number through Brian Lane, who had often used the keyboard player on those Mum and Dad sessions a few years earlier.

'I'd been doing three sessions a day on average,' Rick remembers. 'That's fifteen a week, and I was making about four or five hundred quid that way. I lived in Harrow then. I'd get up at about eight in the morning, get into town for the first session around ten, and not get home until one the next morning.

'Anyway, I'd done about four sessions that day – started at eight in the morning and didn't finish until three the following morning. I got back home and was *really* tired, and I'd just fallen into bed when the telephone rang. Roz picked it up, and I could hear her telling whoever it was that I'd just come in and that I was really tired. I got hold of the phone and this voice says, "Oh . . . hello . . . It's Chris Squire from Yes and . . . er . . . we've just come back from America and we're thinking about having a change of personnel in our band. I was wondering if you'd be interested?" I said, "Do you know what time it is?" and Chris said, "Uh . . . yeah . . . it's half past three."'

Informing Mr Squire in no uncertain terms that he wasn't interested, Wakeman slammed the phone down. Brian Lane subsequently had better luck, and a meeting was arranged at a Mayfair pub.

As Yes's unofficial Personnel Director, Squire cruised over to Rick's house beforehand to give him the cautious once-over, 'and found him to be . . . Rick Wakeman. Sort of an odd personality. Different – and I haven't said this on many occasions – but "aloof and awkward to get to know". Interested in cars.

59

Didn't seem like he was very interested in music, but seemed to be able to do it while he was thinking about who was going to win at the dog races that night. In fact, he had the typical session-man's attitude, an "I'll play this part while reading the evening paper" sort of thing. He knew he was good.'

Off-hand, that doesn't sound like the kind of guy a cautious and conscientious Yes would be willing to take a gamble on.

'Well, you don't always know what you want, though he was the only person I considered,' Chris says. 'Yes were on the rise, Rick was as well, and we had an idea that the marriage would appeal to him. I'd never met him and knew very little about him, but having a name in those days meant a lot. I mean, *Melody Maker* was the bible. The press were saying good things about him, but usually there's some reason for saying it, even if not all the journalists know quite *why* everyone else is saying it.

'I thought this was the sort of man we needed to compete with the Keith Emersons of this world. Later, of course, one realized that a lot of it was, to a certain degree, from being drinking partners with most of the press, but there's no smoke without fire.'

So Yes pulled what Steve Howe calls 'a slight sneaky on Tony Kaye' and secretly met with Wakeman, who was technically still a Strawb, but fading fast. He initially turned Yes down, but by offering better prospects than the £35 a week he was getting from Dave Cousins, the band tipped the balance in their favour.

'We played together, and it was obvious that we were all very compatible,' Steve remembers. 'But then he did a build-up on us. He said, "Actually, when I play on stage, I use a paint roller on the keys, and I rock the organ up and down like *this*." He said some really weird show-bizzy things, even though we obviously weren't show-bizzy at all. I think he was trying to impress us and instil some confidence in us that not only could he play, but he was a good performer on stage. We all just kind of glanced at each other and thought, "What did he say? Paint rollers?"

Rick's overall aura was, to Bill Bruford anyway, 'very glamorous, very hip. There was that early picture of him leaning up against a wall in a boiler suit, and that was a fine image. He looked on top of it.

He wasn't drinking that much. Obviously an up-and-coming young guy. He played moog, and mellotron, and had a burning organ sound. He played it correctly. It cut.'

Wakeman passed the audition, and it was curtains for Tony Kaye – who unfortunately wasn't quite sure what hit him. 'I was under a tremendous hangover from some party the night before, and my girlfriend let Chris and Jon into the apartment,' Tony recalls. 'They came marching in, and I was like *this*, buried underneath the covers and wondering what the fuck was going on. That's when they let me have it. That's when they dropped the bombshell. It was over. It was ironic too, because they'd found me in bed in '68, and they left me in bed in '71.'

Officially, it was Anderson who did all the talking, and as Chris Squire admits, 'Jon delivered most of the . . . he was the verbal hit-man. But the basic idea to replace Clive with Peter, Peter with Steve, and Tony with Rick was essentially mine.'

Above: 'The fish': 'I read a clipping in one of these scrapbooks where I'd said, at the time, that owing to the pressure and the necessity of getting another album out quickly, we'd been rushed into the studio and had to work overtime and separately to meet our obligations. That's what I said at the time. Maybe it was true' – Chris Squire
Opposite: Bill Bruford at Advision. 'If Yes had designed a building, it would have been the most extraordinary kind of horrific Gothic/Edwardian/Modern/Medieval/pseudo-pastiche.
But we weren't. We were designing music'
Overleaf: 'They used to come up with some amazing requests: "Could you go out and get me a piece of chocolate cake?" I mean, *where* do you find a piece of chocolate cake in London at four a.m.?' – Michael Tait

Kaye concedes that the visit wasn't totally unexpected, 'but I didn't want to leave because I know how things change, and the next day it could have all blown over. But they were making it impossible for me to play, though not by anything apart from bad vibes and knowing I wasn't wanted. I was getting paranoid anyway, and if they'd left it up to me, I would have left eventually.'

Meanwhile, Rick Wakeman (who would remain signed to A&M as a solo artiste) was eyeing the three weeks' worth of sessions he'd already agreed to do, and trying to figure out who was Chris and who was Jon. Studio time was already booked, and the golden handshake was barely twenty-four hours old when he was hustled into Advision Studios to start work on the next Yes album.

'The title was no big thing,' Michael Tait says in reference to the band's fourth album. 'Some press guy rang up Brian Lane and said, "What are you calling the new Yes album?" Brian didn't know. Nobody had even thought of a name. He was looking at some photos from that Crystal Palace gig, saw the monitors at the front of the stage and, like all equipment, they had "Fragile" stamped on the back. So that's what he told the guy: *Fragile*.'

Chris Squire might have been slightly wary of Rick Wakeman's studio tan, but it's doubtful if anyone but a seasoned session man could have slotted into Yes and come up with the goods at such short notice.

Yes were a different band now that America had knocked them into shape. The clumsiness, hesitancy, and penchant for overkill had vanished. If *The Yes Album* was the work of a band who were rapidly coming to grips with the studio environment, *Fragile* proved (with Eddie Offord's help) that they'd pretty near mastered it.

The basic model for half the material had been worked out before Wakeman's arrival. When Rick joined, the existing material was overhauled and given a fresh paint job to accommodate his synthesizer and mellotron. But while Yes finally had the means to produce the colour and range they'd been looking for, Rick obviously didn't know their capabilities, they didn't know his, and the five were in the studio long before anyone had figured out the best way to use this new palette.

Then again, that aloofness within the band took some getting used to. 'It was hard,' Rick says. 'When you've got four people who've kind of grown up together, or at least been working together for a while, and they've started to create something their own way . . . I couldn't understand Jon at all, and he couldn't understand me.

'It took a long time. I couldn't believe that they weren't that interested in doing solos – or at least the kind of solos other bands played. I'd sit there thinking, "They can't arrange everything." But you can. And they did. Still, it was easy to get into the music, but very difficult to feel like I was part of the band, just because of the way they were.'

So Wakeman's role was more that of a session man on his first Yes album. Suggestions were made. Rick modified those suggestions and filled in the gaps. As he says, his complete musical integration into the band would take the better part of a year to complete – although Eddie Offord observes that Wakeman 'was nervous in his own way. He even tried a little too hard to please everyone.'

The new line-up took a bit of getting used to on both sides. As Steve Howe explains, 'In some ways, Tony Kaye gave my position in the group a very uncluttered, open field to work in. When Rick joined, I was excited that more things could happen. There *was* more confusion in trying to arrange the music, but more possibilities, so we stretched it further.'

If Yes's earlier music had copped some of its flavour from the Fab Sixties and the dying embers of Psychedelia, *Fragile* was a definite up-market move into what would come to be known as more *cosmic* territory. While the tag would eventually drag the band down like cement overshoes, it's a fair way to sum up – musically, lyrically, and conceptually – the sort of semi-esoteric, highly visual, ultra-progressive streak they were heading into.

Fragile solidifed the band's image, and that cosmic aura was further clarified by what was to be the first of many Yes album sleeves by artist Roger Dean. Concentrating on architecture and furniture design, Dean had studied at the Royal and Canterbury Schools of Art. In 1968, while designing the seating for Upstairs at Ronnie's (part of Ronnie Scott's club in Soho), he was asked to do an album sleeve for the Gun (the same outfit Anderson had briefly belonged to), which inevitably led to more work in that line – probably best typified by the murderous-looking flying elephants concocted for a series of Osibisa sleeves.

Roger and Yes crossed paths early in 1971, and the result was a striking sleeve for *Fragile* – heavily steeped in fantasy and science fiction, which seemed to be a tailor-made visual representation of the band's music.

Labels like 'symphonic rock' began cropping up in the music press around the time of *The Yes Album*, but *Fragile* wasn't quite the next station along that route. Granted, it expanded on the most striking facets of the Yes sound developed over the course of three albums: the dense vocal harmonies; the attention to texture, melody, and mood; the flair for longer and longer pieces of music, and the overall emphasis on *power* rather than bone-crushing heaviness.

But unlike its predecessors, *Fragile* was more of a workshop – its nine tracks more like individual experiments – both to explore the different avenues open to each musician, and to get a clearer idea of what would (and wouldn't) work.

If *commercial* was still a dirty word in the early seventies, Steve and Jon's 'Roundabout' was a fluke, managing to score full marks in the popularity stakes, while remaining true to Yes's new-found status as *Grand Fromages* of the British progressive rock scene. From Howe's shimmering Spanish guitar intro, to Squire's galloping brontosaurian bass, to Wakeman's blazing Hammond solo, to some of Anderson's trickiest wordplay yet, 'Roundabout' *moved* – a masterpiece of hotshot musical engineering.

'Heart Of The Sunrise', on the other hand, was the proverbial oil-painting – an out and out epic, and the longest track Yes had attempted up to that time. Broken down into its components, what was actually going on was often surprisingly spare. But each man's choice of notes, and the careful interweaving and juxtaposing of those notes, created not a high-voltage version of the London Symphony Orchestra but a wide-screen orchestral effect nonetheless.

To a less extravagant extent, the other two band tracks were just as impressive, although 'Long Distance Runaround' and, particularly, the underrated 'South Side Of The Sky' veered more towards out-and-out rock – the threatening feel of the latter underscored by Howe's clanking, sheet-metal guitar work.

The remaining groove space went to five solo spots: Rick's elegant 'Cans And Brahms', Steve's tranquil 'Mood For A Day', Bill's hyper 'Five Per Cent For Nothing', Jon's airy 'We Have Heaven', and Chris's murky, neo-barbarian 'the fish' – which was also the nickname the band had bestowed on Squire because of his marathon stints in the bath.

'The title for "the fish" is one that I got,' Michael Tait remembers. 'Jon rang me up at ten o'clock one night from Advision and said, "I want the name of a prehistoric fish in eight syllables. Call me back in half an hour." I found *Schindleria Praematurus* in the *Guiness Book Of Records*. It's the smallest fish in the world, and by stretching it a bit they made the name fit.'

Tait was also responsible for the title of Bruford's piece. 'He was going to call it "Suddenly It's Wednesday", and I thought "What the hell is that?"' Michael says. 'At the time, we'd just gotten rid of Roy Flynn once and for all, and the deal we'd done was to give him five per cent. So I said, "Right, that's five per cent for nothing." Bill hated Jon for that, because he thought Jon thought it up.'

With the legalities of Wakeman's presence still not totally ironed out, 'Cans And Brahms' was a compromise. Rick planned and partially recorded one of his own compositions, 'Handle With Care', for the album, but found it couldn't be used. 'I was still under various publishing contracts, so I couldn't do anything on my own, which is what I really wanted to do,' he says. 'There was a lot of trouble with *Fragile* over contracts and things.'

Although Squire claims that the solo tracks were partially done to save time and economize on studio expenses, the initial idea came from Bruford. 'There was this endless discussion about how this band could be used,' Bill says. 'Rehearsals were a constant case of, "All right Jon, you've got your point of view, I've got mine, and Chris has his." I felt we could use all five musicians differently.

'So I said – brightly – "Why don't we do some individual things, whereby we all use the group for our own musical fantasy? I'll be director, conductor, and maestro for the day, then you do your track, and so on." That was my plan, but it backfired hopelessly because nobody used the group.'

The five tracks did showcase facets of Yes that might have otherwise been watered down or buried beneath the five-way compromise of the average band track. As Jon Anderson says, 'This group isn't one person shining out saying, "Everybody's getting off on what I do, so the rest of you had better keep up with me." It's a fight sometimes for everyone to get through, but then *everybody* has to shine.'

Those heavily overdubbed and multi-tracked solo pieces crystallized what Yes were aiming to be: a highly sophisticated studio-orientated band, who could take the bare bones of the simplest idea or melody and build it up to colossal proportions, using the studio itself as a musical instrument in its own right.

Steve Howe recalls that 'Roundabout' 'was the first time I'd transposed a bit of guitar from one end of the tape to the other. There are two acoustic phrases in that song, and I took a couple of notes from the first and dropped them in on the second. Tricks like that are easy now, but that was pretty early on, and we were just getting into experimenting.'

Yes were miles from being able to do it on their own, however. That working partnership with Eddie Offord had become a crucial catalyst to the band's growth. 'It was a good, creative, and productive time,' Chris Squire reflects. 'I mean, on "Roundabout", I'd written that bass line at some earlier time . . . in my own inimitable style! Eddie picked up on it, and without saying too much about it, understood how to record that sound and possibly put it across in a stronger way than I was even playing it.

'He knew a lot about studio techniques, and I personally learned more from him about studios and the ideas behind them than I ever will from anyone again. There were a lot of unspoken things that worked because he grasped what we were trying to do.'

Although as Steve Howe adds, 'There were times when we'd ask the impossible.'

But all Rick Wakeman had seen since joining Yes was the inside of Advision Studios. A month-long British tour was pencilled in for October 1971, and Yes split for a week of rehearsals at South Molton, Devon – figuring that the idyllic atmosphere that worked so well when Howe joined was bound to be the same the second time around.

It didn't turn out that way. 'We were trying to relive the past, and you can't,' Chris Squire says. 'When you're trying to relive a memory, it never comes out quite the same. We'd only been down there a year or so before, but a lot can happen in a year. That was a very vague time. It ended up with half the group staying in one place and . . . well . . . there wasn't the same community spirit any more.'

Where did it go?

Chris shrugs. 'By then, we'd done an American tour. America has this nasty habit of . . . changing things.'

63

CHAPTER FOUR

AMERICA

Look how lucky you are. Would you rather work in an office? Or maybe at some car plant, ten to six, five days a week, and get your three weeks' vacation once a year?
BRIAN LANE

At least I'd get three weeks.
CHRIS SQUIRE

Things were happening when Yes flew back to the States for their second tour in November 1971. *The Yes Album* was just outside the American Top Forty and moving up fast, 'Your Move' was doing just as well in the singles charts, and the band were able to ask for (and get) double the money per gig they'd averaged four months earlier.

While Yes opened the show for bands like Procol Harum and King Crimson here and there, most of their time was spent third on the bill to Ten Years After and the J. Geils Band.

'That second tour was gruelling – like an endurance test,' Steve Howe remembers. 'All the cushions seems to have been taken away. I didn't feel any competition with any group we ever played with, really. The only time one can really start feeling the pinch is when you're playing with super musicians like John McLaughlin – which we did later on. Then you worry, "Is our music really good enough to stand up against theirs?" as opposed to thinking, "Well, we're going to knock the shit out of Ten Years After anyway." '

Wakeman, of course, was not only trying to come to terms with being on the road with a strange band in a strange land, but was trying to unravel the mysteries of his newly-acquired stack of keyboards (five in all) that kept conking out at the most inopportune moments.

'I never got the chance to work with the stuff properly before we went on that tour,' Wakeman explains. 'Like the moog. I'd have an hour or two before the show, and I'd be sitting in my hotel room still learning how to work the instrument. When we moved the mellotron about, the octaves went out. The tape frame would bend because the instrument just wasn't built for travelling. It wouldn't hold up on the road, and it was a bloody disaster for a year until we sorted it out.'

Yes landed in England in time for Christmas, but it was back to the slog by the second week of January 1972 – two first-class gigs at London's Rainbow Theatre, followed by a string of shows in Belgium and Holland, then straight back to the States in February for a third coast-to-coast tour, primarily as the show opener for Black Sabbath.

During their two-month absence, *Fragile* had been released to critical acclaim in Britain. Although *The Yes Album* had levelled off at number 34 in

On the road in America, late 1971

America's *Record World*, the new one was leaping up the charts thirty spaces at a time. 'When we came back to England from the previous American tour in December, *The Yes Album* was doing pretty well, but it had gone about as far as it was going to go,' Rick Wakeman says. 'We thought that *Fragile* would need promoting when we got back over there, but by the time we arrived it was number 4 in the charts, and it had taken three weeks to get there. If I remember right, the weekly progression was 151, 51, then straight up to 4.'

Yes weren't the band most likely to succeed any more, but a hot commodity in the rock market-place. Aware that they had a genuine reputation to live up to, the push to get things right on stage was intensified to the point where, even after a good show, they'd be holed up in the dressing room, verbally cutting each other to ribbons for making relatively minor mistakes. 'Some of those backstage dramas were unbelievable,' Rick Wakeman remembers. 'Absolutely unreal. There'd be nights when people wouldn't be arguing over the concert we'd just played, but over something that had happened the night *before*.'

If any of the individual members of the band felt confident that they'd finally made it, that self-assuredness was purely a personal matter. 'About the first and only time I felt that with the band was sitting in a limousine going to the gig in New York,' Bill Bruford says. 'Somebody said the album was number 4 in the American charts, and I thought it was fucking incredible.

65

'Until then, I'd been waffling around. I had no idea what a chart was, or if it mattered whether or not we were in it. But then suddenly it was Andy Williams, Frank Sinatra, Barbra Streisand, *and* Yes. I thought, "Now this is definitely a whole bag of bananas. We're not piddling around any more."

'But with the success of *Fragile*, there was an air of having robbed a bank, in a way,' Bruford continues. 'A feeling that we'd cracked it. There was a lot of self-congratulating going on, as I remember, which I felt was a bit dangerous. I don't point the finger at anybody – I think it's perfectly natural – but then I've never wanted to be a rock star. I've never stood in front of a mirror practising my poses with an electric guitar.

'I mean, I *did* have this feeling of being unhappy in the group, though I didn't know why. I was always nervous that I wouldn't come up with enough goods by Jon's standards, but I didn't have any thought of leaving. There *was* a general feeling that we were going to ride high now, though, and I remember not liking it.'

The months that followed *Fragile* were ones of considerable change for the band. Yes were full-blown stars in England, and only a rung or two lower on the ladder in America. Financial worries were dwindling, and as Steve Howe says, 'It was a time when the people in this band were bettering themselves. Not by getting a new car, but partly through Eddie Offord's influence, which was "be healthy and be fit".'

Offord was a dyed-in-the-wool vegetarian. He didn't touch alcohol, wasn't averse to physical exercise that called for a bit more than adjusting faders on a recording desk, and generally subscribed to the not-illogical theory of 'You Are What You Eat'. To Eddie, monosodium glutamate was a four-letter word. Steve Howe, in particular, was inspired.

'I suddenly felt that I wanted to participate in all that, rather than just be alive,' Steve explains. 'Music was fine, but I had an equally worthwhile interest now, which was looking after myself. Most of the band began to feel the same way, and there was a new lease of life in the group at that time. You could see something was happening. America was happening. The album was happening. *New things* were happening, and the idea of trying to take care of ourselves a little better tied in with that.'

Rick stuck to his sausages and pints, but the rest of the band jumped into the 'no meat/no booze/read label before eating' way of life – shoes and all. Unfortunately, the off-stage, 'part of the furniture' personality Yes had projected for four years was causing problems in journalistic circles.

As Keith Goodwin says, 'Everyone assumed that since Yes led the good life, it was therefore a clean-living, all English-Rose band. This sort of thing gets around, and the goody-goody image stuck, which was a terrible fallacy. A load of crap.'

That conscious effort towards even some tiny degree of self-improvement was going on in more that one area. Bill Bruford, for example, was beginning to write music. 'Jon was always after me to write, for which I'm grateful,' he says. 'He saw no reason at all why the

'I think they knew that once they'd played those early dates in America, it was going to happen worldwide. I don't think Jon ever harboured any doubts that Yes would be huge' – former Yes publicist Keith Goodwin

drummer shouldn't have just as good ideas as the next guy.'

Anderson himself was beginning to stretch out – listening, reading, and picking up new concepts in the classic self-taught manner – taking the trouble to look into things he'd never had time for with the Warriors and during the early growth years of Yes. But then, Michael Tait feels that Jon 'went through a confused space for a couple of years until he could assimilate all this information, and work out what was right, what was wrong, what suited him, and what didn't.'

Jon's sparks of inspiration were being triggered off from all kinds of sources. 'Everything from Marvel Comics, to science fiction, to *Moby Dick*,' Anderson says. 'Then I started picking up books that were talking about *other* things. Hermann Hesse and all. People obviously made suggestions here and there, "Here, try this book."'

On those first American tours, Anderson constantly listened to classical music on his cassette machine, and developed a taste for Mozart, Stravinsky, and particularly Sibelius, 'who's my hero!' he says. 'I mean, Sibelius and Stravinsky were the *kings* of early twentieth-century music. Sibelius encompassed what it really was to have an orchestral feel without feeling any tempo or structure, and right at the other extreme, Stravinsky was composing structures that orchestras had never attempted to do. Sibelius always underplayed the melody, whereas Stravinsky injected melody.

'I think they were the motivation for the tempo changes and the sometimes schizoid rhythmic passages in Yes music. I mean, "Heart Of The Sunrise" probably contained both extremes. We have a very, very simple song in form. I'm singing about love. Love comes, it arrives, and you follow that desire, if you like. It's a physical, mental, and spiritual collaboration of desires, and we joined that with a big orchestral sound. Classical piano, rock rhythms, a slight jazz/avant-garde feel. The Stravinsky influence, I suppose. So that song, and a lot of our music, is a combination of the influence of those two composers.'

During that spring of 1972, *Fragile* remained in the American Top Five for weeks. To nail the sceptics, Atlantic whipped out a shortened version of 'Roundabout' – hacking the tune to pieces in the process, though it did the trick.

'Musically, it was an abortion,' Chris Squire comments. 'Promotion-wise, it worked. It didn't sell *that* many copies, but it got a fantastic amount of airplay.'

By April, the single had reached the outer borders of the American Top Twenty, though Jon Anderson sums up its success as 'a happy surprise, just the icing on the top, because we were doing great anyway'. Although Yes probably

67

could have used a rest, they gathered at the Billings School of Dance in Shepherd's Bush, West London, ('a poxy place with mirrors down the sides,' according to Bill Bruford), to argue over a new batch of ideas for another album.

For Bill Bruford, life with Yes when they were in the studio was a heavy cross to bear. 'I've always kind of been the guy in the back who wants to get on with it and not waste any time, and there was always somebody in the group consuming vast amounts of time and money,' he says. '*Close To The Edge* took a fuck of a long time to record. All those late-night sessions at Advision, leaving at dawn and things. I got bored to tears sometimes.

'I'm a daytime person, and I'd sleep on the studio couch from two until four in the morning, wake up and say, 'How's it going, Chris?' – and he'd *still* be doing the same fucking thing. Or to my ears anyway. He'd have altered the tone on the bass half-a-gnat's, or strung two notes together. It sounded so good at the end, but it used to drive me crazy.

'But that album is absolutely my favourite. No doubt about it. To me, everything I did with the group was leading up to *Close To The Edge*.'

For that matter, everything *everybody* had done over the previous four years had been setting the stage for *Close To The Edge*. That enormous feeling of space and power they'd been chasing was suddenly there. Wakeman had found his creative niche, Anderson's vocals were mature and sure, and the band as a whole positively roared.

Copping a few impressions from those Hermann Hesse books (notably *Siddhartha*), Jon Anderson had collaborated with Steve Howe on the title track, 'a bit of hotel-room singing and playing,' that was fleshed out, stretched in twenty directions, divided into sweeping movements, and wound up sprawling across the entire first side of the album – a thundering, sonic impression of Chartres Cathedral on Easter Sunday morning.

The track's chorus, 'Close to the edge, down by a river . . . ', was lifted from a song of the same name Steve Howe had put together a few years earlier, 'partially about the longest day of the year', Howe says. 'When Jon and I got together to write, we'd each contribute different parts, and that chorus fit best with Jon's song, "Total Mass Retain".'

So there's another, radically different 'Close To The Edge' buried somewhere in Steve's at-home tapes and notebooks, 'and Jon's probably got another song stored away called "Total Mass Retain",' he adds. 'In fact, I finished up another

Above: *Close To The Edge*. 'Precision is ... what can I say? If you're a tightrope walker or a trapeze artist, you can't afford to be without it. Being at the top of the rock and roll tree *is* rather like being a trapeze artist' – Chris Squire
Opposite: New York, late winter 1972: Squire, manager Brian Lane, Anderson, Atlantic Records' boss Ahmet Ertegan, Howe, Wakeman, Atlantic's Jerry Greenberg, and Bruford

song, and the original middle eight was also used in "Close To The Edge". The " ... in her white lace ... " section. It was a sequence I'd had for a long time, though in the song I'd written, I'd used it in a different key. But when you're writing for Yes, the whole integrity of holding on to things disappears. If the lick fits, you use it.'

By that stage, the communal effort was a matter of course, though it caused confusion when the time came to list individual credits on the label. 'It was often a complete guess, really,' Bill Bruford says. 'What you lose on "Sweetness" you gain on "Roundabout". I may have contributed something to "South Side Of The Sky" which I wasn't credited for, but ... it's very vague.'

'And You and I' also pulled together bits and pieces from all over the place, but in contrast to the near-religious spectacle of 'Close To The Edge', its feel was more pastoral. Cloudier. Again etched into movements, underscored by Howe's resonant, brooding 12-string and Wakeman's ethereal, deep-sea mellotron.

Rick Wakeman was slowly beginning to come to grips with Jon Anderson, though he admits that their working partnership was still a bit tight around the collar. Wakeman, accustomed to dealing with highly trained producers and arrangers, didn't find taking cues from the untutored Anderson an easy task.

'There were a lot of musical disagreements,' Rick says. 'But after Jon and I sat down to talk about our problem, we found that we were able to relate to each other with some consistency. He *still* puzzled me, but once we began talking, things started to work out a lot more smoothly.'

If 'And You and I' was an ace example of the cosmic Yes, and 'Close To The Edge' a master stroke in terms of structure, soaring dynamics, and the band's knack for welding fragments together, then 'Siberian Khatru' (*khatru* is supposedly a Yemeni word, roughly meaning 'as you wish') won the Doomsday Stakes hands down.

If, as Bruford feels, Yes had always fancied themselves as a sunny, harmony band, the ominous hurricane velocity of 'Khatru' was a major departure. It was bleak and downright sinister – a roaring onslaught of chilling, atonal mellotron, blazing guitar and drums, and a relentless bass line.

Anderson was concentrating on the pure sound and visual patterns of his words here, exploring the possibilities of open-ended free verse. In the end, 'Siberian Khatru' ranked among the most intense nine minutes and fifty seconds the band would ever come up with – a powerful finale for the album, that boded well for the future. Yes knew it too, though during those long evenings at Advision Studios, a metaphorical rope-ladder was slowly being lowered from an upstairs window, and no one noticed that Bill Bruford had left the room.

For Yes, Bruford's exit was like getting run down by a bus. Nobody saw it coming.

From Bruford's point of view, the move was a long time coming. He'd run out of aces, and it was time to head for the door. '*Close To The Edge* was just being mixed, and I was thinking about how I didn't want to do that again – three months in the studio,' he says. 'I had the feeling that I'd done my bit with the band. I couldn't improve on *Close To The Edge*.

'I didn't *have* a better idea, and it goes back to this rehearsal thing of constantly improving your playing to stay on Jon's good side. They wanted me to astound them all the time, which I could seldom do, even though that's a great place for a drummer to be in: "So long as it's interesting and we've all never heard it before, you can do it, Bill."

'But I didn't have anything to top that, and I wasn't going to sit in a rehearsal room anymore, getting nervous because I might not come up to scratch.'

Along came Robert Fripp with the suggestion that he join King Crimson. 'His phrase was, "I think you're ready to play with King Crimson now," ' Bill says. 'It wasn't so much that he made me leave Yes. I was about to leave anyway, but he was there to catch me when I fell.'

The fact that Yes were beginning to rake in the big bucks didn't hold much sway. 'People find this very silly, but I'm not very keen on the glory bit,' Bruford continues. 'That's not why I was in Yes. But I do see myself as having very few formative years in which to get a good idea together on my instrument. Any time you spend in rock bands not progressing is wasted. I see it as a matter of survival. You can't afford to hang around.

'I want to scratch this rumour that it was artistic martyrdom. It wasn't. I wanted to play more instrumental music. I didn't want to do these vocal harmonies and this business with the bass – you know, with Chris spending half the day just tuning it.'

Yes had already gone through two major personnel changes in four years, but Bruford was the first to split under his own steam – a blow Anderson seemed to take personally.

'Bill was the hardest change to take,' Jon explains. 'No. Not the change. Just the fact that Bill wanted to leave. We didn't know a thing, though in fact, only two days before he left, I woke up and said to Jenny, "I think Bill's going to leave." I had no idea, I just felt something.'

Dream or no dream, 'It hit me like a ton of bricks. I couldn't believe it, because after *Fragile* and *Close To The Edge*, I thought, "Here we are at last." I couldn't change his mind though. I really tried very hard. It seemed crazy. There was something that he wasn't getting out of the band, and I said, "Put it in if it's not there. I'll try if you will, but don't leave."

To Bill, who'd always operated on the premise that he was just as expendable as Clive Bailey, Tony O'Riley, Peter Banks, or Tony Kaye, the reaction came as a surprise. 'I was really sorry to upset Jon, but I think he understands that I wasn't personal,' he says. 'It wasn't the group's fault in any real way. It was my particular state of development. I'll say this, though – leaving Yes is the most famous thing I've ever done.'

With three back-to-back American tours looming, not to mention a stack of European gigs, Bruford offered to hang on until the end of the year. Jon politely refused. 'I told Bill, "If you're leaving, you can't really go on tour with us, because we'd have it in the back of our heads that you're going to move on."'

Besides, Anderson and Squire already had a good idea of who was going to be offered the job. The guy's name was Alan White, he was a friend of Eddie Offord, and like Rick Wakeman he'd played on more sessions that even he could remember.

It's getting to the point where Alan White thinks twice before opening his mouth. A cool drink at the hotel bar, a few exchanged pleasantries with whoever's standing, sitting, or face-down-on-the-carpet next to him, and suddenly it's, 'You're *English*? *Really*? You're kiddin'! Gee, ya sound like ya come from *L.A.*, or somethin'.'

Accusations that he's a Californian rightly get up his nose. Alan's been spending a lot of time at the Malibu house he shares with his lady, Rory Flynn, but he's what they call a Northern lad – even more Northern than Jon Anderson, which is saying quite a bit.

But that accent, the surfer's build, and the easy-going West Coast vibe are deceiving. Alan knows exactly what's going on, though in a business full of shell-shocked drummers, he's not the type to start punching waiters in Chinese restaurants. No hassling. Very little arguing. A bottle of beer, a pool table, a bit of hot sun, and he's content. A handball court, a shooting range, or two laps around the block, and he comes alive. Rent him a fast car or book him into a hotel with a gym, and he's in seventh heaven.

As a musician, he's lived up to the classic line by having done more in fifteen years than most will in a lifetime, though the trail leading to Yes and Malibu was a long one, starting out in the grey environs of Durham, up Newcastle way, where Alan was born on 14 June 1949.

'There was some industry up there, but it was a big mining area,' Alan

Above: Bill Bruford
Opposite: Anderson, Howe, Eddie Offord, and Squire at Advision for *Close To The Edge*. As Bill Bruford recalls, 'We were in there for a long time. It felt like forever'

explains, adding that his father was a clerk, 'and drove lorries, buses, and things like that. He did a lot of different jobs. Storekeeper. That kind of thing.'

His father (like his grandfather) played piano, and with an uncle who played drums, music was in the family from the start. Alan was already taking piano lessons by the time he was seven, but by twelve, his interests had shifted to the drums. 'I played piano very percussively,' White explains. 'My uncle told my parents to buy me drums for Christmas, and it progressed from there.

'My uncle played drums in dance bands at the local Mecca ballrooms. He was well known, too, but he got killed a year or two after I got my drums, which I suppose made me even more determined to be successful at it. He was a big influence.'

Not that Alan was totally sold on the idea of being a musician, but by his early teens he was putting in a full day at school, playing semi-professionally on a regular basis, and doing a newspaper round on the side. 'I used to get up at six, deliver my papers, come home, have breakfast, go to school, come back, have tea, then go and play until one o'clock in the morning,' he remembers. 'Workingmen's clubs. Dance halls. Seven nights a week. Maybe eight.'

His group called themselves the Downbeats (later the Blue Chips), and their cover versions of Beatles, Searchers, and Gerry and the Pacemakers hits made them popular in the area. 'Everybody was a lot older than I was,' Alan says. 'I was really small up until fourteen or fifteen when I started growing. I used to get written up in the local papers – The Youngest Drummer In The North At The Club A Go Go In Newcastle – and that's when I started to realize that maybe there was a career in this.'

Alan laid low for a while to study for his school exams, but even then he was clocking up four nights a week behind the drums, 'and I was actually earning more money than my teachers were at school'.

In 1964, the Blue Chips won the area final in the *Melody Maker* amateur group contest, with the chance to go to London to compete with dozens of other groups from around the country. The judges included Brian Epstein, Cilla Black, and Ringo, and the Blue Chips made it down to the last twenty finalists. 'We were shitting ourselves,' Alan says. 'Did about three songs. All the other groups had busloads – tons – of fans, and we had one guy who'd come all the way down from the North to watch us.'

The Blue Chips won, and with a small fortune in new gear and a recording contract with Pye, went back to Durham as heroes. The subsequent handful of Blue Chips singles did nothing in the charts, the group opted to stay up North where the money was good and they fell apart. 'One guy wanted to change the name again,' Alan White says. 'Another one ran off with the lead guitarist's wife . . . '

Alan packed it in and signed up for courses at the Ferryhill Technical School with the intention of learning 'something useful', but wound up joining Billy Fury's nine-piece backing group, the Gamblers, instead.

He spent the next three months playing dreary clubs in Germany, his first extended trip away from home, 'during which time I grew up *very* quickly. I was doing five three-quarter hour spots a night, and seven at weekends. Not strip clubs – that was more the type of thing that Jon was playing. In fact, I was playing the German clubs the same time the Warriors were over there. I learned a lot about music and endurance.'

Back in England, the Gamblers did a three-week cabaret stint with Fury, 'which was funny, playing things like, [sings] "I believe, when I hear a baby cry . . . the falling leaves . . . ". It was another experience. I was being opened up to all sides of the industry while I was young.'

With an Anglo-Indian singer named Alan Marshall (destined to sing on White's first solo album), Kenny Craddock (who'd later form Lindisfarne), and a handful of others, Alan helped assemble Happy Magazine, who recorded a couple of records with Alan Price as producer. White ended up going on the road with Price's own band and played on several of his hit singles, including 'Simon Smith And The Amazing Dancing Bear', 'Don't Stop The Carnival', and 'Tickle Me'. 'It was the beginning of my "moving around"', Alan says. 'From that point, people kept offering me jobs. Lots of session work.'

Within a year and a half, Alan rejoined Happy Magazine (still keeping up the sessions), and their name changed to Griffin – a period White looks back on as the most depressing of his career. Griffin shared a house, and since Alan was the only one making any money, he took it on himself to keep the seven-strong group from starving, 'so I could play the music I believed in.

'I'd had enough of playing old standards, and I was selling my record collection to buy cans of beans. It was that bad. I used to buy tons of cheap vegetables and make these great big stews to keep us all alive. I used to think, "What am I doing here?" I could have been playing cabaret and living comfortably, but what about the rest of the

Above: Alan White in his early teens – 'The Youngest Drummer in the North'
Opposite: After joining Yes, Alan had barely four days to get himself together before the band hit the road in the States

guys? I was keeping the family alive. It was that kind of group.'

Griffin played what could loosely be described as progressive soul. Luckily, John Lennon spotted them in a club, and White was invited to go to Canada on twenty-four hours' notice to join Lennon, Yoko Ono, Klaus Voorman, and Eric Clapton in the Plastic Ono Band.

'It was incredible,' Alan remembers. 'We played in front of 20,000 people. Rock and roll, and that was it. Nobody had ever played with each other before. We just went and did it.'

The *Live Peace* album came out, Alan got a cut of the profits, and the sessions started rolling in: Ono, Harrison, more Lennon.... 'I remember one day when I was fourteen years old, some old guy in a workingmen's club came up and said, "You'll play with the Beatles one day, you will," but I never thought much more about it. I made about fifty albums in two years, but I was still playing with my band, Griffin. We rented a house in Sussex, and I went out there in between to play this music that I hadn't stopped thinking about.'

Around the same time, White got involved with Denny Laine in Balls, 'one of the original supergroup trips,' including ex-Move bass player Trevor Burton, and managed by the Move's manager, Tony Secunda. Balls spent nine months making an album with Stones' producer Jimmy Miller (out of which only one single, 'Fight For My Country' appeared). They went to Germany where, Alan says, 'We all took acid to play our first gig. It was a total experience, but it didn't work on stage at all. I did the one gig, then I left them.'

After that, Alan did a ten-week stint with Ginger Baker's Airforce, sharing the stage with three drummers and, from the way it looked, half the population of Western Europe. 'Things got a bit out of hand,' White laughs. 'It was a fifteen-piece band, with Baker, Graham Bond, Stevie Winwood, Chris Wood, Trevor Burton, Jeanette Jacobs, Rick Grech, Phil Seaman, Denny Laine....'

Later, a handful of sessions for Terry Reid led to a working partnership that spanned a year and a half 'on the road in England, doing four or five gigs a week,' followed by a studio-only membership in Bell and Arc – part of the 'family' built around Griffin. 'I was leading a very comfortable life,' Alan says. 'Yet I still had this band, who were still basically living hand-to-mouth.'

To save on the wear and tear of commuting between Griffin's communal house in the country and the London studios, Alan started crashing at Eddie Offord's flat. Inevitably, he wandered down to a Yes recording session one day while they were miming to their newly-completed version of Paul Simon's 'America' for a promotional film.

He cruised down to watch them again while they were rehearsing 'Siberian Khatru', prior to the recording of *Close To The Edge*. 'Bill was being a bit stroppy around then,' he recalls. 'He was in a really weird mood. He got up and said, 'I'm sorry, I have to leave,' and

73

walked out at about five o'clock one day. Everybody's going, 'Jesus Christ, what are we going to do about this?' They were into recording and Bill just leaves.'

With Bruford gone for the evening, the session turned into a semi-jam, with Alan picking up the sticks for 'Siberian Khatru'. 'I didn't know what the reaction was, but I was playing a lot of complicated time signatures, which is what I'd been doing with Griffin,' he says. 'And we swung! We had a good blow and somebody obviously made a mental note there.'

White joined Chris Stainton's All Stars for a British and European tour backing Joe Cocker after that, and remembers that Chris Squire came to see them at the Rainbow Theatre in London, 'possibly to see what I was like on stage, though I never asked him'.

A phone call from Tony Demetriades (who was handling Offord's affairs) was the first thing inkling Alan received that Yes want him to join. 'I said, "You're joking," because it really *was* out of the blue,' he says. 'We didn't really have totally compatible styles. I knew right away that if I joined, which I wasn't sure I'd do, we'd obviously both have to bend a little.'

Yes were fairly desperate at the time. The start of that American tour was less than a week away and they needed someone fast. Anderson and Squire turned up at Offord's place for a talk, though White didn't jump at the bait right away. 'The money *was* a thing, though happiness in music meant a lot more to me than that,' he explains. 'But Jon and Chris said, "Look, either you join the band, or else we're going to throw you out that window."

'Eddie lived on the third floor, so I joined the band.'

With four days to go until the first stop on the tour, Alan pored over Yes albums and rehearsed virtually round the clock. On 30 June 1972, he made his Yes debut in Dallas, Texas. 'That first gig was great,' he remembers. 'I didn't make any mistakes, probably because my adrenalin was so high. The *second* gig is where I made the mistakes. And the third gig. And the fourth . . . . '

Yes hit the States hard over the following months – as headliners now. They criss-crossed their trail dozens of times to strengthen the impact *The Yes Album*, 'Your Move', *Fragile*, and 'Roundabout' had been having on the nation's FM airwaves. To pave the way for *Close To The Edge* (which would also hit the Top Five there by the year's end), Atlantic put out another single, 'America' – a highlight of the band's live gigs – which settled just outside the Top Forty.

A harder, more rock-orientated drummer than Bruford, White led with his bass drum in contrast to Bill's tendency to concentrate on his top kit. As Jon Anderson says, 'Alan gave us that swing, if you like, which we'd always felt we'd had in a sense, though it didn't always shine through clearly. When Alan came along, there it was, and he was also willing to do what Bill could do, so it was twofold. He could swing like crazy, yet he wanted to learn all the intricacies of percussion.'

Those tricky changes and time signatures involved more concentration than most of the stuff he'd played in the past, and then there was the matter of Chris Squire and his bass.

'I told the band we'd have six months

Above: Backstage at Crystal Palace, London, 1972
Opposite: Gold albums in New York for *Close To The Edge*
Following page: Alan White with Yes at Crystal Palace: 'For me, playing live is what this band is all about'

each way,' White says. '"If I don't like it in six months, or you don't like it...." I wanted us both to be happy. It was like a marriage, and it was good for me. It brought more contrast to my life – being settled down, as it were. It's great to play with different people all the time, but it was even better to be in a steady position, have a steady income, not have to worry about money, and have a direction in music that was satisfying.'

By now, Yes were touring in style. In the course of twenty-four months they'd gone from a pair of rent-a-cars, shared motel rooms, and commercial flights, to limousines, star-class accommodation, and a private jet.

Regardless of the long months spent on *Close To The Edge* and that back-to-back series of tours, Rick Wakeman was a solo artist as far as A&M Records were concerned. The boys in the front office had been making discreet enquiries as to when a Wakeman album might be expected.

So, while *Close To The Edge* was still on the drawing-board in February 1972, Rick had nipped into Trident Studios to partially redesign 'Handle With Care', the keyboard piece that had originally been earmarked for *Fragile*.

Howe, Squire, and Bruford were on it. With the addition of second bassist Les Hurdle, percussionist Ray Cooper, and session-singers Liza Strike, Barry St John, and Judy Powell, the piece was rechristened 'Catherine Of Aragon' – the first of a series of tracks based on the lives of the six wives of Henry VIII.

Wakeman had hit on the concept during his first Yes tour when, in the market for something to read on the plane, he picked up a paperback called *The Private Life of Henry VIII*. That book led to more books on the king, though Rick became more intrigued by the diverse stories of his wives: the three Catherines, the two Annes, and Jane Seymour.

Having a clear story line to work from is something Rick claims is essential to his compositional method. It stems from those early piano lessons he took with Mrs Symes. 'Most of the classical music I was learning from the nineteenth century had no titles,' he says. 'It was always Brahms' Fourth, or Mozart's Symphony No 9, and when I was learning a new piece, my music teacher always told me to try and imagine something. A boat going down a river. So I was always taught to form pictures in my head.

'When I first got my contract with A & M, I thought, "Magic!" – until I sat down at my piano. I couldn't think of a bloody thing. The ideas were there and my playing was okay, but it just didn't hold together. Then I realized that all I really had to do was take that original idea of my music teacher and turn it around. Instead of playing the music and seeing a picture, I'll look at the picture first, then fit the music to it.'

Wakeman's treatment of Brahms' Fourth on *Fragile* had made his general method clear, and the new album was essentially an extension of that idea and that way of working.

Apart from the atmospheric 'Jane Seymour', which focused on Wakeman's work on the 240-year-old church organ at St Giles' Cripplegate, City of London, his approach was modern rather than medieval. Pivoting around grand piano and Hammond organ, and although classically-based, it veered more often than not towards the jazz, rock and jazz/rock end of the spectrum.

In contrast to the dramatic build-up that had become part and parcel of Yes music, the tracks on *Six Wives* tended to cruise along on an even keel without really leading anywhere – a showcase for Wakeman's musicianship, but a letdown in terms of scope.

Still, the album would sell millions in the end – its impact in Britain sparked off by Rick's appearance on the BBC's *The Old Grey Whistle Test* in January 1973, a week prior to its release. As the story goes, ITV had scheduled a tits-whips-&-decadence documentary on Andy Warhol for the same time slot, which had garnered so much advance publicity that it was sure to cop most of the country's viewing millions.

Conveniently, outraged journalist/broadcaster Ross McWhirter succeeded in getting a court injunction against the showing of the Warhol film. Andy got the bum's rush at the last minute, England reached for the dial to see what else was on, and since there were only the two BBC channels to choose from, many spent the remainder of the evening with Wakeman and Henry's wives on the *Whistle Test*. A keyboard star was born, and by the year's end, *Time* magazine would rate Rick's album as one of the best of 1973.

Over the course of five albums, Yes had gradually risen to that slightly holier-than-thou status of the *studio* band, presumably more at home behind a mixing desk than in front of a packed house, despite the fact that they'd spent most of the four years of their up-and-

75

down existence trying to find the backstage door.

To some critics, the recorded Yes had become a bit *too* polished, precise, and obsessed with the wonders of the studio. The live Yes was something else completely. A reversal of the old 'good in the studio/lousy on stage' theory, they were actually, fifty, if not a hundred, times better in person – which was why *Yessongs*, a triple album that included all the material from the only recently-released *Close To The Edge*, was wheeled out of the hangar in spring 1973.

But it had its drawbacks. The production job on *Yessongs* was fairly diabolical – thin, weedy, and sounding as if the band was calling in from a phone booth in Grand Central Station, New York.

With Bruford, and later White, on the drum riser, weeks' worth of tape had been recorded on the road in America, although Eddie Offord wasn't always around to supervise. Even when he was, he says, 'I'd gotten so involved with the P.A. system that when it came time to do a live album, I couldn't sit in the truck outside *and* sit in the hall at the same time. I didn't actually record most of that, though I have to say that I wasn't very happy with the quality on that album.'

In terms of electricity, however, *Yessongs* is probably the best album the band have made to date. Yes's razor-edged energy was staggering, particularly on the more rock-orientated tracks like 'Siberian Khatru', 'I've Seen All Good People', and 'Roundabout', which left the more studied and postured studio versions standing in the shade.

'That's not unnatural,' Chris Squire says. 'The energy on a live album is generated because of the audience, and unless you can get an audience in the studio you're never going to get that on a studio album. A combination of the audience *and* the live band make the show, not one or the other alone.'

But it's not just the energy – the band were actually playing better on *Yessongs*. The dynamics and sudden mood changes which sometimes came across as slightly stiff and incomplete on the original versions (e.g. Anderson's 'Sharp! ... Distance!' bit on 'Heart Of The Sunrise') were carried through on stage with remarkable power, even aggression. It wasn't hard to spot the bum notes, and the vocal harmonies were occasionally sloppy around the edges, but that excitement was there.

Alan White had only been in the band for three months when most of the live material was recorded, and he's not particularly crazy about his performance. 'It was a bit unfair,' Alan explains. 'I didn't really know the music fully. I hadn't grasped every subtle dynamic possibility so that it came across well on stage. It was all right, I guess, but I wish I'd been in the band a bit longer.'

Above: *Fragile*, 1972

Right: Yes on stage, November 1973

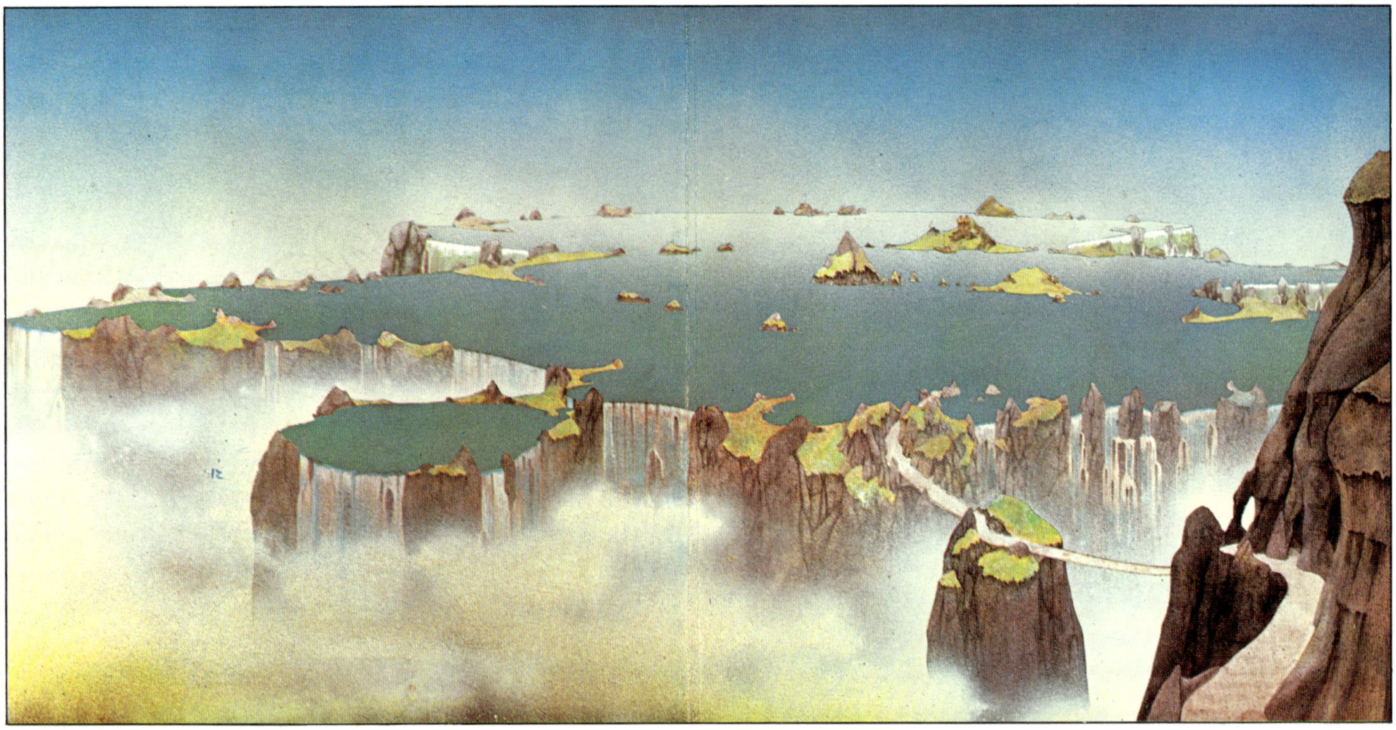

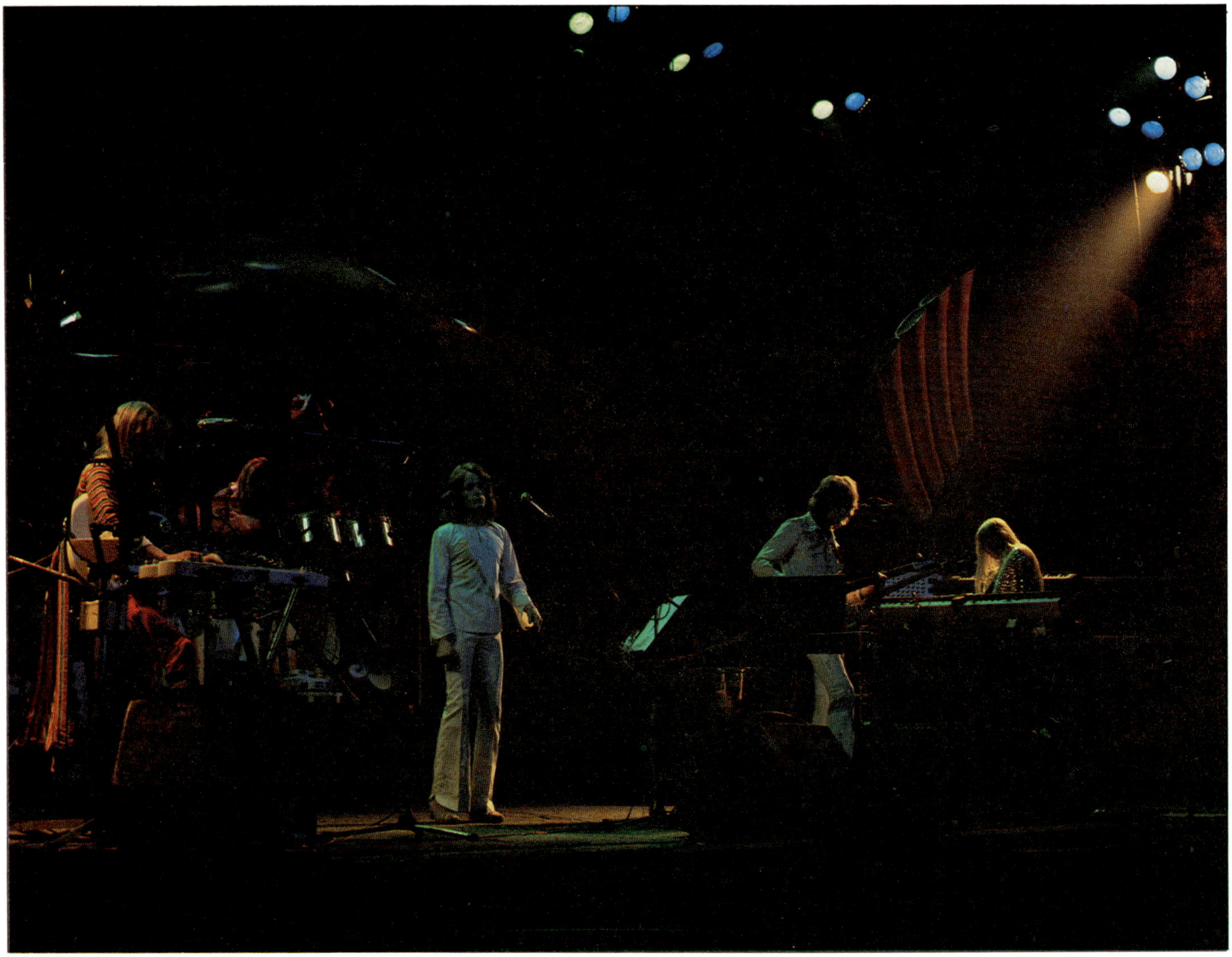

Opposite above: *Close to the Edge*, 1972

Left and this page: Yes on tour in the U.K., 1973

Top left: Jon Anderson

Above: Rick Wakeman

Top right: Alan White

Right: Chris Squire

Far right: Steve Howe

79

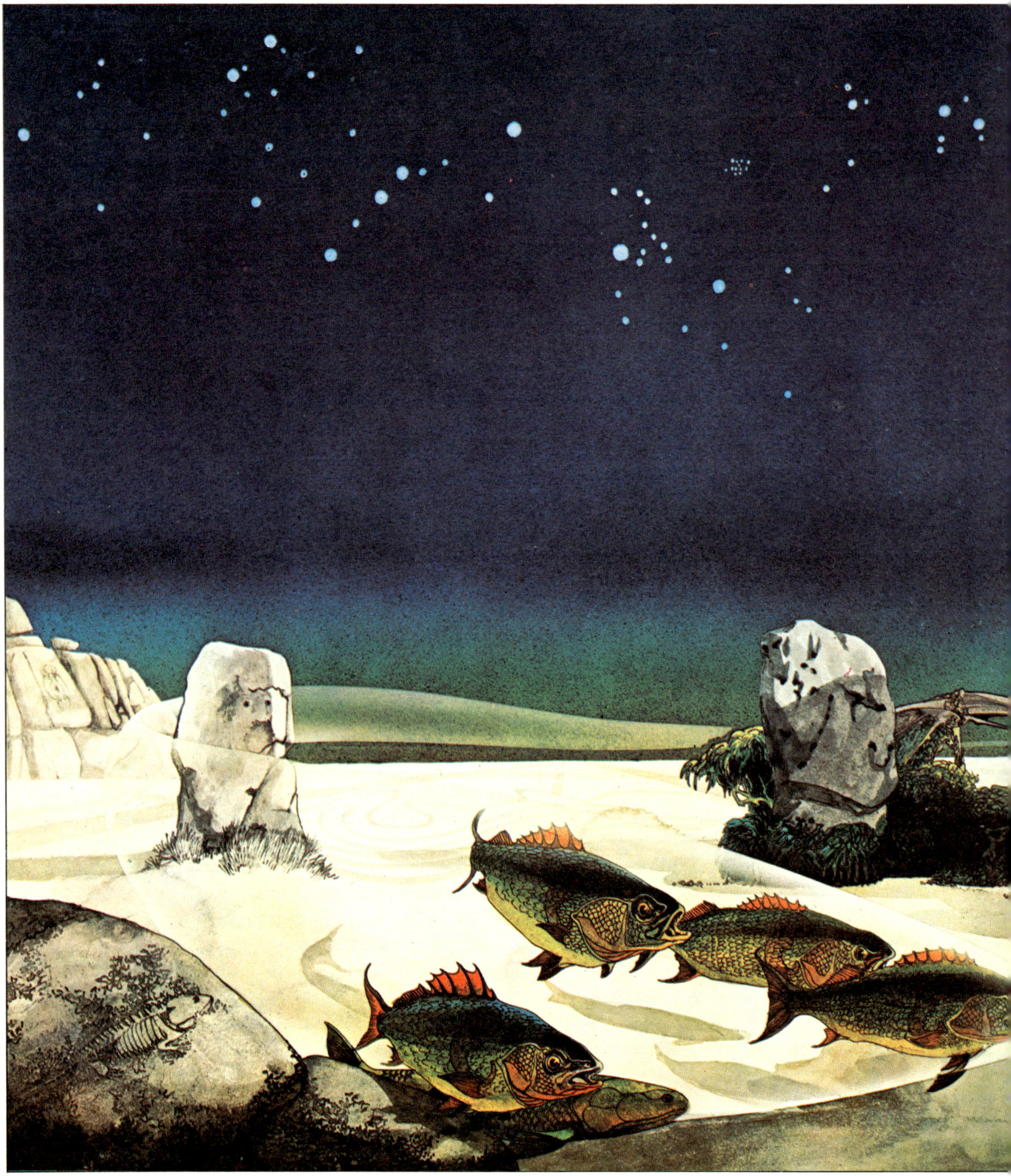

Tales From Topographic Oceans, 1973

82

Opposite above: Chris Squire, with Jon Anderson in the background

Opposite, bottom left: Jon Anderson (foreground) and Steve Howe

Opposite, bottom right: Steve Howe

Top: *Relayer*, 1974

Above: Patrick Moraz

Right: Rick Wakeman

83

Top: *Drama*, 1980

Middle: Lake Geneva, Switzerland, spring 1977

Above: On tour in the U.S., 1979

Left: The current line-up. Left to right: Geoff Downes, Trevor Horn, Chris Squire, Steve Howe, Alan White

CHAPTER FIVE

DELUSIONS OF GRANDEUR

My role wasn't just as an engineer/producer. I also kind of kept the peace between them. A mediator.
EDDIE OFFORD

We've never agreed on anything, really. We just agree with having compromises.
STEVE HOWE

'It was a very car-marked time,' Steve Howe says of mid 1973. 'People in this band were going off into all sorts of Grand Diversions. We were doing what we considered to be a humble, down-to-earth, look-at-life record, and there were four Rolls-Royces waiting outside so Rick could have a look at them.'

A year had gone by since the completion of *Close To The Edge*. While success had finally found Yes, and *Yessongs* was deservedly selling like hot cakes (certified gold on American advance orders alone), Jon Anderson had been itching to get back into the studio.

The arguing was getting louder, however. Although everything looked cool on the surface, the success of *Fragile* and differences in outlook had created serious cracks in the band's foundations. The most that was ever heard about it at the time was in the form of a few vague rumours in the rock press, but Jon Anderson and Chris Squire had locked horns over issues – a period Michael Tait remembers as 'very tense. I never felt like "This is it, they're breaking up." Not like the Cuban Missile Crisis. But it was a very shaky time.'

For a moment, anyway, there was a real possibility of a Yes/Squire split.

'To make points with music, you have to be helpful to one another and definitely not set up barriers,' Jon Anderson says cautiously, by way of explanation. 'To work towards a very harmonious sort of sound is the law of the land with this band, and I think it was broken on a few occasions.

'It's hard to explain. Earlier on, still being a non-musician in the band, I'd found it very difficult to appreciate why Bill and Chris had so many frustrating moments. A time finally came when I decided that my weight *should* be heard. It was a time when I felt the music was suffering because of this ... inner conflict.'

In a way, it tied in with Bruford's comment about that self-congratulatory air within the band during that post-*Fragile* period, complicated by differences in opinion as to where Yes should head next.

'Obviously, when the group became successful, everyone went, "Hey!"' Jon says. 'That's why these conflicts came about. Push and pull is fine, but the only way I can describe it is that if there'd

85

Left: The 65-foot *Topographic* balloon – $40,000 worth of hot air and fabric
Below: Steve Howe – 'There was a lot of talking in the corridors about the music. Out came the guitars and ideas on the stairs between the control room and the loo'
Opposite: *Topographic* at the Rainbow, London. 'The press missed the point. The first night *was* a disaster. By Thursday, Friday, and Saturday, the music *was* happening, but nobody came back' – Jon Anderson

been a little more help at times, things would have turned out a lot better.

'But I wouldn't say it was just me and Chris. It was a combination of everybody. I'd try to be the mediator, and at one point I had to put down the law to Chris. That if he couldn't be more attentive to everyone's opinion, of everyone *wanting* him to be a good guy, then he could leave.

'The funny thing is, everybody will talk about what *I* do, but when it comes down to it there's only me who ever talks to somebody who looks like they're going to leave. When everybody's told me, "I can't stand working with that guy any more," when the time came for that guy to leave, *I* was the one who had to go and tell him.'

But, as Keith Goodwin observes, the

skirmish probably marked 'a teething time. A make-or-break period between Jon and Chris. A hurdle they had to pass. A seven-year itch.'

As Squire reflects in retrospect, 'The most important contributing factor to Yes's success during the previous year and a half, particularly in the case of *Fragile*, was the equilibrium existing in the band during that period. I was only trying to maintain that balance.'

After twenty rounds in the ring, the dust cleared, and Anderson and Squire were both still standing. 'Chris is a stalwart in this troop of people,' Jon says. 'We've had our ups and downs, but I think I've learned that it's important that there *are* ups and downs.'

So the hatchet was buried, the incident relegated to past history, and Yes got down to the business at hand. After seeing that they could get away with a lengthy rock opus like 'Close To The Edge' without putting their audience to sleep, Jon had set his sights on bigger and better things. As he explains, 'I wanted to try something really extravagant, in the sense that it would take a lot of learning, a lot of preparation, and a lot of time.'

Logically enough, he felt the piece should revolve around some sort of Grand Concept – an ongoing theme to glue it all together the way Wakeman had copped his inspiration from Henry's wives. On the road in Japan that spring, Jon had been checking out Paramhansa Yogananda's *Autobiography Of A Yogi*. Its description of the four-part Shastric scriptures caught his eye – covering, as they did, virtually every aspect of man, mankind, and for that matter, Life Itself.

The idea sounded risky. An anti-Yes faction had appeared in the press since *Fragile*, armed with accusations that Britain's Brightest Hope of 1968, 69, and 70 were slowly but surely disappearing up their own collective posterior.

If those Shastric scriptures were a nebulous piece of esotericism to build an album around, Anderson didn't take much notice. He convinced Steve Howe that it was a workable idea, and the two began spending their off-duty moments on tour holed-up in the one or the other's candle-lit hotel room, throwing random ideas around that slowly gelled into four distinct sections.

'They were very simple,' Jon remembers. 'Guitar and vocal. I had a couple of chants there at the beginning, which went into a song, then into another section, then into another song, then into the next bit, and so on. We mapped it out on a very sketchy basis.'

By the end of the tour, the third and fourth segments were still vague, but the first and second had been organized, scribbled down in notebooks, and put on cassette tape during one marathon effort in Savannah, Georgia.

Confident that they had the bare bones of their idea sorted out, the two laid their plan on the rest of the band, whose initial reaction was, as Anderson puts it, 'slightly confounded, I think'.

Or, as Chris Squire explains in more graphic detail, Steve and Jon steamed in with their cassette outline of their Epic Concept for Yes's seventh album, 'and Rick walked out of the room'.

To put it mildly, *Tales From Topographic Oceans* caught the people at Atlantic Records with their pants down. 'It was a traumatic experience for all concerned,' Phil Carson says. 'Here's a group whose last album had done sensationally well, suddenly presenting you with a double album that's only got four tracks on it. For any person working at any record company, that's difficult to understand, especially in the case of the people who actually had to go out and sell the thing.

'But that's the statement Yes wanted to make at that point in time. They were the artists. I guess with Ahmet and Neshui's understanding of jazz musicians

Above: Chris Squire – 'On *Topographic* we lost the balance between guitar, keyboard, and bass. It wasn't there'
Right: Steve Howe

over twenty-five years, they helped the rest of Atlantic to see the light.'

While all four sides showed Yes in their broadest, most cinematic, glory, it was obvious by the middle of side one that there was little, if any, clear cut structuring in the music. From all indications, Yes themselves had only the foggiest notion of where they were going while recording it, despite the two months they'd spent rehearsing at ELP's Manticore Studios in Fulham. The Anderson/Howe tapes formed the skeleton, but perhaps more than any previous Yes album, *Topographic* was largely ad lib.

Granted, 'The Revealing Science Of God' and 'Ritual' (sides one and four) showcased some of the finest stuff the band had yet produced. Many of the melody lines in those Anderson/Howe song fragments were downright haunting and the brilliant flashes of musicianship (like the Arabic guitar figure that precedes the 'What Happened To This Song' segment) blazed with an energized, primitive majesty that picked up precisely from where *Close To The Edge* had left off.

On the other hand, some of the crucial qualities that originally made Yes great seemed to be on vacation. Squire's normally monumental bass work was reduced to a low, inaudible rumble, Wakeman sounded tired and subdued, and the band as a whole seemed unusually listless and passive, with only Howe's guitar work really shining through.

While a track like 'Close To The Edge' was built up by degrees, there was little of that forward and upward movement on *Topographic*. An occasional kick up the backside from White and Squire got it airborne, but the music was largely horizontal. It didn't go anywhere, and when it did, the band had a peculiar tendency to steer it down a blind alley, or kill it off prematurely – as if for the sake of getting on to the *next* idea.

The most effective side was the last, 'Ritual', which made a valiant, cohesive stab at capturing the old Yes power and grandeur with a minimal amount of introspective wallpaper-gazing. Virtually every effective melody, riff, and motif that had appeared earlier on returned for a final reprise. Squire and White stepped to the foreground, and the music finally took off in a welcome blaze of life, building up through the exquisite 'Nous Sommes Du Soleil', through a driving Squire mini-solo and a slightly overdone percussive segment, then back down to a perfect, subtle conclusion.

It was inevitable that Yes would one day go the whole hog with a towering *Meisterwerk* to end them all. Despite some riveting moments, they didn't quite get there with *Topographic* – possibly confusing quantity with quality, and constant variety with High Art.

'Yeah, there were times we shouldn't have put that extra piece of music in,' Jon Anderson partially agrees. 'But at the time, you don't know these things. You only do it out of a sense of desperation. "Where's it going now? Let's put this bit in because I've got it ready and it'll fit really nicely." I could hear the damn thing in my head at certain times. It was frustrating at times, but at other times a revelation.'

Jon admits that it took a bit of prodding to keep going, 'and everybody in tune and on top of it. In any group of people, you can't all possibly be thinking the same thing at the same time. I was striding along in leaps and bounds, jumping through hoops and standing on my head. I was trying out all sorts of things like percussion, and for me, working on that album was a very energized sort of schooling.

'It was like trying to get everybody in Yes to go back to their roots and start again: "This is a new way of making music. We've got to find a feel, give it energy, make it move." If you listen to it on that level, it *is* a damn good album, though it took a lot of energy from everybody, and it took a little too much from some of us. It was a bit of a Yin/Yang situation, a push and pull situation. All I needed were stalwart boys, you know. Guys who'd stand by the idea, but it wasn't a hundred percent, even while we were making the album.'

Above: 'I wanted to write the liner notes. I didn't know if I had the talent, so I had this guy write it down for me. It was a bit ... high brow ... but the guy was an amazing character' – Jon Anderson
Opposite: Michael Tait
Overleaf: 'Rick was the worst hurt by the reaction' – Steve Howe

It's well known that the slowly simmering hotbed of discontent was Rick Wakeman – who, it's safe to say, had no interest in Anderson's basic literary concept to begin with. All that remained was the music, and with no clear-cut battle plan to go by, Wakeman, more than anyone else, had been wandering around in the dark. 'Experimentation is fine, but it's something you should do in your own time as you're writing and rehearsing the music, until that experiment is proven in your own mind,' Rick says. 'Once you've finished experimenting and know where things are going, *then* you can put that music on record.

'My whole problem was that the music wasn't proven in my own mind. It wasn't worked out. It wasn't comfortable. So there was no bloody way I was going to stand up and say, "This is a great Yes album." No way.'

Michael Tait claims that Yes floundered around for the better part of four months, 'and Rick didn't do anything except play darts. The frustration level was so high that at one stage, Jon said, "I want you to build a bathroom in the middle of the studio. You get sheets of plywood and stick tiles on it, so I can get a bathroom sound." He wanted that echo, and I said, "Jon, it won't work. You need concrete walls. Let's just put a mike in the loo." But he made me do it, we did it, and it was useless. All those white tiles.'

Then there was Eddie Offord, 'and his waste-bin full of two-inch tape,' Tait adds. 'He was always out of his brain. Edited the crap together and threw away the good bits. You'd look at the master and every six inches was an edit. It was all Scotch-taped, and Rick would still be in the bar, throwing darts . . . .'

Wakeman wouldn't be the only one disenchanted by what was going on. Unwisely, Yes embarked on a full-scale British tour before *Topographic* was even released, and gently proceeded to cram all four sides of the album down their unsuspecting fans' throats. As Chris Squire says, 'Let's just say it didn't go down very well at all.'

By the time the band checked in to London's Rainbow Theatre for a then-unheard of run of four sell-out nights, the album was out, and so were the critics. Oddly enough, many of the daily papers were impressed, with *The Times* spouting things like ' . . . the third movement alone ... will be studied twenty-five years hence as a turning point in modern music', though the more cautious *Guardian* curiously observed that 'only Jon Anderson, whose high-pitched and carefully-modulated voice must make him the Mel Tormé of rock singing, seemed at ease and in control.'

The rock press didn't have kind words for anyone, and their reviews were almost unanimous in their savagery. In *Sounds*, the album and gig reviews respectively sported YES: WISHY WASHY TALES FROM THE DEEP and YES: CLOSE TO BOREDOM for headlines. *Melody Maker*'s Chris Welch, one of Yes's staunchest allies, axed both with YES – ADRIFT OF THE OCEANS and YES – OVER THE EDGE.

Ironically, Yes had just been voted Best Band in both the international and British sections of the *Melody Maker* readers' poll, while Wakeman had walked off with top honours for his keyboard work.

At the time, Anderson went to extravagant lengths to defend *Topographic* in the press, though as Keith Goodwin says, 'I know he went through an awfully long period of self-analysis – wondering whether he was right to have put it on record. On the surface, the rest of them said, "Well, who cares?" but I think the criticism cut pretty deeply for all of them.'

Steve Howe claims he didn't quite see what all the fuss was about. 'I was convinced that side one was immensely commercial,' he says. 'Although it was long – it was twenty-eight minutes long when we were working on it – once you got past the introduction, it was very much a side for the audience. Asking questions. Pointing things out. Suggesting things. It was a lot of fun for most of us, but as soon as the critics got hold of it ...

'But, yeah, after *Topographic*, I think all of us went through a period of questioning things. "Oh ... you think it's a load of rubbish, do you?" It started affecting us. Like, Rick saw the papers, and they said, "Rick doesn't play enough", so he thought he didn't play enough. You get caught up in it, even though your better judgment might tell you to ignore it.'

Jon began having doubts, 'but only because people around me doubted it, I suppose. One or two people would say, "Well ... it *is* a bit ... " and I've listened to it sometimes and thought that it really *is* a load of rubbish, yet I've listened to it at other times and thought, "Now this is nice. It hangs together so well." '

But then it was largely Anderson's lyrical contributions that drew the lion's share of artillery fire – the obscurity of his writing style, compounded by a mishmash of miscellaneous revelations and Cosmic Truths that were piled on top of the original concept.

To paraphrase Tony Kaye, nobody knew what the hell he was talking about. Looking back on it, Anderson agrees that some of it was slightly off-the-wall. 'The books I'd been reading about inner realization influenced me,' he explains. 'There were a couple of gurus – Yogananda was one – and then there was Vera Stanley-Alder (*The Finding Of The Third Eye*), who's quite a marvellous writer. But there were a couple of people coming along and saying things that really *were* a load of rubbish, though I was really in there at the time. It was a large-scale commitment, so when anything was said to me back then, I tended to think it was part of The Whole. I thought the music would carry the idea to the guy who works on a farm, the guy who works in a bank ... '

The critics never came round to Jon's point of view, though the disjointed concerts and lousy reviews were soon forgotten by the public. While it's been suggested that *Topographic* sold largely on the backs of its predecessors, it would eventually climb as high as number 11 in the *Billboard* charts. Most American reviewers were, if not ecstatic, then at least more tolerant.

Topographic holds together better now than it did in late 1973. Although it might have been a prime case of Yes being slightly ahead of their time, there was a lesson to be learned from its comparative failure.

'It was trying to run before we could walk,' Chris Squire says. 'Or, we'd learned to walk, but hadn't had much practice, and now we were trying to walk *and* run, all in the same moment. Sure, the idea was logical to an extent, but the realization of a work of that size, and how big an undertaking it was, wasn't fully appreciated by everyone concerned. It missed with a lot of people because of that. I realized, even at the time, that there could have been a lot more done to make the album hold together a bit better. I wouldn't have cut it down, I just would have spent more *time* – but then that's my penchant, as you know.

'Everyone has to go through a learning process, and if that's what it takes for some people to learn then .... Some members of the group just missed the point of what Yes is all about and *why* people like the group, that's all. I mean, the album could have been incredible.'

While Yes were still feeling the sting of those reviews, Wakeman made plans to slot his next solo outing into the brief lay-off period before the band's February 1974 American tour. This time, it was going to be a musical adaptation of Jules Verne's classic science-fiction epic,

Journey To The Centre Of The Earth – an idea Rick had worked on before *Six Wives*, but shelved due to lack of available cash.

If *Six Wives* had been modestly ambitious, it was almost kid's stuff compared to what Rick had up his sleeve for *Journey*, with plans calling for not only a small armoury of keyboards and a five-man electric band but also the sixty-eight-voice English Chamber Choir and the full might of the 100-piece London Symphony Orchestra.

To top it off, it wasn't going to be a painstakingly laid down studio job, but two do-or-die, warts-and-all performances in front of a packed house at the Royal Festival Hall.

Brian Lane and the bigwigs from A & M weren't overjoyed from the start, and in certain respects it was an almost suicidal caper. For one thing, that five-man band (Ashley Holt, who'd worked with Rick in the Ronnie Smith Band, Garry Pickford-Hopkins, Mike Egan, Roger Newell, and Barney Jones) were all but unknown – several being members of a loose-knit pub band Wakeman occasionally jammed with near his Buckinghamshire home.

Then again, the preparations – from early planning stage to the actual Night Of Reckoning – were forcibly geared to span a matter of weeks. Rick had to sell several of the vintage cars in his growing collection and take out another mortgage to cover expenses. When word came down that the L.S.O. wanted double pay if both gigs were recorded, he was forced to take the considerable risk of taping only one.

Although actor Richard Harris turned down the offer to serve as narrator, Yes's Hemdale affiliation saw company director David Hemmings himself manning the peacock throne and microphone.

On the evening of Friday 18 January

1974, Rick Wakeman, shattered from six dress-rehearsals with an ulcer and a mouthful of teeth that were killing him, climbed into his silver stage cape and placed his neck on the line. 'For the first time in my life, I was nervous as hell,' he says. 'I suddenly realized that it was all down to me. I wasn't sharing the responsibility any more.'

Nobody seemed to be out to score any points on the cleverness scale, and while more flash could have been injected through more exotic arrangements and pacing, the basic no-frills simplicity of the music was no real mark against it.

The album would hit number 1 in the British charts in no time flat, cop its fair share of gold records, find itself nominated for a Grammy in the States, and win awards from magazines and rock papers left, right, and centre. Not surprisingly, a few home truths were beginning to click in Rick's head, though it was still a bit too early to judge the outcome. If Wakeman already knew, he wasn't telling a soul.

The *Topographic* American tour was the flashiest Yes had undertaken up to that time. Definitely in the major league now, the band were riding the crest of the wave with three Top Five albums and four heavily-aired singles in their wake, not to mention the healthy showing the new album was making on the sales front.

The show itself was a visual dazzler, with Michael Tait's superb lighting system and the Dean Brothers' elaborate stage setting outdoing virtually every other rock show in existence at the time.

But out in the $5 seats, from Miami to Atlanta to Baltimore, *Topographic* in the flesh wasn't faring much better than it had on that first night at the Rainbow Theatre. Those hockey rinks and basketball arenas might have been packed to the rafters, and tickets for the Madison Square Garden shows in New York had sold out without any advertising, but crowd reaction was mixed and restless. Too much *Topographic*, not enough of the old stuff, and though nobody booed, more than one bored ticket-holder headed for the exit before the end.

Emergency measures were taken, sides of the album were dropped from the set, then reinstated, then dropped again or switched around with Yes classics in varying running orders to streamline the show. Although Yes were only performing half the new album by the end, it wasn't enough to ease off the behind-the-scenes friction. From his conversations with friends and journalists, it was obvious that Wakeman wasn't a happy man. Two sides of *Topographic* were two sides too many, and his grumbling was getting louder.

'It was just too long,' Rick says. 'It was like baking a huge cake that nobody's ever tasted before and asking them to eat the whole thing at once. It went gold on the day of its release, and a lot of Yes's supporters bought it and came to the gigs, even though it wasn't what they wanted to hear. I felt that blind support like that was dangerous.'

It wasn't just the length that had Wakeman bitching in the wings. Through on-stage repetition, night after night, his

Above: Chris Squire
Opposite: Vangelis Papathanassiou

94

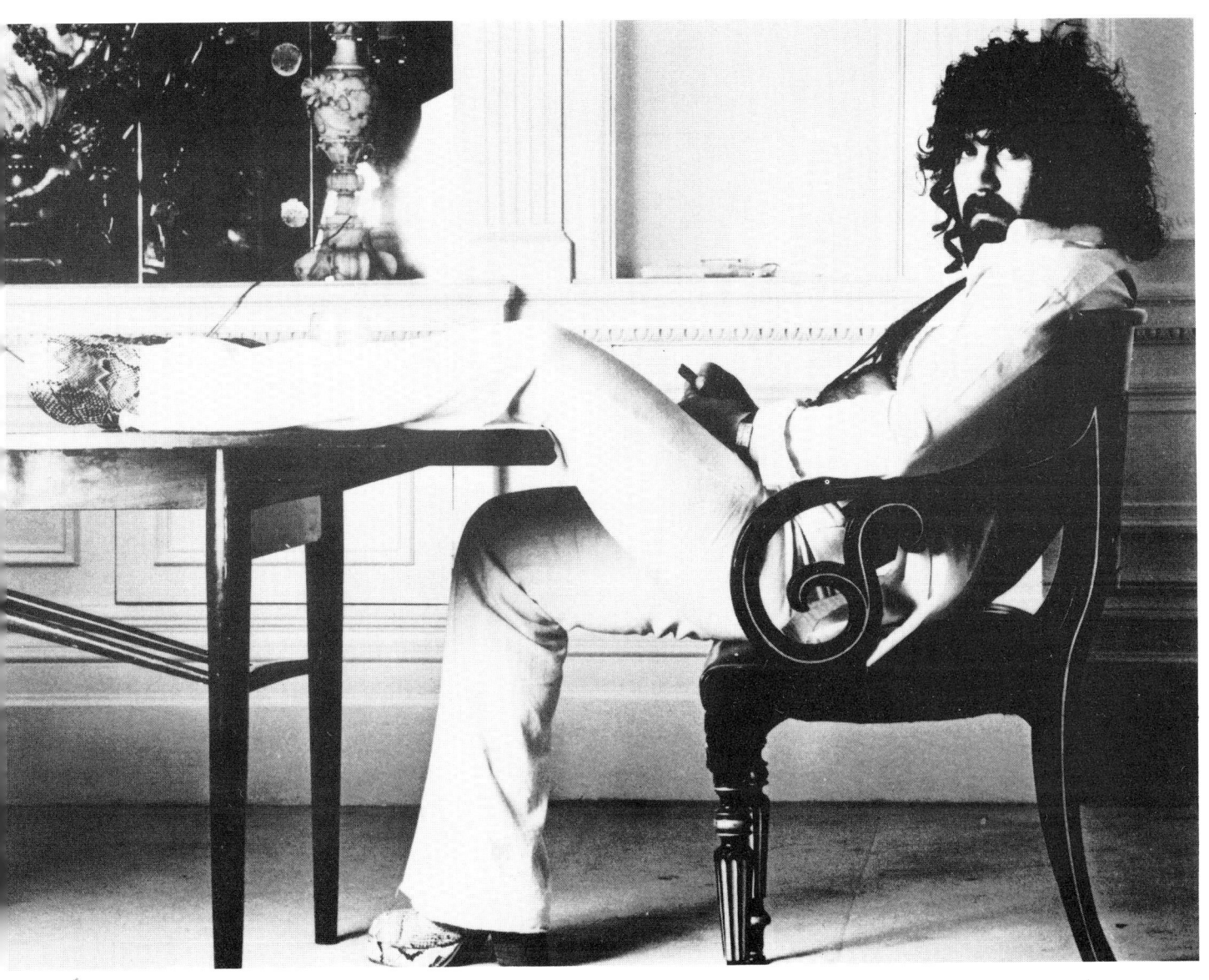

confusion and disappointment over the music was turning to an all-out hatred. Anderson, for one, was pissed off with the keyboard player's lackadaisical attitude, though Wakeman didn't particularly care. As Rick explains. 'From a musician's point of view, the easiest way to explain it is that music, any music, is really give and take. You put a lot into it and you take a lot out. Ideally, it's fifty-fifty.

'But if you know that you can't naturally give something to it, then it's obvious that you won't be able to take anything out of it. That was the problem, and that's what was happening during that tour.'

Jon Anderson was well aware that things could lead to yet one more Yes member legging it over the garden wall. But as he explains. 'I think it was a question of, "You can either stick with us, or . . . ." I didn't want to have to defend the album within the ranks of the band. You know, "Come on Rick, of *course* it works. Give it time."

'He had his own career happening anyway, but as a collective unit that wasn't something we were very aware of. It was a separate thing. We knew we could carry on without him, though at the time I felt it would be a shame if this happened over a piece of music. But I didn't want to set something up and then just pull it apart because one person disagreed with certain parts of it.'

It wasn't until after the band had taken the tour across Europe that Wakeman finally lowered the lifeboat. Back in Britain, he split for the seclusion of his Devon farmhouse for a thinking session. Anderson may have been defending *Topographic* to the death, but as far as Rick was concerned, 'I thought, "If that's the direction the music is going in, I'd rather get out."

'The thing is, my whole musical life had been based on frustration. When I went to the Royal College, I got frustrated when I realized that I wasn't going to make it as a concert pianist, and then I got frustrated again when I realized I wasn't going to get anywhere as a teacher.

'So I did sessions for a while, which frustrated me creatively, so I joined the Strawbs for a ludicrous amount of money compared to what I was making in the studio. After fifteen months of that, more frustration led me to Yes, and then it was suddenly frustration time again. I realized it was time to move on.'

With his mind made up, Wakeman shipped off a 'Dear Brian' telegram to

95

manager Lane, and the dance, as they say, was over.

'He did it all the wrong way, for a start,' Keith Goodwin says. 'The first people he told were me and Brian Lane. Then Brian had to go and tell Jon, whose first reaction was, "Well, why is it that you and Keith know before we do?" I think that's one of the big aspects of Rick's departure that really got up Jon's nose.'

Actually, the telegram wasn't quite the final word. The official Yes/Wakeman split dragged on for a while longer, and Steve Howe says that it was a fairly off-and-on situation. 'It was *not* clear-cut that Rick was going to leave, believe me. He left, and he came back. All in the course of a couple of weeks. It was, "Is it going to happen? Isn't it going to happen? Is Rick leaving?" '

In some ways, Howe feels, 'Rick left the group because we *were* getting more into the vegi thing and all. Those "Oh ... but we don't do *that* any more" kinds of changes. Rick wasn't changing so fast and was feeling, "Well, I still like hanging out with my mates round the pub." Maybe he stayed the same, while we were finding new interests.'

Then there was the increasingly erratic behaviour of the guy who'd inspired the whole health kick to begin with: Eddie Offord. 'It got to the point where Eddie was all that was bad about where we were going,' Howe explains. 'I think Rick almost felt that Eddie was leading us and would somehow affect us very badly, because Eddie *was* in a pretty bad state at the time.'

On the other hand, Wakeman's open criticism of the Yes way of doing things didn't endear him to certain corners of the band. 'It wasn't made easy for him to stay,' Chris Squire says vaguely. 'People were very touchy. Things shouldn't have gone that far, but they did in those days. We were fairly immature.'

An attempt was made to patch things up in London with a band meeting on neutral ground at the Holiday Inn. As it turned out, 'Somebody didn't turn up,' Steve says. 'So we said, "Well, maybe it's gone." But it was never really official somehow. It was strange. Almost like saying goodbye to somebody at a station, never realizing that it's the last time you might ever see them.'

If Wakeman's exit left an uncertain Yes stranded on the platform, the condition was only temporary. Within weeks, they were hidden away outside London at a studio called the Barn –ostensibly to hammer out new material, though the burst of activity was undoubtedly in part to thumb their noses at Rick and the critics, while bolstering post-*Topographic* morale.

In Paris at the end of the final tour with Wakeman, Jon had tracked down a Greek keyboard virtuoso named Vangelis Papathanassiou, whose work (notably with the continental jazz/rock fusion band Aphrodite's Child) Anderson particularly admired.

Loud, bearded, and tipping the scales at well over 200 pounds minus his gaudy jewellery and trinkets, Vangelis looked

Above: Patrick Moraz
Opposite: Yes in August 1974 during a break in rehearsals for *Relayer* at the Barn

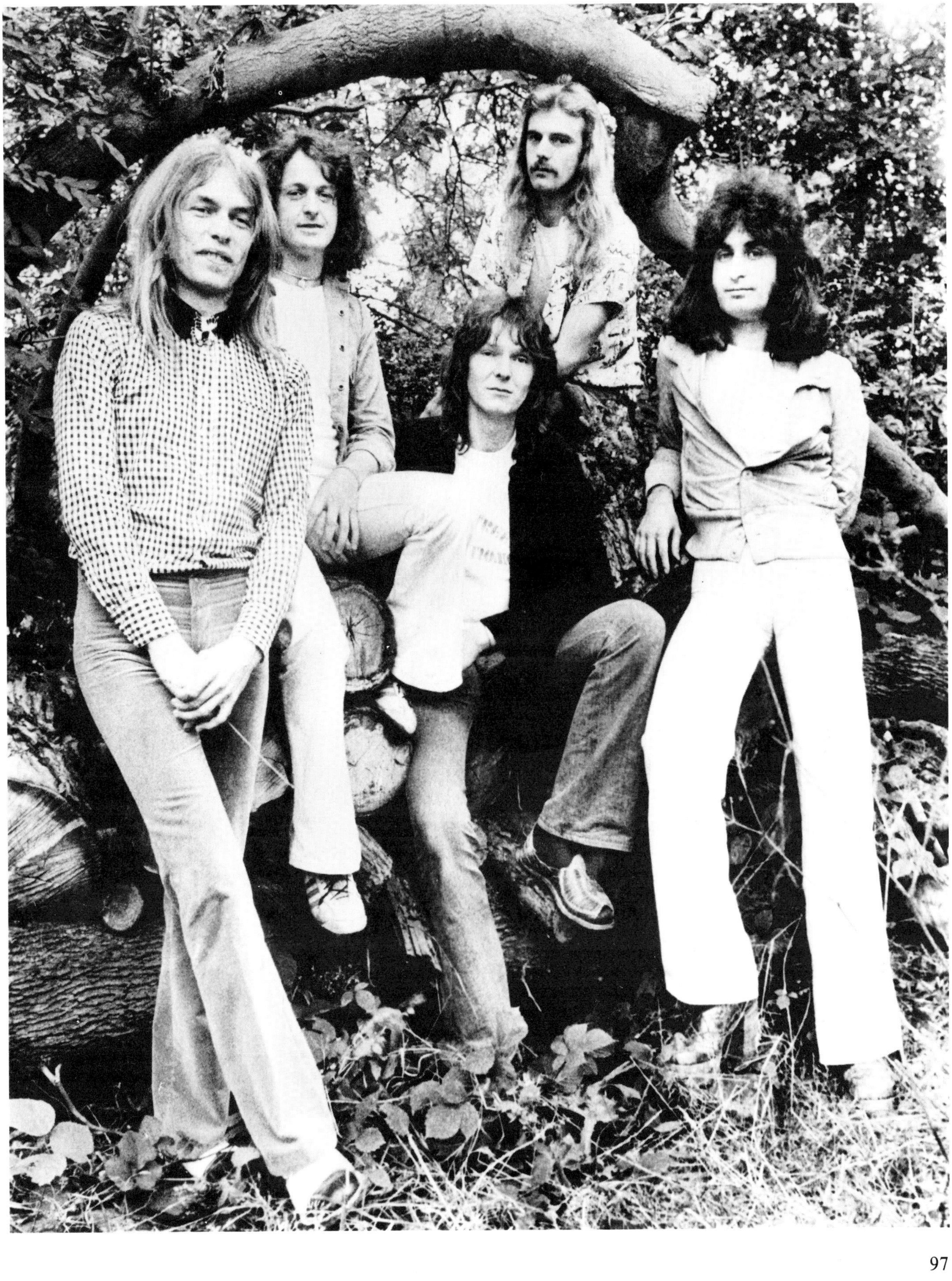

more like a wrestler, a slave-trader, or a Greek restauranteur than an accomplished musician. But when Yes regrouped their forces and kicked off the quest for a new man, Vangelis was the first to get Anderson's call.

'We dragged him over to England,' Jon says, and at first, Papathanassiou seemed to be just what the doctor ordered. He wasn't a carbon copy of Wakeman, and Anderson saw him as someone who could hold up his end, while helping to shift the music in a new direction – out of the quagmire that Jon wasn't quite yet admitting the band had stumbled into with *Topographic*.

Squire says that all and sundry were 'very excited' over the potential arrangement, though over the next three weeks the Greek proved to be a bit of a handful.

'He was pretty overpowering,' Steve Howe laughs. 'We could see the musical possibilities right from the beginning, but we were a bit confused at the time. He was very non-committal, and we weren't too sure if he was going to stay.

'We played great music for half an hour and were sure he was the right man. "Okay, let's try this song now, Vangelis. We've already worked this bit out, so just play along." But he couldn't understand anything we said, he wasn't used to working with a group. He was an entity, a sound, and that entity was called Vangelis.

'He had all sorts of hidden talents,' Steve adds. ' "AH! THE DRUMS!" and he'd get on the drums and play like hell, like fury, for ten minutes. Like some

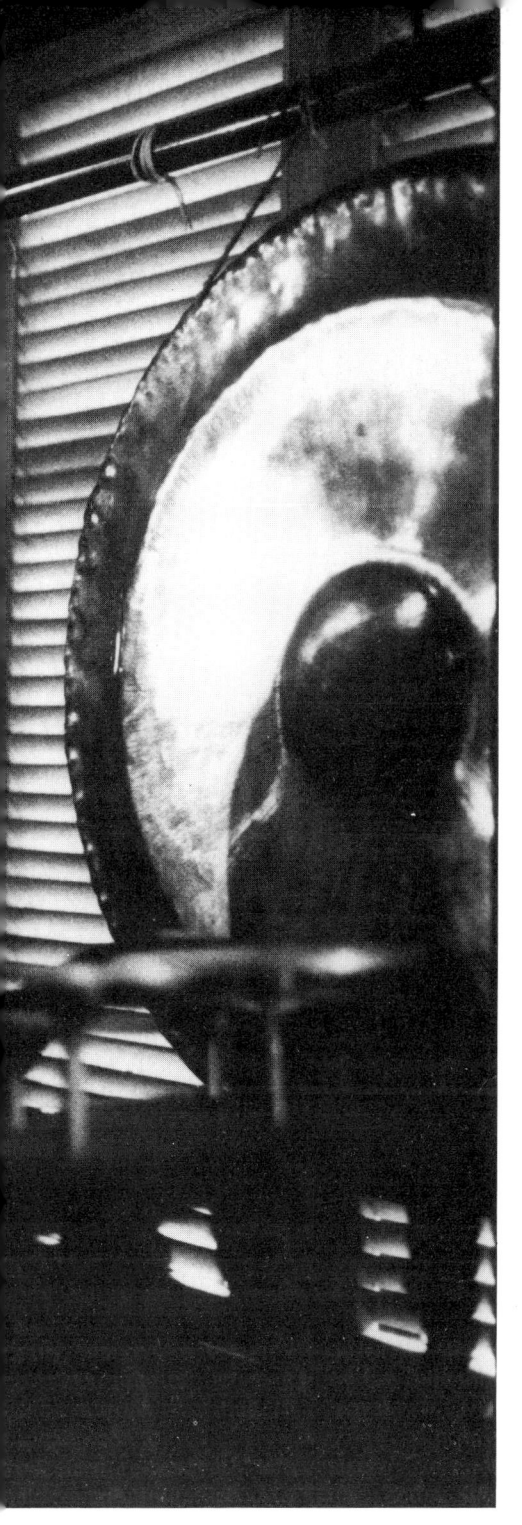

Alan White in Squire's behind-the-garage studio, September 1974

virtuoso at a drum school. "AH! VERY GOOD DRUMS, HAH?" and he'd crash away at them some more – a bit like the drummer on *The Muppet Show*. Everybody greatly admired him, but it was like, "Uh ... could we play this *song* now?" '

Exit Vangelis Papathanassiou – though not without regrets. But as Alan White adds, 'It never would have worked. For an album maybe, but never permanently.'

For the moment, Yes seemed set to carry on as a four piece, which Chris Squire admits was 'a possibility. It would have produced simpler music, but then that was exactly why Rick left. So it would have been a great contradiction of terms in some ways. To have done it would have been a backtrack statement.'

All told, they checked out something like eight people over the next six weeks, amidst rumours that the band were about to settle for Nick Glennie, an unknown musician then playing with another Lane-managed band called Wally. 'I wanted Keith Emerson!' Steve Howe says. 'We tried out people we knew. People we didn't know. Jon's friend. Everybody's friend. Jean Roussel came down, but he had a go at us. He criticized us. Thought I was an out-of-tune guitarist, so it was, "Oh. Okay. Bye-bye." "Bring in the next one." '

While the trial, error, and bickering was going on, a three-piece London-based progressive band called Refugee was going down for the third time. Lee Jackson was on bass, fellow ex-Nice man Brian Davison was on drums, and a Swiss wanderer by the name of Patrick Moraz handled keyboards.

Patrick Moraz is in Miami, sitting in a hotel room at the Coconut Grove. He's getting ready to split for yet another airport with his wife, and their sixteen suitcases are staring him in the face.

'I can't keep dragging all this fucking luggage around like this,' he says, sounding like an Ancient Swiss mariner with a dead albatross for a necktie. 'You wouldn't *believe* what I pay in excess baggage.'

Moraz likes to call himself a 'rock and roll gypsy', and in Patrick's case, the shoe fits. Trying to track him down takes on all the trappings of an international manhunt – phone calls, telegrams, more phone calls, false leads, and rumours. He's in Paris when he's supposed to be in New York, in Rio when he's supposed to be in Paris, in Switzerland when everyone *thinks* he's in Rio, but then he might be in L.A. after all, only nobody's sure where he's staying, though he's probably already split for London anyway, and he'll only be there for half an hour before hopping a boat to . . . .

Moraz has been cruising around the globe for half of his life. It was once rumoured that he was actually born in an airplane on 24 June 1948 – thereby making him not a citizen of any particular country but a Citizen Of The World. It's a nice touch, though Patrick claims he was too young to remember. 'You could still leave it in question,' he says. 'I don't mind. As far as I know, I was born in Switzerland. On the ground.'

There's something 'intense' about Moraz – friendly and hospitable in the European way, yet prone to whack the stereo up full blast while standing in the middle of the room, hollering his explanation of the finer musical points of the piece over the din. Pointing. Gesturing. Conducting. Psychologically shaking you by the lapels until you *understand* what it's all about.

Maybe it's the accent, but he gives off an unmistakable aura of class and breeding – the kind of guy who was probably born with bread in his pockets, and lots of it.

'I come from a plain, normal family in Switzerland,' he corrects. 'They were very modest, they weren't well off, though they were very artistically orientated. You've heard of Paderewski, the great violin player? My father was his road manager. He was also a tap-dancer. He's tap-danced with Maurice Chevalier and Fred Astaire. He used to play a piano behind a cinema screen too, but only the black notes, because he didn't really know how to play piano.'

Moraz began studying piano and violin when he was five, although three years later, 'I threw the violin out the window during the winter in Switzerland' and decided to stick with the ivories. He'd been weaned on classical music – Bach, Beethoven, and the rest – but picked up on European pop and jazz by his early teens.

At the government-financed religious boarding-school he went to, Patrick discovered a pipe organ in the chapel, and also formed a rock/jazz-orientated big band with his classmates.

At seventeen, Moraz unexpectedly struck it rich after buying a lottery ticket.

He won the grand prize, over $40,000, earmarked to finance the rest of his education – though it didn't quite turn out that way. 'I spent the money,' he says. 'It took about six months for me to do it, too! I gave presents to everyone.'

He landed a brief stint as a scuba-diving instructor in Spain, just down the beach from Salvador Dali's place, and moonlighted during the evenings playing vibes with a local resort club band. 'Then in 1964, I went to learn English in Bournemouth in England,' Moraz says. 'I was a cook in a school, and I used to earn £4 a week, so I started giving Latin and French lessons so I could buy my way out of that fucking job.'

During the same period, he took on a part-time gig playing organ in a church – 'not an actual job, but I did a deal with the church to get a percentage of the collection'.

It still wasn't enough to put him through University, however, so in the time-honoured fashion, he started selling carpets and encyclopedias door-to-door. Finally, with an economics and political science degree from Geneva University in his pocket, he went to New York to work on economics reports at Columbia University, returning a short while later to take on a job as an administrative director for an import/export firm in Africa, 'which was doing these oil deals all around the world'.

Although it was in the background, Patrick's part-time musical career was still going strong. As the kingpin in a slick club and jazz festival outfit called the Patrick Moraz Trio (later Quartet), he was making enough cash at his straight job to keep his fellow musicians going. As he explains, 'We used to meet in Europe at weekends to play some gigs, then I'd go back to Africa and my job during the week.'

He spent two years down there, and in late 1968 decided to devote all his time to music. 'I didn't want to become a professional musician until after I'd finished my studies,' Moraz says. 'I wanted to make sure I could do something else if I had to.'

By April 1969, Patrick was back in Switzerland with his trio/quartet, secure with the cash he'd saved, and living in a Montreux villa on the shores of Lake Geneva. As it happened, Yes were also in Montreux in April of that year for the Golden Rose Festival, playing a one-night stand at the casino down the road. Moraz, it seems, had dubbed himself the festival's unofficial Social Director. 'I was throwing parties every day for all the bands,' he says. 'One night was Yes's night. They were playing with Rory

Above: Steve Howe – 'This photo was taken in Holland when Chris and I were promoting our solo albums.'
Chris Squire – 'Actually, it was New York. I think'
Opposite: Patrick Moraz during the reception for the Roger Dean Exhibition at the New York Cultural Center

Gallagher and Taste, so I threw a party for them.

'I didn't know them, but I briefly met Chris, and Jon, and Tony Kaye, and Peter Banks. They were all there, though they didn't really know who was throwing the party. The villa was well known for all the jam sessions, you know. It was kind of an in-place, and I used to do it for all the Festivals in Montreux.'

Later that year, Moraz joined Peter Lockett, Jean Ristori, and Bryson Graham in Mainhorse – a British-based progressive band who worked on-and-off around the Continent, but never played a single gig in England during the two years they lived there. With no manager and a début album that sank without a trace, the band disintegrated in early 1972. Moraz took off for the Far East on an eight-month trek with the eighteen dancers and six percussionists of a Brazilian dance company. 'We went everywhere,' Patrick recalls. 'Hong Kong, Thailand, Japan . . .'

Composing film scores became Patrick's main occupation during the first half of the following year. In the space of twenty-four weeks, he composed the music for fifteen European films – subtitle jobs like *The Middle Of The World, The Invitation,* and *La Salamandre*. 'That was also the time when I learned about synthesizers more deeply,' he says, and by the dawn of 1974, he was back in England as one-third of the progressive bass, drums, and keyboards-galore outfit called Refugee. When their first and only album appeared, several critics pegged the band for the Hall Of Fame, though within a few months, 'It wasn't happening to everybody's liking. We had a few management problems, a few personal problems, and it didn't look like it was really going anywhere.'

In August, as Refugee were falling apart, Brian Lane turned up on the other end of Patrick's telephone line. Wakeman was gone, and the Swiss keyboard-player had unknowingly become a candidate for the parking space. 'Yes had probably heard of me, and some close friends of mine were close friends of Yes as well,' he reasons.

For Yes, the situation had reached a critical stage. The auditions they'd been conducting were tiring, disappointing, and in the end a waste of time. As Jon Anderson recalls, 'We just couldn't seem to find the man who could replace Rick. Someone who had a similar talent. A wide keyboard spectrum. We still wanted that colour.'

It stands to reason the Moraz should have jumped at the chance to join Yes – an established band, with a huge following, who were generally playing the kind of music he'd admired and played himself for years. When he turned up at the Barn to audition, the band were impressed with the 'European flavour' of his keyboard work. Moraz himself was sceptical. 'I found their new music very interesting and certainly very well played,' he remembers. 'Very flash. I was into that then.

'But I thought the vibe was very strange. There was so much difference between them, and they were very . . . cool. It was not an instant click, like, "Oh yeah!" At the end of the day, I didn't want to go into the band. I thought, "What the hell am I doing here? This isn't for me." The music and the vibes weren't the same kind of thing I was used to. Eddie Offord was very strange. They were *all* very strange.'

The band gave him tapes of the stuff they'd been working on, which he listened to carefully that night along with some of the older Yes albums. 'I was acquainted with their music anyway,' Patrick says. 'I could have played "Roundabout" by heart. By the next day, I'd analysed the tapes and I really liked them. I realized it *was* the kind of band I wanted to get into. I knew they were stuck somehow and I thought I could help, at least for a while.'

So Patrick Moraz stepped onto the keyboard platform, and preparations for the eighth Yes album continued. The band had put down so much material as a four-piece that Moraz was often only asked to fill in the blank spots. While he wasn't, a rumour had it, told exactly what to play straight down the line, Steve Howe admits that Moraz was, by necessity, 'directed' a bit more than if he'd been there from the beginning. 'Occasionally, we said, "It needs a bit more here," so I suppose he was pointed a bit into the Yes way of doing things. But he could play the music we wanted to play, and he seemed to have this endless ability to improvise.'

Patrick was thrown in at the deep end,

Above: Alan White for Ludwig drums
Opposite: Howe on *Beginnings*. 'The people around me told me what they thought I wanted to hear'
Overleaf: 'I'd never actually played in America before' – Patrick Moraz

and had to memorize all the new music (including the imposing 'The Gates Of Delirium') within a week. Over a period of six years, however, Yes had refined their way of working in the studio to a slow science of sign language and monosyllables that was all but incomprehensible to outsiders. Not surprisingly, there were times when Moraz couldn't understand what they were going on about.

'I had to learn their vocabulary,' he says. 'It was like when you go into a new country, you have to learn the language. Even if you are already familiar with it, it always takes time to learn it the way the people there actually speak it.'

Staking out his own territory was easier said than done. 'Everybody is trying to make a musical statement within the framework, within the musical pattern,' he explains. 'So, of course, to accommodate everybody's ego within one musical framework takes time.'

With that end of things still only partially sorted out, Yes began recording down at Chris Squire's as-yet-unfinished studio, using Eddie Offord's new, super-duper recording desk.

More than anything, *Relayer* could probably cop the prize for the oddest Yes album of all. If the band were nervous after the critical murdering of *Topographic*, it didn't show. But though the new music was often powerfully brilliant, it was just as often uneven and coldly aggressive in a startlingly un-Yes-like way.

Technical is the key word. While Yes had always sweated overtime to be precise and technologically adventurous, there was always that underlying flavour of something older in their music. They were a modern electric band, but their influences and subtle colourings stretched back over the centuries – something that always came through on their albums.

With most of *Relayer*, however, the focus was nerve-shatteringly futuristic – all stainless steel and glass, hard as nails and almost robotic in places. In a sense, the new Yes was a plutonium-powered, science-fiction band, with the Wonder Of Modern Technology burned into every groove. Patrick Moraz and his 'European Approach' may have accounted for part of the sudden change (and, as he suggests, 'The production was terrible.'), but the Yes on *Relayer* seemed not quite flesh and blood. There was a cold, alien edge to their music now, an over-attention to flash and slick jazz/rock pyrotechnics that bordered on self-indulgence, despite the tightness of the act.

Jon Anderson had initially visualized the album as a long-winded musical adaptation of Tolstoy's *War And Peace*. But whether he saw the light on his own, or was talked out of the idea at gunpoint, the basic theme was condensed into a mini-epic, 'The Gates Of Delirium', which took up the whole of side one.

At times during the charge and battle sequences, the band's power was spine-chilling. But there was an awful lot of fancy window-dressing cluttering up the view. Much of the track seemed to be a semi-organized jam that meandered as much as it impressed, with Anderson's vocal presence unusually understated and subdued from start to finish.

Moraz's urban, progressive jazz influence particularly came to the fore during the opening bars of 'Sound Chaser'. Drums, bass, and keyboards lurch through a Chick Corea/Return To Forever speedfreak overture, setting the pace for Howe's unaccompanied lunatic guitar solo – ten thousand notes per second, with gypsy mellotron melodrama courtesy of Patrick. It was impressive, but the rest of the track seemed to be blowing for the sake of it. Lots of wiggly synthesizers and guitar, interspersed with heavy breathing and satanic cha-cha-cha's.

Like the prelude to 'The Gates Of Delirium', the serene 'To Be Over' (by and large the most traditionally 'Yes' track on the album) could have easily turned up on *Topographic* – strange, because Anderson was still touchy about the reviews. Howe's graceful lines on steel guitar, in particular, were understated but effective. The track proved that Yes could ease off on the amphetamine intensity and concentrate instead on ambiance and atmosphere.

So *Relayer*, while excellent from a distance, was oddly disappointing over all. There was little warmth, and the impressive drive and aggression in the music was cancelled out by the suspicion that Yes were trying too hard to be something they're not. Whether it was a simple case of everyone overdosing on Mahavishnu Orchestra albums, or whether the band were over-reacting to the aesthetic failure of *Topographic*, *Relayer* sounded forced – too derivative of the jazz/rock fusion music in vogue at the time.

Like the *Fragile* era, the months surrounding *Relayer* had been months of considerable change for Yes. After what Steve Howe calls 'an awfully long, drawn-out saga – real Peyton Place' the band's contract with Hemdale had finally expired. Yes left, and Brian Lane came with them, buying back the rights to their songs (which had been signed away to pay the bills) at what Lane calls 'a bargain price'. Under the separate but interlocking umbrellas of Yes Music and Sun Artistes, Yes and Brian set up shop on their own.

Once again, the band had cleaned up in the British and international section of the *Melody Maker* readers' poll, with individual awards for Squire, Eddie Offord, Anderson and Howe (as composers), and the now-departed Rick Wakeman.

An American tour was organized to coincide with the release of *Relayer* – the first of several mammoth treks with Moraz that would get longer and longer each time around. 'I had to learn material from eight records,' Patrick says. 'I think we only had two rehearsals before we went to America, and one of those was actually *in* America.'

During 'The Gates Of Delirium', Moraz tackled seventeen changes of keyboards in the first twenty-two bars. As he says, 'In one go, I went from the seven keyboards I had in Refugee to the

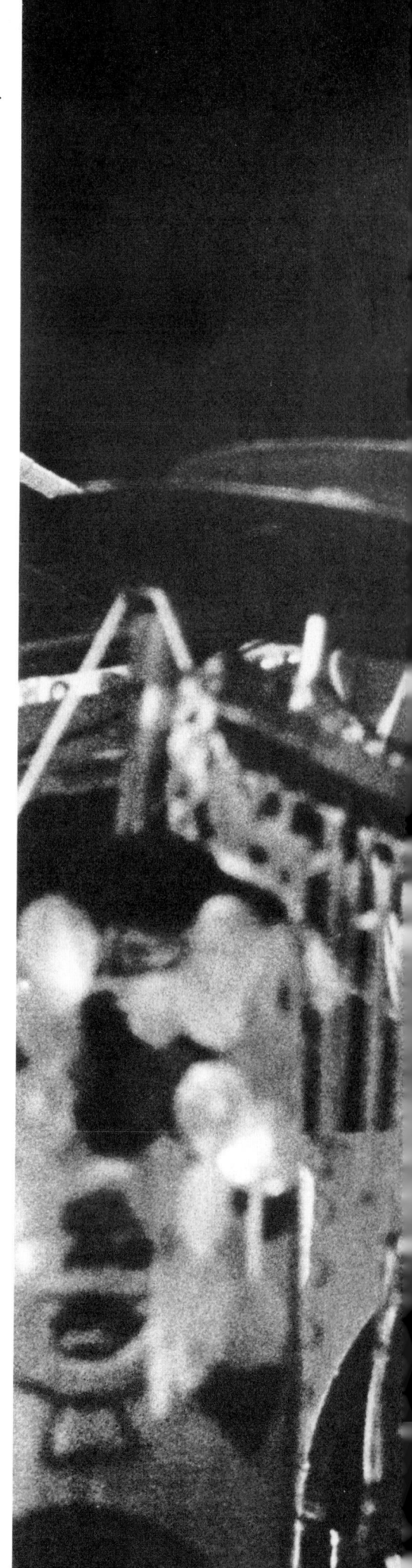

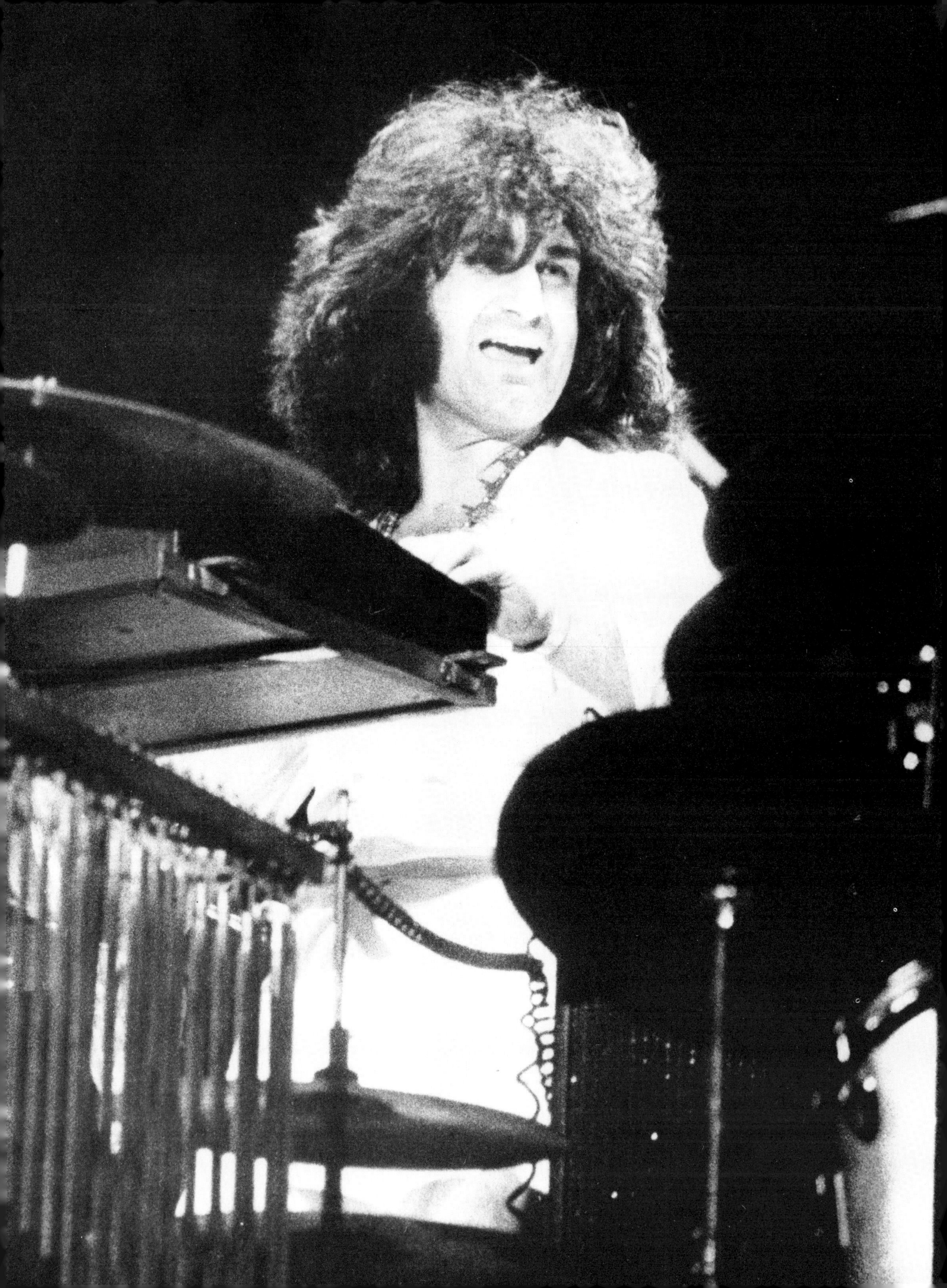

fourteen I played with Yes. It was difficult, especially at that time because it was a turning point in keyboards. They had all these new synthesizers, but they were all monophonic, so you needed a lot of them to get the effects.'

Eddie Offord, who was on what proved to be his final Yes tour, thinks Moraz overdid it. 'He took on too much,' Offord says. 'All those keyboards, keeping them in tune, and playing all the parts he was supposed to play. It was a phenomenal task, and I don't think he could quite cope with it.'

Patrick slowly started to get the hang of things. More time, another album, a bit more road work, and he'd probably have it down pat. The only snag was that the Yes calendar wasn't quite mapped out that way. Atlantic had scheduled the release of *Yesterdays* (a retrospective album containing tracks from the first two albums, plus 'Dear Father' and 'America'), and three weeks of British gigs were already lined up for April and May of the new year. But instead of recording another album, the first quarter of 1975 would be set aside for the solo albums everyone had been thinking about for ages. Anderson and Howe had planned one as far back as 1972, for example, when they'd intended to collaborate on an album with musical director Johnny Harris (one side of Jon's songs, the other devoted to an orchestral version of Steve's 'Mood For A Day'), but the idea never got past the talking stage.

This time, the Master Plan called for everyone to start and finish their projects at more or less the same time. Jon Anderson ran into technical problems with his – leading, in part, to the cancellation of a Far East tour. But between October 1975 and June 1976 all the solo albums were put on the market.

Steve Howe's varied stockpile of self-penned tunes formed the basis for *Beginnings*. His solo vocals on several of them might have been better left unsung, and hotshot soloing may have been curiously absent, but the instrumental tracks (particularly the pastoral, nine-minute-plus title track) bore the hallmark of someone who was comfortably at home behind a set of guitar strings. The album was flawed (a fact Howe is well aware of), though it did give him the opportunity to display an even wider range of guitar facets than he'd been able to with Yes. In that sense, it served its purpose.

Not surprisingly, Chris Squire took the neo-pagan, wide-screen approach with *Fish Out Of Water*, pulling all the stops for that 'epic feel' that Yes had been after from the start. With Squire's spectacular bass work as a centrepiece, the album's scope was immense, riding a wave of symphonic-scale orchestrations (courtesy of Chris's formed Syn compatriot, Andrew Jackman) – arguably adding up to the most musically successful of the five solo projects.

Virtually every keyboard instrument and musical gadget in the catalogue turned up on Patrick Moraz's i, along with a squad of top-notch session men, Patrick's tap-dancing father, and an army of Brazilian percussionists. The complex, often crazed, end-product was at times powerfully inspired, at times cacophonic, and at times straight *Dr Who* – orchestrated with as much care as a symphony. The album may have appealed to more specialized tastes, but

Above: Alan and Patrick in New York with Atlantic's Barbara Carr and Jerry Greenberg during the promotional tour for *Ramshackled* and **i**

Opposite: The band in Chris and Nikki Squire's Surrey garden

pointed out the degree to which Patrick's potential hadn't been tapped on *Relayer* – a situation that would almost inevitably cause problems in the near future.

Alan White took the 'family' route with *Ramshackled*, bringing in a crew of musician friends he'd worked with over the years. Although the gas was turned up under the rhythm section right from the start, the album was undoubtedly the most eclectic of the crop – the most un-Yes-like of all, running the full gamut from funk, to jazz/rock, to suburban reggae, to ethereal.

Jon Anderson's *Olias Of Sunhillow* was the only real 'solo album' in the strictest sense of the term. Armed with a sci-fi tale inspired by Roger Dean's *Fragile* starships and Vera Stanley-Alder's book, *The Initiation Of The World*, Jon locked himself inside his home studio with some thirty-odd musical instruments. The resulting album was an organic, swirling, sonic poem of synthesized space sounds and multi-tracked voices – limited in instrumental expertise and a bit 'samey' in places, but mesmerizing at times just the same.

As Atlantic prepared to release the first of the solo albums, a long-delayed, three-year-old feature film of Yes in action rolled out of the vaults. Shot by film-makers David Speechley and Peter Neal, the seventy-five-minutes *Yessongs* was a celluloid record of a younger Yes on stage at the Rainbow in 1972, racing through material from *The Yes Album*, *Fragile*, and the newly-released *Close To The Edge*.

'The guys arrived with cameras on the day of the show,' Michael Tait recalls. 'They just turned up and said, 'Uh... we're here to film the concert.' No one knew anything about it. No preparations had been made. We were playing in the dark, and it was a joke. Pathetic.'

Even so, *Yessongs* was destined to go down a storm, particularly in America, where it would rank respectably among the fifty highest-grossing films over a two-month period. In Chicago during the last week of December 1975, it pulled in more money than *Jaws* – then the hottest film in the country.

In the end, none of the five solo albums acquired legendary status. All sold reasonably well on both sides of the Atlantic, all made the middle-to-upper regions of the American charts, and as Steve Howe says, 'The people who bought them were the people they were intended for' – even if most of those people were already dyed-in-the-wool Yes fanatics.

All the albums helped siphon off some of that excess creative steam, however, and perhaps pointed a way out of the blind alley Yes seemed to have marched into with *Relayer*. The fact that nobody in the band suddenly became A Legend In His Own Time was of little importance, and it was probably better that way. As Howe admits, 'It would have been very exciting if one of the albums had done really well, but it *possibly* would have affected the stability of the group. At the time, of course, we all said that it wouldn't, but...'

107

CHAPTER SIX

MUSICAL CHAIRS

Famous? I'm not famous. Sometimes people come up to me and say, 'Hey, Steve.' Other times, they stop me outside the hall and ask me if I want to buy a Yes T-shirt, or a Yes poster, or a Yes badge. Or even a ticket to the Yes concert.
JON ANDERSON

'We had Jean Ristori mixing for us,' says Steve Howe, remembering 1976. 'It was an era of technology that baffled me. I saw everybody getting more and more equipment, and I kind of wondered whether everything might have been getting just a little bit out of hand.'

That Bicentennial summer saw Yes back in America. In the midst of one of their most gruelling tours yet, they played to an estimated crowd of 100,000 in Philadelphia and later reluctantly co-operated with the cameras for *Yessongs II* – an on-the-road, cinéma vérité project that would never be completed.

It was autumn before the band finally got down to mapping out their next album. Although Yes had spent nearly sixteen weeks during the previous year rehearsing new material minus Anderson (who was still grappling with *Olias*), most of it was eventually scrapped. Bored with London studios and with the taxman eyeing their wallets, the band split *en masse* for Mountain Studios in Montreux, Switzerland (where every day is Sunday) to start all over again.

Unfortunately, serious problems were brewing. Again. After a Yes album, a solo album, and several huge tours, Patrick Moraz was dragging his feet. Although he'd spent his first year with the band urging them to become 'more outrageous and percussive', his enthusiasm had waned. As Jon Anderson explains, Patrick 'got to the point where he just wasn't playing like he was involved. His sound wasn't too good, and that reflected his vibe. He's a lovely man, a gentleman, but it was obvious that he just wasn't getting off on what we were doing.

'He's a moving person. A gypsy. He wanders from one thing to another. A very good player, but temperamental. He's a Cancer. Very romantic and very strong. And he knows what he likes. But a group can only survive if the parts of that group have the right amount of talent and energy to fit it all together, though they don't *necessarily* have to be going in the same direction.

'The direction is achieved afterwards, not beforehand. It's the interaction of the people within the band that creates that direction. So if you've got one person who isn't putting in enough energy, then somebody's got to work overtime to keep it together.'

For Moraz, that initial suspicion that he and Yes just weren't suited to each

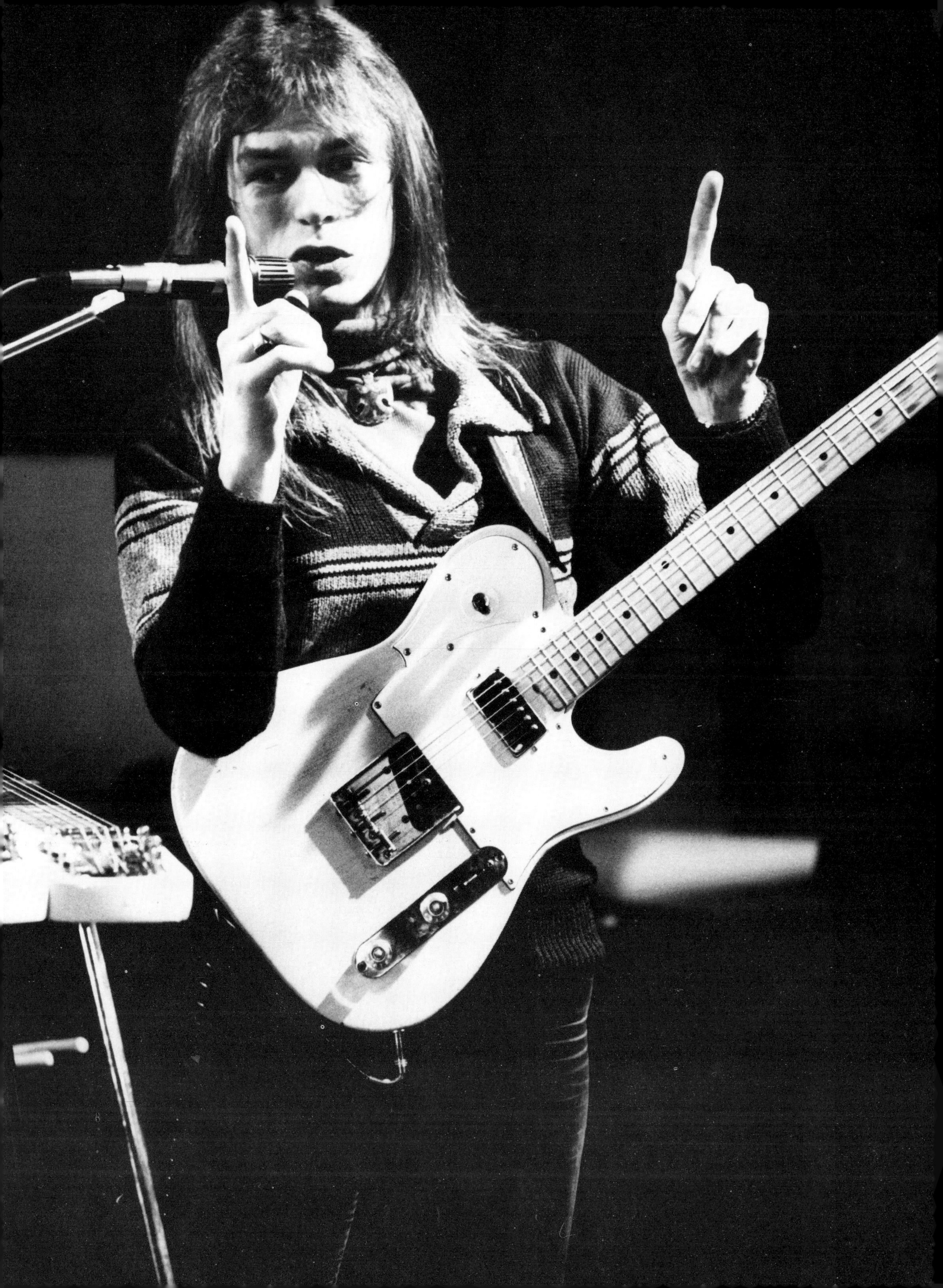

other had proven itself. 'When I was working on my solo album, working with people like Alphonse Mouzon and Jeff Berlin, they could understand my music and ideas so fast, and even write them down,' Patrick says. 'I suddenly realized that I was with musicians who could play exactly what I wanted, and *fast*, whereas with Yes it would have taken ages. Yes weren't into the music I tried to get them to play, and that threw me off a little bit, you know?

'I really enjoyed working with Chris – he's a very interesting musician. I think all of them are excellent musicians, but I also think that good musicians should be able to play virtually every kind of music, and be able to understand it quickly and play it fast. With the right intention. The right spirit. I didn't find that at the time, and that's what made me start wondering about what I was really doing there.'

To a certain extent, the problem was rooted in that lack of clear communication. 'The best way to describe Patrick is that he's Swiss,' Alan White says. 'Psychologically, he was a foreigner, and there's a link in there someplace. He didn't fit in.'

Steve Howe agrees, but with reservations. 'I never quite saw it that way,' he says. 'Once he joined the group, he joined the group. But what we didn't realize when he joined was that we really needed an *English* person who could understand when we'd go "Whoooooooossssshhhhhhh". The rest of us were so at home with each other that we never accounted for the fact that Patrick wasn't used to the way we talked, the way we worked.

'He often misunderstood us, which was nobody's fault, but then again, there was a lot of pressure put on him because he had to live up to where he was.'

Moraz claims that the problems stemmed from more than just a simple lack of communication, explaining that he felt hemmed in by the rest of Yes, and that he wasn't given enough to do. 'With Yes, I realized that they always keep the keyboards very subdued in the mix,' he says. 'Whether there's a keyboard player there or not doesn't really matter, unless it's Rick Wakeman, because he has that charisma. But I never felt there was an important relationship between the keyboards and the other instruments in Yes. I had no responsibilities.'

There's the suspicion that Anderson made him nervous. 'Well, you know how difficult it is to work with Jon,' Patrick says. 'I got really pissed off at times. In some ways he's a genius, in other ways not. He's a genius in terms of simplicity in lines and ideas, but he's a very difficult person to work with. He doesn't give way. Everything's up to him.'

Above: Patrick Moraz
Opposite: J.F.K. Stadium in Philadelphia on 12 June 1976. The biggest Yes gig to date
Previous page: Steve Howe during tour rehearsals at Lee International Film Studios in London, April 1976

Jon Anderson admits that he cracked the whip over Patrick's head in the end, but feels the tactics were necessary. 'In all honesty, I liked Patrick so much that I *would* shout at him,' he says. 'If I didn't like the guy, I wouldn't even bother talking to him. He made me nervous, and I appreciate that he got more nervous as I got more nervous.

'There was that time the *N.M.E.* quoted me, and that was a quote if I ever saw one,' Anderson goes on. '"Get your finger out, or get out." If you're playing football in a team and you're letting them down, get out. If you're not playing music well, get out. If you're not interested any more, get out. If it's obvious that you're not really helping, then it's time to go.'

By mutual agreement that it wasn't working out, Moraz quietly left, and still maintains that the original decision to split was his. 'I have no regrets,' he says.

'The two years I was with the group was good experience, and we all benefited from it.'

Or as Steve Howe adds as a postscript. 'It was Patrick's dream to play with Yes. And he did.'

In the two-and-a-half years he'd been away from Yes, Rick Wakeman hadn't been cooling his heels. He'd co-produced an album for Wally with deejay and *Old Grey Whistle Test* presenter Bob Harris, and, within weeks of his departure from the band in June 1974, presented an open-air, almost instant replay of *Journey To The Centre Of The Earth* at South London's Crystal Palace with his five-piece band, 'The New World Symphony Orchestra', the English Chamber Choir, and two inflatable plastic dinosaurs that rose from the knee-deep lake in front of the stage.

The gig informally confirmed that the

shock/horror Yes split was the real McCoy, and that Rick was now a card-carrying Solo Artiste. However, the strain of getting the show organized took its toll.

'I woke up the morning of the concert and felt really horrible,' he remembers. 'I couldn't move my arms, but the doctor came around and gave me a couple of jabs of morphine so I felt okay. I went to Crystal Palace, did the concert, and everybody told me later that it was really great, but I have no recollection of actually being on stage at all.'

Within a couple of days, Wakeman had lost nearly thirty pounds in weight. 'I felt terrible again, and this time the doctor called an ambulance. I was in such a state that they wouldn't even let me walk downstairs. The next thing I knew, I was on a stretcher being carted off to hospital.

'Four doctors were waiting there.' Rick continues. 'I thought, "Hmmmmm . . . this is a bit funny." I had no idea of how sick I was until they wheeled me through a door marked CARDIAC ARREST UNIT. Then I absolutely freaked.'

Officially, the then twenty-four-year-old Wakeman had suffered a mild heart attack, and spent several weeks recuperating in a hospital bed.

Despite heavy warnings from the cardiac specialists, Rick took *Journey* on the road in America early that autumn. With an electrocardiograph machine waiting at each port of call and a suitcase full of heart pills, Wakeman touched down in twenty-two cities in twenty-five days in a rented Lockheed Electra, with 118 musicians, singers, and technicians in tow – all of which depleted Rick's bank account considerably – to the tune of $243,000.

After a Far East tour, he jumped into a project he'd started working on in the hospital – a new vinyl extravaganza in the *Journey* tradition, based this time on the exploits of King Arthur and his Knights of the Round Table. Once again, he hired half the musicians in Britain to play on the album.

While the project was technically ambitious, Wakeman's MGM-style musical impressions of Guinevere, Sirs Galahad and Lancelot, Merlin, and Arthur himself were, like *Six Wives* and *Journey*, obviously aimed at a wider audience. While Yes had always semi-consciously geared their music to a

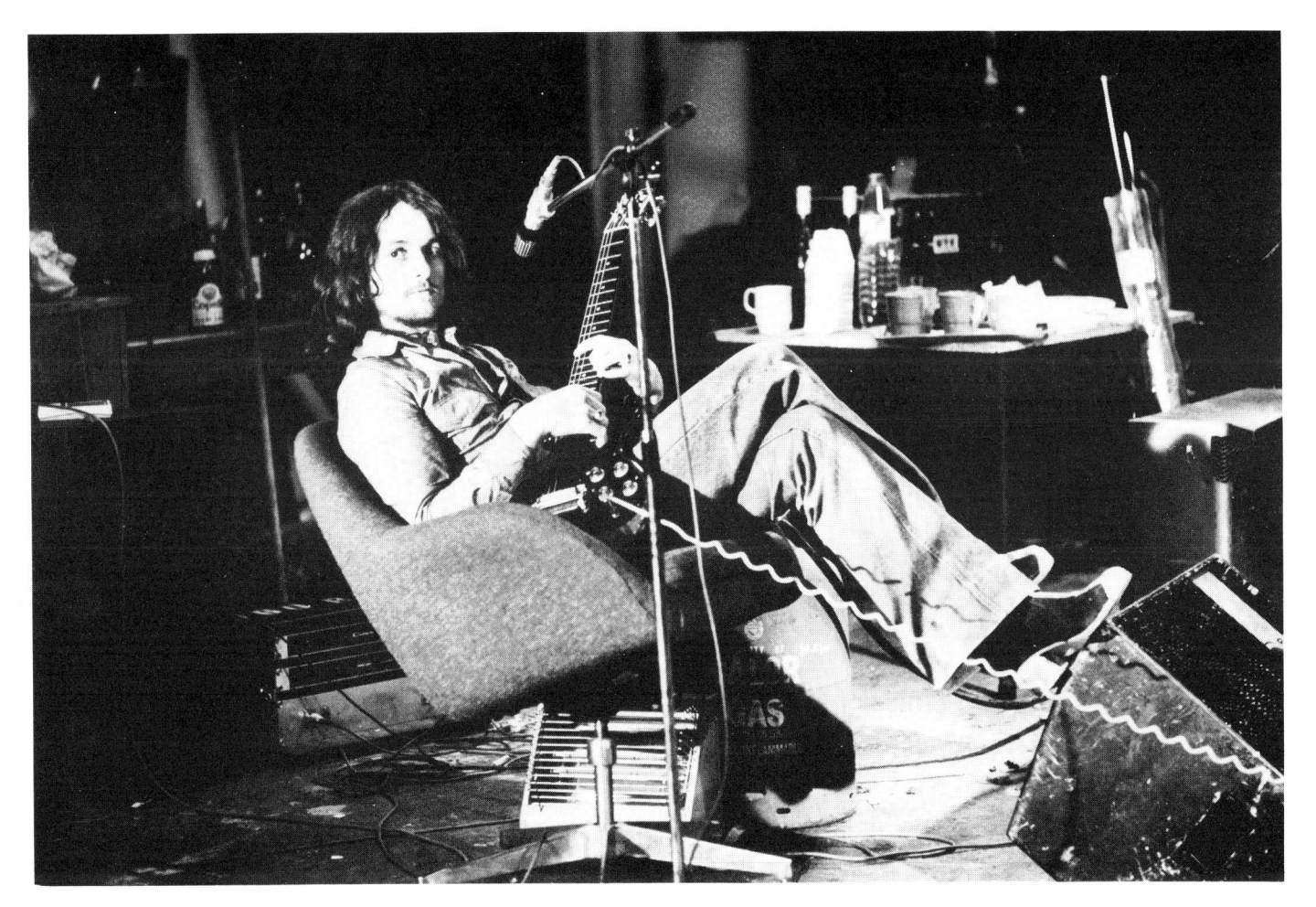

Above: 'I've always been into the artistic side of all this – the album sleeves and single sleeves, the booklets and the tour programmes. Those are the things I wish I'd gotten more involved in' – Jon Anderson
Opposite: Chris Squire doing a sound check in Jackson, Mississippi, 5 June 1976

specific, open-minded cult audience, Rick seemed set on creating Modern Classics For The Common Man – clear-cut, uncomplicated stuff that anyone with a working set of ears would be able to comprehend.

But in the aftermath of his concert successes with the flamboyant *Journey* concerts, Wakeman was caught in the slipstream of having to outdo himself the next time around.

His original scheme to hold a medieval pageant near the Cornish site of Arthur's legendary Tintagel Castle was axed by the local authorities, so Wakeman was forced to opt for second best with three nights at the Empire Pool, Wembley. On ice.

Actually, there were a mere nineteen skaters in Rick's Arthurian ice spectacular, but the elaborate stage setting, with the now-obligatory band, choir, and symphonic-sized orchestra, unravelled a few more threads from the shirt on Wakeman's back. The shows were packed solid, but expenditures exceeded profits. With the financial sting of that expensive American tour still fresh, Rick had to chalk up another $120,000 to experience.

Although he subsequently toured Brazil and the Far East on a slightly less elaborate scale, the era of Wakeman's Big Productions was over.

For the rest of 1975 he kept a low profile, shelving plans for another epic called *Suite Of The Gods,* but producing and arranging the score for Ken Russell's *Lisztomania* – which features Rick's first and possibly last acting role as Thor, the Norse God Of Thunder.

1976 rolled round, and there wasn't an orchestra in sight for Rick's next album, *No Earthly Connection* – just a roomful of keyboards, the six-man English Rock Ensemble (with vocalist Ashley Holt held over from the earlier band), and a theme revolving around Wakeman's long-standing fascination with UFOs. In music *and* words.

That, in itself, was enough to cause a few raised eyebrows, because after all the stink over *Topographic* and the inability philosophically and artistically to see eye to eye with Jon Anderson, Rick was suddenly churning out song lyrics conspicuously Andersonian in style.

Wakeman and the ERE hit the road, playing British city halls and cinemas considerably smaller than the Empire Pool before heading out onto the Continent. Earlier on, Yes had been approached to create a original score for a proposed film of the 1976 Winter Olympics at Innsbruck – though, as in the case of a film called *Peace* which they'd been asked to collaborate on as far back as 1971, the band turned it down.

Since Brian Lane was still managing Wakeman, the request was naturally forwarded, Rick agreed, and later spent five weeks writing, producing, and playing – gearing his music to the various Olympic events features in the film, which eventually went out under the title of *White Rock*.

But as Wakeman had discovered time and time again, the drawback of being a Solo Artiste was that *everything* was his responsibility. By the summer of 1976, the workload and the strain were both physically and mentally drilling him through the floorboards. The crunch came when the accounts from the European tour had been checked, and Rick was informed clear out of the blue that he was roughly $700,000 in debt.

Faced with hard reality, Wakeman disbanded the ERE and unloaded several of his outside business interests, including the Fragile Carriage Company – the car-hire firm he'd built around his stunning collection of vintage Rolls-Royces.

The situation was so tense and rife with paranoia that he was on the verge of severing business relations with Brian Lane, until A & M Records agreed to fork over the record royalties that were due him ahead of time, thereby pulling Rick out of a financial nose dive that could have crippled his career for years.

Not surprisingly, a wiser Rick headed for higher ground and an even lower profile, casting his lot in with none other than Bill Bruford and ex-King Crimson/Uriah Heep bassist John Wetton.

In theory, it should have worked, but a news leak in *Melody Maker* during the second week in October partially pulled the plug on the whole caper. With the three-piece band still in secret rehearsals and a pile of contractual hassles still to be ironed out, the announcement caused chaos among the managers, music publishers, and record companies involved. Although Bill Bruford claims that the problem 'could have been sorted out in time if Rick had really put himself into it', the unnamed, six-week-old Wakeman/Bruford/Wetton triumvirate faded into oblivion before they'd even climbed down off the drawing board.

So when Brian Lane's partner and tour manager, Alex Scott, flew into England from Montreux (followed by Lane a few days later), Rick Wakeman was 'resting', with no band on the horizon and no plans for a tour or another album in the pipeline. He'd crossed paths with various Yes members on a few occasions, but hadn't had anything to do with the band since that early summer of 1974 – though, as he says, 'After I left, there were so many legal problems and hassles that, in a way, I'd never *legally* left the band.'

He hesitantly agreed to meet Yes in Switzerland, knowing that the verbal

Above: Patrick Moraz – 'I never played my best with Yes'
Opposite: Rick Wakeman

broadsides they'd fired at each other during the *Topographic* chapter were still fresh in everyone's minds. While the initial claim that he was *solely* brought in as a session man has always been hard to swallow, the Moraz situation had left the band stranded in the studio with neither the desire nor the patience to start hunting for another man.

Bringing in Wakeman, even on a temporary basis, was a matter open for debate. 'I didn't necessarily think it was the best move to make,' Jon Anderson says. 'I was a bit wary. I didn't want the same thing to happen again. I just didn't want any aggravation on that kind of level at that point in the band's career. We didn't need that, and I just wanted someone who'd really put his full energy into it.

'But that first meeting was strange after not seeing Rick for so long. It started out, "Hey! Everybody okay?" with everybody smiling on kind of a semi-forced, formal level. Friendly, but weird, you know? At the beginning we were all pretty wary, but by the time we finished we were all very happy. We were all beaming for twenty-four hours.'

Wakeman ran an ear over the rough demo tapes the band had been working on, and decided the stuff was definitely up his street – in his words, 'Magic'. When he later took some of the music for a test drive at the studio, the direction was clear. As Alan White says, 'Rick was *there*. I could feel the enthusiasm. He was really getting off on what we were doing.'

When Atlantic's Montreux office threw a small party for Yes, the subject of Rick coming in on a full-time basis was brought up. As Steve Howe explains, 'We felt he was playing good, had moved along a little bit, progressed a bit, had some experience that would be valid to us, and therefore hadn't totally wasted his time since we last saw him. But then again, we felt that his style of keyboard playing came across very well in the group, and that's what we were offering him, really.'

For the second time in five-and-a-half years, Rick Wakeman joined Yes. Although all of them went through a period of trying to shrug off the verbal mudslinging that had gone on a couple of years before, Yes put their heads down and got to work immediately, even it it did take them another six long months to finish the album.

'When we decided to get together again and set all our gear up, it was really . . . it's hard to explain,' Rick says. 'We hadn't playing a note together in three-and-a-half years, but it was like we'd only just done a concert a couple of days before. I *had* to leave when I did though. If I hadn't, the frustration would have just stayed inside, building up, and that wouldn't have been good for any of us. I think there was also the problem that the band became very successful all of a sudden – over the space of about six months with *Fragile*. We were all suddenly on a plateau where nobody had time to think, and we never really got the chance to know each other.

'The irony of it all is that Jon and I realized that we were really after the same thing. It's just that with our different backgrounds and influences, we were trying for it in our own way. That goes for the others too, I think. I've said this before, but if you can imagine this big sphere, with all of us on one side trying to get around to the other side . . . we might go in different direction to get there, but we're all aiming for that exact same place on the other side. It's like flying from Australia to Los Angeles. There are lots of different routes, and they all end up in L.A.

'But when somebody says "Yes", you think of the music and not so much of the people in the band. It's like with the great composers – Bach, Beethoven, Brahms. Not that I'm making a comparison, but if someone says "Beethoven", you don't really think of this deaf, grey-haired old man sitting at a piano. You think of his music. And that, I think, is what Yes are all aiming for.'

But as Jon Anderson remembers, 'Rick said, "It's great to be back. I've been through a lot," and I said, "It's good to have you back, but I've got one thing to say: I haven't changed. I'm still the same kind of character. If it's not happening, I'll tell you. If it is, I'll praise you as much as the next guy."

'So I was on the level and . . . blunt. That's my upbringing, to say what it really is. If it's black, it's black. If it's white, it's white. Let's sort it out and get on with it.'

Anderson, Howe, Squire, Wakeman, and the band as a whole pulled in eight awards in the *Melody Maker* poll that autumn, though Wakeman was back in the band for weeks before anyone outside the Yes camp got wind of it. At the time, Steve Howe says, 'There was a lot of poppycock talk about how we didn't want to make Patrick look disgraced or make it look like Rick had come back for the money. We tried to hold up announcing it as long as possible so Patrick could get himself ready in what he wanted to do.

'I think all Rick and I said to each other was, "Oh well, let's carry on from where we left off." It's the greatest lesson you can learn to actually become friendly with your enemies – especially, of course, if that enemy is a friend who you've fallen out with.'

Jon Anderson's view of the late 1976/ early 1977 Yes and their tenth album, *Going For The One*, is fairly concise. 'We'd gone full circle,' he says. 'We were beginning the next cycle.'

In a way, there was nowhere else to go. While the period between the summer of 1974 and the autumn of 1976 had seen concert attendances soar to an all-

Opposite: 7 January 1977. Steve Howe at Mountain Studios in Montreux, Switzerland
Above: Since Mountain's proper studio was far too small, Yes took over the Casino downstairs

time high, and *Topographic* and *Relayer* score well in the charts despite the fact that what could be called the 'Yes Vision' had not been realized, the band sensed that they'd played themselves into a corner. All had learned a lesson or two from the *Topographic* episode, and largely perceived the stainless-steel futurism of *Relayer* as an ultimate dead end.

The only way to go was *backwards*, or at least to try and rekindle some of the life and spontaneity that had characterized, say, *The Yes Album* – that pounding rock energy that had been unconsciously pushed out of the studio door as the symphonic-scale productions moved further into uncharted territory.

In other words, Yes began to suspect that maybe they *were* in danger of vanishing up their own posteriors – but far from a cop-out, *Going For The One* really did sound like the start of another era. The New Yes.

Sure, there were the trademarks. Anderson's 'Wonderous Stories', with Wakeman's polymoog cascading like a waterfall, had that timeless, ethereal quality that had become the hallmark of his song-poems over the years – an aura shared on a more epic scale by the graceful, melancholy 'Turn Of The Century', underscored by Rick and Steve's wistful piano and Spanish guitar.

But it was on the remaining tracks where Yes nearly blew a gasket. For one thing, bass and drums were back with a vengeance after four years of being buried in *Topographic*'s basement or lost in the confusion of *Relayer*. Instead of homing in on flash and blinding technique, however, the rhythm section's focus was on *power* now – a roaring, rock-steady omnipotence that torpedoed the band's rediscovered dynamism into gear.

From the start of Alan's count-in, 'Going For The One' was a wired, head-spinning shift in direction – a jump-start for the new phase, even if it was a bit too shrill and frantic to join the ranks of all-time Yes classics.

On the other hand, 'Parallels' reached those heights with ease. One of Squire's tunes that was originally destined for

Fish Out Of Water, it's volcanic bass line and cathedralesque organ easily put it in potential 'Roundabout' class. A majestic, driving piece of Squirean grandeur, it captured the essence of Yes, while capitalizing on their rediscovered taste for hard-edged rock.

In the lyric departments, Anderson made a noticeable attempt at clarifying his imagery. His style on 'Turn Of The Century' was ornate but told a story, while one gently self-mocking section from 'Going For The One' was proof that Jon doesn't take himself as seriously as many would assume.

'I don't think I'd want to write a really commercial, top ten hit song,' Jon says. 'I don't know if I *could* do it, actually – though I'm not sure what the next step is. In a way, maybe I'm a better singer than a writer. I know that I write in a certain way, in an identifiable style . . . and it's called "twee"! But the funny thing is, if you look at the lyrics to, say, "The Gates Of Delirium", *they're* not twee. At least I don't think so, yet "Soon" is a very, very twee sort of thing. When I first wrote it, I thought, now that's right near the knuckle. "Soon, oh soon", it will arrive. The Second Coming. Or soon peace. Or soon love. But why not? That's what I believe.'

But some of those very early Yes lyrics were a bit suspect.

'Yeah, some of the stuff on *Time And A Word*.'

Or, 'she puts the sweetness in, stirs it with a spoon'.

'Yeah,' Anderson moans. 'Well, that was the first thing I ever wrote with the group, and those lyrics just came. In fact, most lyrics that I write just . . . appear. I think they all need a great deal of attention always, but they seem to flow when they're ready to come out. I don't want to deny that or hold back. If I start thinking, well, somebody's not going I like this line, so I'd better change it, unless it comes pretty instantly, I don't think there's any point in denying what's naturally flowing out. It's like the air you breathe.'

Yes hadn't completely purged their flair for *Ben Hur*-length extravaganzas out of their systems by any means. The fifteen-and-a-half-minute 'Awaken' was proof that they had a new understanding of how and how not to build a better epic.

If 'Close To The Edge' had been neo-Christian in its church-like magnificence, 'Awaken' was positively pagan – real human-sacrifice stuff with barbarian chanting, looming bass, Ghenghis Khan guitar, and earthquake drums, hurtling along like a thunderstorm. Steve Howe, in particular, outdid himself with a typhoon of an electric 12-string solo that blew the lid off of just about everything he'd done before.

But there'd been changes made since the last time around, and not only in the switch from Moraz to Wakeman. After a seven-year stretch with the band, Eddie Offord had long since ridden off towards the horizon for health, but primarily creative, reasons. Although the band produced *Going For The One* on their own (aided by engineer John Timperley,

Above: Jon Anderson
Opposite: Squire's triple-necked bass, built by Wal, was inherited from Wakeman's English Rock Ensemble

who'd worked, like Eddie had later on, with ELP), there's the impression that Offord's sometimes erratic but unique flair was missed.

'He felt very much like the sixth member of the band in the studio,' Steve Howe admits. 'It was a nice working situation. Nothing got out of hand in the early days, and there was a lot of pushing from Eddie to get things right.

'I think the only time we could tell the real difference was when we did *Going For The One* with Timperley. Chris and I really realized what Eddie had been doing for us, because we suddenly had somebody who wanted to do the "right" thing for us – but that wasn't what we wanted! John Timperley almost had to relearn engineering from our point of view, which was sort of impossible.'

Yes considered asking Eddie back to do *Going For The One*, though the idea was never carried through. 'Not that we've lost by not having Eddie,' Steve says. 'His last words about us in the *N.M.E.* were that he felt like he was trying to produce five producers.

'In the end, he knew his scene and he knew ours, but we were verging on his a little too much. It got to the point where on *Relayer* certain things were talked about, but if Eddie didn't want to do them he suddenly found that he'd been overridden. We didn't really leave him his bit of say any more.

'At the same time he was becoming more and more unreliable,' Howe adds. 'On tours, Eddie could do that crowd over, but he could also let us down and give us a shit sound. We did manage to keep a good rapport, even though he was leaping around like a maniac half the time, but it got to the point where we didn't think it was very funny any more.

'Mind you, Eddie Offord was *unique*! In the studio, he'd come in, do headstands around the room, pull out a bottle of whisky, roll a joint, and say, "Just give me a couple of minutes and I'll be ready." He was a great personality.'

While the band were still in Montreaux, Wakeman (on the verge of splitting from his wife, and now based in Switzerland as a British tax exile) recorded *Criminal Record,* assisted by White and Squire. Musically, it never caught fire. But then, since Yes had last put out an album of new material in 1974, the musical climate (particularly in Britain) had changed dramatically. Where the giants like Yes, Led Zeppelin, The Who, and ELP had gone unchallenged for years, disco and new wave were suddenly in the spotlight, capturing the media's attention virtually overnight. While it didn't drastically affect record sales (in fact, most of the superbands were selling more albums that ever), the sales pitch for much of the new music hinged on the assumption that audiences were tired of the rock dinosaurs and the lifestyle and musical values they represent.

Maybe so, but it's doubtful whether it cost Yes any fans, particularly among that hard-core element that makes up such a huge percentage of their audience. With Rick back in the band, any confusion or disappointment over *Topographic* and *Relayer* was forgotten, with the result that the new Yes on *Going For The One* hit the number 1 spot in the British charts soon after its release. 'Wonderous Stories' – the band's first British single since 'Sweet Dreams' and released purely as a shot in the dark – moved into the Top Twenty in the album's wake.

In the States the single went almost unnoticed, yet the album shot to number 7 in *Cashbox*, aided by the already-in-progress, fifty-one date Yesshows 1977 tour (supported by Donovan) where, in Philadelphia alone, 40,000 tickets were sold in less than a day.

But as Michael Tait has mentioned, it wasn't only on the musical front that Yes were aiming for something simpler. With Roger Dean out of the picture over differences in opinion with the band, Hipgnosis had designed the *Going For The One* sleeve, the elaborate stage settings were gone and, image-wise, one of Yes's strongest links with their past was severed.

With a further thirty-three dates in Europe and Britain (including a record-breaking six nights at the Empire Pool, Wembley), Yes were virtually crawling on and off the plane by the time they hit the home stretch. Steve Howe had achieved one of his dreams by being voted best guitarist in the *Guitar Player* readers' poll. Yes had once again been voted best band in the international section of the *Melody Maker* readers' poll (with Jon and Chris piling up more awards between them), and continued to show up strongly in magazine and newspaper polls around the globe.

By mid February 1978, the band were already rehearsing at Sound Associates, off London's Queensway, sifting through more scraps, fragments and rough tapes for the album that would mark their tenth anniversary: *Tormato*.

Yes laid down enough new material during the *Tormato* sessions for an album and a half, though as Steve Howe suggests, it was possibly due to necessity as much as choice. 'Yes had hit quite an indecisive time,' he says. 'When we give ourselves lots of choice, we can eventually come up with something pretty good. We don't like having too little choice, you see. We start feeling hemmed in.

'Very often, we change the arrangements half a dozen times,' Howe explains. 'Like we'd be working on "On The Silent Wings Of Freedom" and somebody would say, "How were we doing this bit last week?" So somebody pulls out a cassette tape, puts it on, and three voices say, "No . . . that was the week before."

'We go on and on like that, and nobody can remember exactly how that bit went, so we have to go off and arrange it *again*. A piece we've already arranged. It's a real comedy sometimes.'

That eats up a lot of time and cash, Even after the arrangements have been fought over, and the tracks laid down and roughly mixed, each component goes through a murderous nit-picking process until they meet with the band's – and particularly Chris Squire's – near-fanatical standards.

'Yeah, maybe I do take a long time,' Chris concedes. 'But I can name a lot of albums that, if they'd had that approach to them, would have been a lot better. That includes Yes albums too. Precision is *always* worth it because the "joy and spontaneity of the moment" is usually only valid for the moment and the ensuing period around it.

'Usually, that sort of music becomes very invalid in retrospect, and I'm not looking for that. When I make a record – and a Yes album is just as much *my* record as it is everyone else's – I'm thinking about something people will be happy to put on in fifty years' time.'

Yes do seem to take their polishing process to extremes – which is why their albums appear weeks, or even months, after their originally scheduled release date – and test pressings are more often than not sent back to the cutting lab three or four times.

'But this is the age of emphasis on

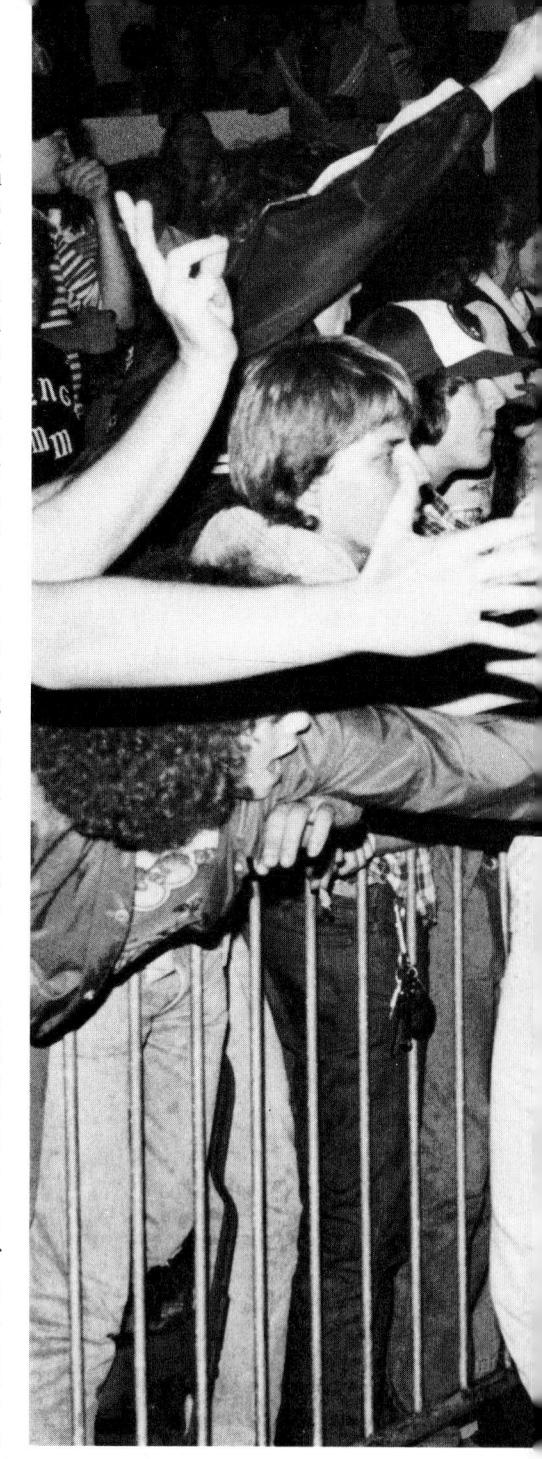

Madison Square Garden, New York, 6 September 1978

excellence,' Chris argues. 'One doesn't have to live up to it, but if you don't there are other people who will, and you always lose out in the end.

'With a group... well... *this* group, we work on the premise that we all have a vague idea, a different idea of what we want to do, so by the time we sort it out ... *that's* where our time goes. With "Parallels" and "Onward", which I presented on a simple demo tape – voice and piano – I tried to impress on everyone else from the start as solid a direction as I saw it. This tempo, that sort of feel. If you don't *know* what you want from the beginning, you're only wasting time. Personally, I just wish we'd spend more time rehearsing before we go into a studio.'

Alan White agrees that Yes often take things to extremes, but in contrast to the methodical Squire, he's 'a great believer in the moment. The liaison between instruments *is* like a conversation. If you've got the stuff written in your head and *then* play it, that's fair enough. But if you work it out on the spot and go for something spontaneous, you can often come up with better music in the end.'

As Steve Howe says, 'There's two extremes to deal with. Jon's is that we should record in three weeks, Chris's is "Don't tell me how long it takes, just tell me when it's right." In my experience, Chris is more right than Jon, but then we've made records we've thought were good, in long *and* short periods of time. *Relayer* was done very quickly, and I thought it was a reasonable album, while *Going For The One* took forever, and I honestly don't think it was that great.

'So in those two extremes, you've got a good example of the crazy mismatch in this group – the inconsistency to be tight and together when it comes to doing a

121

major project. We tend to stretch out: "Should we start at one or two o'clock? Chris can't make it until three...."'

While the Yes Of Old tended to share common musical interests, approaches, and goals, their work as it swung into the eighties was becoming more and more of a tug-of-war between five often radically different point of view.

As *Tormato* showed, the logical answer was to streamline the basic model. No novel-length concepts. No six-day solos. No extraneous doodling, floss, or insulation. The new album sported no less than eight tracks (nine if you count 'Future Times – Rejoice' as two) – unheard of since the days of *Time And A Word*.

As Chris Squire explains, there was never any intention to do another 'Close To The Edge', or even a follow-up to the long 'Awaken'. 'It's not easy to work on extended pieces,' he says. 'They need an incredible amount of foresight and arrangement, and the knowledge to encompass them so that they come off well.

'To a lot of people, the longer pieces we've done tend to be repetitious anyway. You could have said the same thing in half the time – or at least that's one critique of previous Yes work – which I agree with to a certain extent.

'I listened to one of the live tapes of side four from *Topographic* the other day, and I really enjoyed it. But there *are* certain points in the middle where you think, "Fucking hell, it does go on, doesn't it?" So by the time it gets to the end, is its relevance to the beginning really in anyone's mind any more? That's the trick. It should be. There should be some cohesion.'

That seemed to be the Master Directive for *Tormato*. The album was largely recorded at Advision, their old stomping ground, and the most successful tracks leaned towards Cinemascopic fire and brimstone in the best Yes tradition. But that strength was distilled into a series of compact, carefully balanced micro-epics that did make some of their earlier marathon tracks seems slightly prehistoric.

From Wakeman's opening polymoog fanfare to the final apocalyptic growl of Squire's bass, 'Future Times – Rejoice' churned with that awe-inspiring grandeur usually reserved for the tail end of the band's epic-length spectaculars. This time, the band came *in* with a monumental roar, shelving their traditional slow, lengthy build-up to concentrate on the main event.

'Release, Release' ripped along at 100 mph – like an electrified Anglo/Puerto Rican take-off of 'America' from *West Side Story*.

'Don't Kill The Whale' was unique in that it was the first Yes track with a clear-cut, topical message behind it – a fair stab at something a bit more 'accessible', but possibly a bit *too* un-Yes like to appeal to their older followers. On the other hand, the post-psychedelic/galactic commando fluff of 'Arriving UFO' was definitely the one wrong move Yes made on *Tormato* – an embarrassment that,

Above: Chris Squire during the recording of 'On The Silent Wings Of Freedom' at Advision, April 1978
Opposite: London, 1978
Overleaf: 'Future Times' – Alan White in Nashville, 16 September 1978

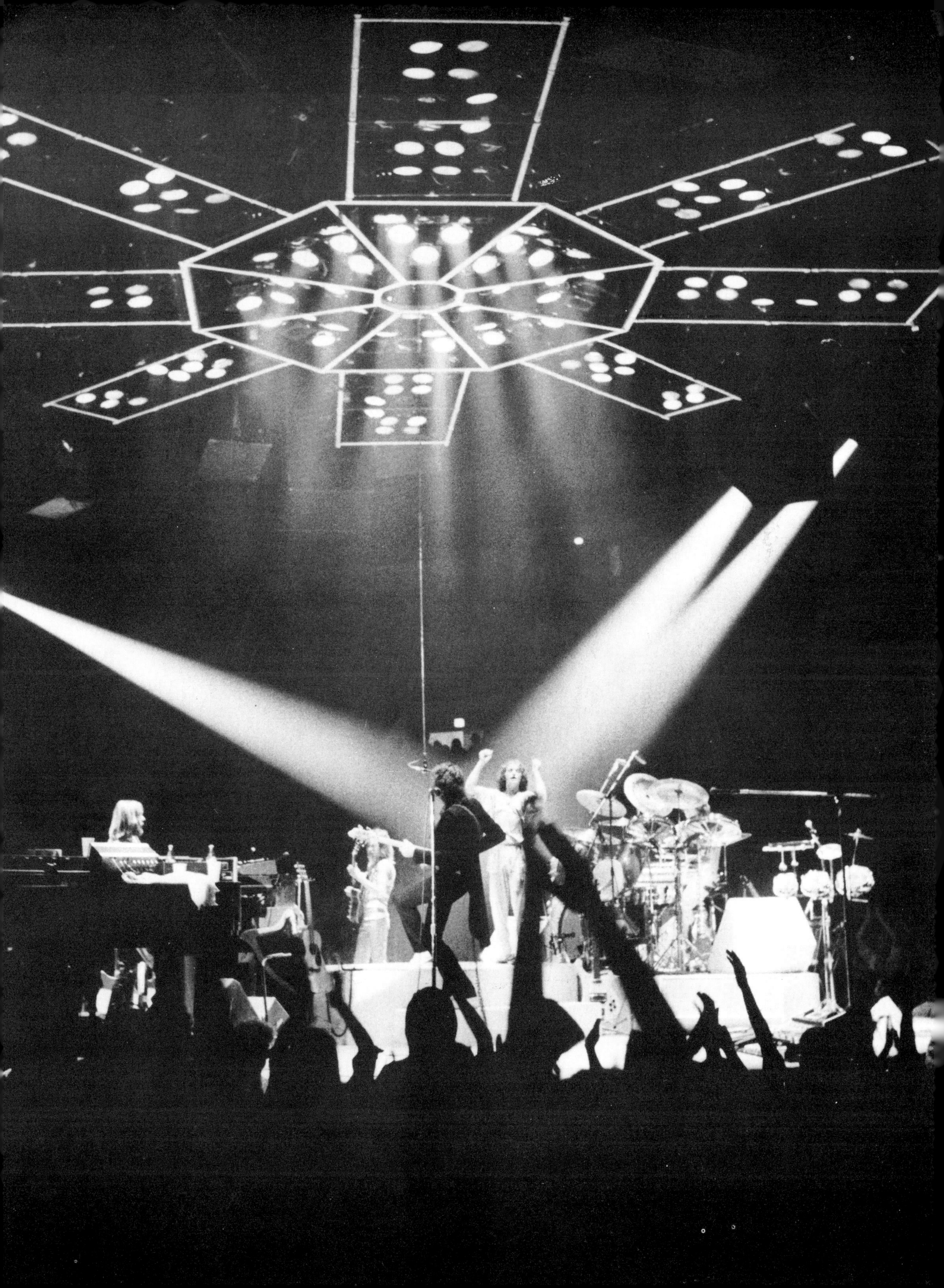

compared to a track like 'Future Times – Rejoice', was a bit like editing a cartoon into the middle of *The Ten Commandments*.

During the neo-baroque 'Madrigal' and the funfair fantasy of 'Circus Of Heaven', Anderson's lighter touch held sway – the former highlighted by Rick's shimmering harpsichord intertwined with Steve's gentle Spanish guitar, the latter by young Damion Anderson's closing commentary on his old man's visionary rambling.

But if the contrast between those serene Andersonian interludes and those fiery micro-epics tended to water down *Tormato's* impact a bit, 'On The Silent Wings Of Freedom' – with Squire's bass storming in, twin barrels blazing – was loaded with hit-and-run energy. Loud, brash, and aggressive, it came close to re-creating the power of Yes on stage.

The material came off better live, and the 1978 U.S./U.K. tour saw the potentially risky Yes In The Round concept work like a charm. That circular stage brought more of the audience closer to Yes, and as Michael Tait has noted, Yes closer to their audience – mirrored in Anderson's new-found self-assurance. 'I've lost all that nervousness,' Jon says. 'In the early days, I *was* kind of unsure of myself on stage, but it was more energy than anything. I get mesmerized by what's going on. The lights. The sound. The event. At times, it can get fairly spacey up on that stage.'

Although *Tormato* went to number 10 in the *Billboard* charts, aided by favourable reviews on both sides of the Atlantic, a hit single never materialized. 'Don't Kill The Whale' was released in both Britain and America, but the fact that it was neither conceived as a single nor particularly representative of Yes meant that it never attracted much interest outside of the band's immediate following.

On the other hand, Chris Squire feels that, 'Yes are, and probably always will be, an album band, though we might even get around to making a hit single one day. But then we're also aware of the responsibilities we face when we go in to make music for the people who respect the care Yes put into something, and don't necessarily appreciate us because of our hit potential. It's *those* people who've stayed with us for all these years, and ultimately it's *those* people who come first. They made us what we are.'

124

CHAPTER SEVEN

DRAMA

Everybody was a little confused.
RICK WAKEMAN

'It still seems to be expanding,' Steve Howe says over the phone. 'It's getting bigger all the time. Whenever we do a tour, the kids *do* seem to be younger than the last time around, but the energy level coming from those kids is that much higher. You can feel the excitement. It's electric.'

Six months after Yes stepped off their circular stage at the Empire Pool, Wembley, in October 1978, they stepped back onto the same stage in Kalamazoo, Michigan, for the first leg of a gruelling three-month trek, concentrating on the small American cities they'd missed during the previous autumn.

In the interim period, Rick Wakeman had whipped up a double solo album, *Rhapsodies* – a deliberate attempt at breaking out of the established Wakeman mould. No theme, no concept, shorter tracks, and an overall style geared more to the demands of the Top Forty market, best typified by a subtly nose-thumbing disco rendition of George Gershwin's 'Rhapsody in Blue'.

Steve Howe had been busy as well, laying down tracks in London for his second solo album. In the long run, *The Steve Howe Album* was closer to the sort of thing Steve should have been doing right from the start. He'd obviously learned a lesson from *Beginnings*, since out of the second album's ten tracks, only two featured vocals (including Claire Hamill's contribution to 'Look Over Your Shoulder'), and finally allowed the guitar to shine through.

Down in the studio behind his garage, Chris Squire spent the early summer of 1979 holed up with Nigel Luby and *Tormato* engineer Geoff Young, grovelling through several years' worth of tour tapes in preparation for a double live L.P, *Yesshows*. The completed project (with a sleeve designed by Roger Dean) would be shelved just prior to its scheduled release when the band couldn't agree on the finished mix.

On the other hand, both Howe and Wakeman performed separately as solo guest artistes at the Montreux Jazz Festival that summer, and Rick later took the moonlighting bit one step further by clocking up five nights at the Venue – roughly London's equivalent to New York's Bottom Line.

Jon Anderson (rumoured to be working on music for a proposed ballet, as well as a solo project with Vangelis) turned up in

125

a group of seasoned British jazz/rock musicians (including Jack Bruce and Alan Holdsworth) for a one-off performance at a London musical instrument trade exhibition.

So if 1978 had seen Yes in a transitional period, 1979 possibly marked the start of a branching-out process that will carry them well into the eighties. The trouble is, the internal changing and rearranging that had been part and parcel of the Yes story from the beginning still wasn't over. The biggest blow was yet to come.

'Dreams?' Jon Anderson says at home, trying to revive himself after a late night out. 'Yeah, I did have certain dreams. It would be easy to say that sure, I knew *exactly* what I was doing all along. That's a great line. Zappa said that once, and I thought it was amazing: "I've known what was going to happen for the last seven years." Oh yeah! Of course, Frank! But then he's that kind of character, and he can probably *prove* that he planned it all.

'It's been a long road, you know? We've tried a lot of different things over the years, and some of them didn't work. You've got to let it flow through, and flow with it.

'On the odd occasion, once a year, I'll sit and think about where things are going. At times they do seem a bit chaotic, but then most everything in this business is. It's corny but, as you know, I'm fully into the musical journey. I'm into finding out what's possible, and that need and that want is still there. The need to do something different from the way everybody else does it, and the want to move forward. In some ways, I don't even feel as if we've really gotten started yet. It takes time.

'But Yes have always been a *group*,' Anderson emphasizes. 'I'm really into the old low-profile number, and I think that's the best way to live. It causes less problems, but then I'm not opposed to spelling out what I think if someone does something that isn't, first and foremost, for Yes.

'We haven't had an easy time, especially with the press. Sometimes the things we've tried have fallen apart, and the things we've said have been a little bit misquoted. You see, we did one of the things which is *not* the thing to do in this business, and that's been to go our own way, which has bugged a lot of people.

'But who says you can't make a piece

Above: Rick Wakeman in Switzerland, early 1979
Opposite: 'Jon, more than any other member of Yes, is conscious of music twenty-five hours a day'
– Keith Goodwin

of music that's over three-and-a-half minutes long? Who's the damn fool that says music is time? Music is money? Music is hit singles?

'In a way, I suppose you could crystalize the whole Yes story by saying we were the band of '68, but it took us until at least 1978 to fucking *be* it. It took us ten years to cover the ground everyone said we were going to cover in twelve months, but then *we* never said we were the band of '68, *they* said it. For better or worse, it took ten years for the people who supported us at the beginning to be able to say they were . . . .'

In early 1980, Jon Anderson parted company with Yes. Six months before, or the exact same day, or three weeks afterwards (depending on who you're talking to), Rick Wakeman did the same.

In the months following Yes's 1979 American tour, Anderson and Vangelis Papathanassiou had gone into Nemo Studios in London for a series of ethereal, impromptu afternoon jams – later released as *Short Stories*. 'We just sat down and made music,' Anderson recalls. 'The music on the album is all first takes. A week later, I came back and re-sang the songs, having re-worked the lyrics which were originally spontaneous.'

Although the pair's efforts were rewarded with a chart single in Britain and America ('I Hear You Now'), the main focus of Jon's life was still, presumably, with Yes. Faced with another round of rehearsals and recording for the follow-up to *Tormato* (and typically unable to agree where to work), Yes found themselves in Paris, 'because it was halfway between London, Switzerland, and the South of France,' Chris Squire says drily.

'It was a compromise,' Steve Howe adds.

'Yeah. Nobody particularly wanted to go there.'

The musical push *seemed* to lean toward heavier music. But something, as all agree, was definitely wrong.

'We'd been together as a group for twelve years by then,' Jon Anderson reflects. 'Nine to ten months of the year. Every year. After a while, things didn't seem to gel. It can either become a catastrophe or there's got to be a change. You *can* make a really bad album – which wouldn't have been the best thing to do for the band – and just say, "It doesn't matter." But everything *always* matters with this group. That's why there was a little bit of friction, a little bit of doubt as to the musical side of the album.'

Yes were tired, and as Rick Wakeman explains, 'I think everybody knew that the line-up, as it was, had between three and five years to run. I had hoped it would run for the five years. It became obvious in 1979 that it couldn't.'

Total lack of interest was finally creeping in. As rehearsals started, both Anderson and Wakeman began making themselves scarce – leaving Howe, Squire, and White to their own devices. 'The continuing three-piece – Chris, Alan, and myself – had a couple of very happy days just pissing about with different licks,' Steve Howe remembers. 'Playing new things for each other. Heavier things. Then Jon and Rick walked in, and everything seemed to go

127

to pieces. We were suddenly playing these airy-fairy bits of music again.'

Evidently, Jon's new material was straying even further into the whimsical style of 'Circus Of Heaven'. But were his songs really that awful? Or had the rest of Yes finally grown tired of the cosmic approach?

'Fifty per cent of both, I think,' Steve says. Although, as Mr Squire feels, 'The usual darting around was the most annoying thing. We ended up rehearsing seventeen songs badly instead of doing a good job on six.'

Brian Lane had talked the band into bringing in an outside producer, Roy Thomas Baker, early in the game – which only clouded the issue. Tracks were recorded, but will probably never be heard. 'Roy basically had a hell of a difficult group to work with,' Steve Howe admits. By mutual consent that it wasn't coming together, Baker made his exit within weeks, and Yes were in limbo.

'It was inherent in the music,' Howe says. 'The feeling that Chris and I weren't really doing anything. We'd started to get some good things together, but as soon as there was something to hold on to, Jon would fire the criticism, "We're playing too much rock and roll. It's not subtle enough. Not gentle enough." '

Back in England for Christmas, Yes opted to complete rehearsing and recording in London early in 1980. 'At the time, I suggested we should have a break,' Jon explains. 'I thought of a year, Rick thought of six months. Everybody was a bit disheartened because we hadn't finished the album. As a group, we'd

Above: Steve Howe
Opposite: Chris Squire, on stage at Madison Square Garden, 13 June 1979

played some great music, but at that moment we didn't seem to collectively know what to do with our musical ideas.'

Anderson split for Barbados to work on new lyrics, while White, Howe, and Squire resumed rehearsals at Redan studios in London. And Rick Wakeman?

'We never saw him anytime that year,' Steve Howe says. 'He was going to rehearse with us for a week, go back to Switzerland, we were going to record the backing tracks, and he was going to come back and record his parts later. Nobody liked the idea very much. It was becoming more and more . . . fake.'

As Wakeman admits, 'I have faults. Everybody has faults. Everybody knows them. Yes tried to put up with everybody's little idiosyncrasies . . . That's part and parcel of any group – the same as any business. Not everybody in the office likes each other, but you sometimes have to work together to produce something really good.'

But as Rick discovered, 'It's a bit like a football team. When you have the same team together for such a long time, you can actually run out of manoeuvres.'

When Anderson returned from Barbados, his new lyrics weren't exactly what the rest of the band had in mind. 'He was really just hanging in,' Steve Howe comments. 'He faded into the background.'

But Jon *must* have noticed the writing on the wall by then.

'I think he was aware, but he was oblivious to the consequences. Even if it *was* that bad, he still thought we wouldn't go on without him.'

As Chris Squire hints, the music wasn't the only sore point. 'There are always outside aggravations – financial problems, personal problems, people making stupid decisions – all those things have always been around. But then, we wouldn't have stayed together for over ten years if we hadn't been able to get over those, and the thing that kept us getting over those was the music.

'It seemed, at the time, that Jon just wanted to have this void, a sort of floating, heavenly approach to everything – which obviously wasn't very current, to say the least.'

The final break was, as usual, a hazy item to most of the people involved. While nobody admits that Jon was forced out, nobody denies it either. 'We never said anything,' Alan White explains. 'It was just obvious. A day came down when he questioned a lot of financial things. Steve told him what he thought of him. It all came out in the wash, basically. And Jon left.'

Meanwhile, Rick Wakeman was home in Switzerland, supposedly unable to set foot in Britain since he'd used up his tax exile's quota of 'free days'. 'He could've come to England,' Chris Squire says with a trace of annoyance. 'He kind of used it as an excuse all the time. He always *thought* he was going to make the album. We'd send him the backing tracks, he'd put a few little lines on it, and that would be it.'

Wakeman, it would seem, just wasn't interested any more. 'Jon, to me, was an integral part of the band,' Rick explains. 'Very important. The music we produced *was* Yes, and when Jon went, I thought, "That's not a fifth gone, that's a great big chunk. If we want to carry on as Yes, and call it Yes, then I think we're in for a lot of trouble." '

Suddenly, Rick Wakeman was 'ex-Yes' for the second time – though what went down is, again, difficult to fathom. 'Brian Lane called Rick and took care of it,' is Chris Squire's cryptic response. 'It was a bit like the way he left the first time. Nobody knew whether he was still here or not. And then he wasn't.'

But although Wakeman immediately went ahead with plans for his own record label, Moon Records, a solo tour, an album based on Orwell's *1984* and – at the end of 1980 – a new band with ELP's Carl Palmer, he'll probably always be most identified with Yes. So will Jon Anderson, who followed *Short Stories* with *Song of Seven* and will continue his part-time collaboration with Vangelis, with the books, ballets, video projects, and longer works he's been talking about for years.

'I'll survive, and so will Rick,' Jon says. 'For all the fans of Yes as it was, all that I can say is that I want to try to do my best in the music I'm involved with at the moment, and I hope the culmination of each artiste doing his best is going to take away the frustrations of Yes fans.

'I'm sure there are a lot of fans who'll feel that we've let them down, and that things didn't go the way they expected – but we feel exactly the same. We didn't expect it. *I* didn't, certainly. I had visions of another ten years of Yes. But I'll always be in Yes. The idea of what Yes was – and *is* – will always be inside of me.'

Above: 'We never seem to allow enough time to rehearse. It may not look like it from the audience, but the first few shows are usually, from a technical standpoint, chaos' – Steve Howe
Opposite: Chris Squire, Madison Square Garden, 13 June 1979

Yes were three now, and actually considered remaining that way permanently, with Squire presumably taking over on lead vocals. Howe and White agree that it *might* have worked, but as Chris says, 'Then we ran into these guys. Trevor and Geoff.'

'This is the first time I've ever been a lead singer in a band, though it *is* a good place to start,' Trevor Horn muses, so hoarse from hitting the high notes that he can hardly speak. Slumped in an armchair during a break in tour rehearsals at Mike Tait's Pennsylvania workshop, he methodically cleans the lenses of his round spectacles, returns them to the bridge of his nose, then stretches wearily. Being in Yes, he's finding out, can be a bitch at times. His vocal cords are already out to lunch and the 1980 American tour hasn't even got under way.

'I've been a Yes fan ever since *The Yes Album*, so their music was implanted deep inside my consciousness years before I ever met them,' he says in a broad Northern accent, not dissimilar from Jon Anderson's. 'Jon, Alan, and I come from the North of England,' he explains, thinking of his 'just above working class' childhood, deep in the Durham countryside. 'My father is a dairy engineer, but he's a bass player as well. Used to play professionally in a dance band up there.'

It's the classic scenario: pre-pubescent delusions of grandeur, a cheap guitar by the time he hit his teens, and a reverence for the early Beatles which bordered on idolatry, 'though my earliest influence was probably Dionne Warwick. I thought she was dynamite.

'I had a group called the Outer Limits when I was fourteen. I was lead singer and played lead guitar. We were a terrible little group – Rolling Stones stuff – "I'm Your King Bee, Baby". All that crap. Then we got a lead singer who played harmonica like what's-his-name in the Yardbirds, so we were suddenly doing "For Your Love".'

Moving down to the Midlands and college by his late teens, Horn spent his evening soloing around the Leicester clubs. 'I used to do a Bob Dylan act and say, "Name any Bob Dylan song and I'll sing it for you." That was my gimmick.'

He quit college for a day job, but couldn't quite hack it. 'I thought I'd become a musician, but the only way to earn money was to join a dance band, so I joined one for a while, reading the charts and playing bass guitar.'

Trevor drifted through loads of dead-end musical jobs after that, just to pay the rent. 'I gradually got into sessions as a bass player, though it was nothing noteworthy,' he says, adding that he used to sing on Top Forty cover LP's ('As Seen On TV' or in the bargain bin at Woolworth's) 'doing Brian Ferry impersonations'.

At twenty-two, he'd gone on the road with Gary Glitter, then got fired in Manchester 'for getting drunk, and getting into a fight with the police, and getting locked up for the weekend. I haven't had a drop since then. I'm a teetotaller.

'But I've been into loads of other things since then. Built a little studio with this guy, and decided I wanted to become a record producer. I used to work with this disco singer called Tina Charles, too. I was her musical director – organized a band for her, organized the tour, played bass, made all the announcements. Come to think of it, that was right around the time I met Geoffrey.'

Out on a sun-baked highway, somewhere in rural Pennsylvania, Geoff Downes is trudging along the soft shoulder, side-stepping rusty beer cans, en route to the local witch doctor for something to straighten his plumbing out. 'It's the food,' he winces, referring to Yes's wholesome-but-gut-loosening nightly communal meals. 'It's going to take a while to get used to it. Like everything else in this band.'

Downes is from Manchester – the son of a church organist father and a mother who played piano. He'd sung in the church choir at six, started piano lessons at seven, and switched to organ at eleven – though with no aspirations to wind up at the Royal College like Rick Wakeman or Tony Kaye.

As he explains, the Beatles rounded the bend, closely followed by psychedelia, 'and I knew I wanted to be in a band. I'd started playing bass by then, so I formed one when I was twelve – Technicolor Dream. I was a bit too young to afford a Hammond C-3, but I'd gotten interested in directing what I'd learned on keyboards into a rock band. I borrowed a Farfisa eventually, then got myself a Hammond when I was about sixteen. At the time, Keith Emerson was *the man*. He was my hero.'

He passed through several local bands during that era, though they were 'nothing spectacular'. When an audition for the vacant keyboard spot in Caravan ('they seemed like the ideal English melodic/rustic rock band') came to nothing, Downes shipped himself off to music

Above: The Buggles. ' "Video Killed The Radio Star" took a ludicrous amount of time to do. When it was finished, we were sick to death of it' – Trevor Horn
Opposite: Vangelis Papathanassiou and Jon Anderson

college in Leeds. 'I wanted to be a rock keyboard player,' he says. 'But I wanted to be making a profession out of what I was doing, without having to do gigs. I've hardly done a gig in my life – playing in sleazy nightclubs six nights a week. I never really wanted to do that shit.'

After finishing college in 1975, Downes split for London, moving to a room recently vacated by a friend. 'The girl living in the next room was Chrissie Hynde. She was practising the guitar at the time, which was a rather unpleasant experience. I had my keyboards set up in my little room, and it was a bit of a battle to see who could play the loudest.'

The odd jobs continued, musical or otherwise, until Geoff began getting offers for sessions – 'things you get paid for and then never hear of again'. He started composing jingles, and wound up doing that nearly full time for two years. Television and radio. British Gas. ICI. Berger Paints. Allied Carpets. 'I started producing my own jingles, so I was writing them, producing them, and playing on them. We got so cynical about it, but it also makes you commercially aware.'

Geoff had met Trevor Horn while auditioning for Tina Charles' band. 'I was the only one who took a moog along to the audition, and Trevor phoned me up later and offered me the job – but only if I'd bring the synthesizer with me.'

The tour ran its course, the band split up, but the two musicians kept in touch. Sandwiched in between his jingle activities, Downes explains, 'Trevor and I started making tapes. He was really into keyboards, and he'd get these tacky production jobs to do. Demos and things. Gutter Publishing Ltd. He'd sit behind the recording desk, get some no-chance singer in, and record a couple of tracks which would invariably spend the rest of their days on Gutter Publishing's shelf.'

That was in 1976, and the pair spent the next few years refining their art, tinkering with new equipment, effects, and recording techniques. As Geoff recalls, 'We used to get so bored doing these lousy songs people would give us that we started souping up the arrangements. The arrangements started taking over.'

That was the beginning of the Buggles. As Trevor Horn recalls, 'We'd been producing other people's records for three years and had gotten absolutely nowhere. I was broke. Nobody knew who I was. In 1978, I produced fifty tracks, and my total earnings – total profit – for that year was £3,000.'

Geoff Downes was making a decent living from his TV and radio jingles, Trevor goes on, 'but we had these songs kicking around. Things we'd written. One Tuesday afternoon, we were sitting in Geoff's flat in Wimbledon, and I said, 'Look, we've *got* to do something. How? Let's use *everything* we've learned over the past few years.'

Realizing that a hit single was the quickest route to the Big Time, they ploughed every resource, every studio trick they could think of, into a handful of demo tapes – aiming for 'the infallible single'. One of the tracks was 'Video Killed The Radio Star', co-written with one Bruce Wooley during an earlier, unsuccessful effort to get a band off the ground.

Impressed by Horn and Downes' 'perfect radio arrangement' (Geoff: 'I'd learned a particular sort of mixing for radio and TV which was designed to cut through'), Island Records gave them the go-ahead to record an entire album.

'We had this idea of making the perfect pop album,' Trevor says. 'Ultra clean. Everything thought out. Very machine-like, though we never thought about the ethics of it.'

They dubbed themselves the Buggles. 'It came from the Beatles,' Horn explains. 'It started out as "The Bugs", but then I thought "Buggles" would be even more repulsive. We got incredible pressure to

Above: *Drama*. Alan White in New York City, September 1980
Right: Trevor Horn

change the name. It embarrassed the record company.'

The then-managerless Buggles met up with Brian Lane. 'My wife's brother is John Sinclair,' Trevor says. 'He produced an album for Brian by a group called the Curves. My wife manages her brother, and she told Brian about me and the Buggles.'

'One-hit wonders,' was Lane's initial verdict, but after hearing rough tapes of the Buggles' album, he offered to manage them.

'I was a big Yes fan,' Trevor says. 'I thought, "Wowee! Brian Lane! I've read his name on all the Yes albums." In talking to him, though, we began to realize that things were not well with Yes.'

Inevitably, Horn bumped into Chris Squire at the Yes office. 'I mean, I was pretty knocked out. *Chris Squire*! He asked me about studios, because Yes were looking for one to record in. It turned out that he had the Buggles album and was really into it.'

135

By this time, album and single were doing landslide business. The Buggles found themselves in the same London rehearsal studio as Squire, White, and Howe, whipping up material for a follow-up Buggles album and preparing to take their act on the road.

Chris Squire – the gears in his head obviously beginning to turn again – invited Horn and Downes to his Surrey home. 'We sat and talked for a while,' Trevor recalls. 'I had this song I'd written while I was on holiday, "Fly From Here", and I thought maybe I could hustle it onto the next Yes album. I played it for him, and Chris said, "God, you sound just like Jon Anderson." '

A further invitation was extended, and Trevor and Geoff sat in on the next Yes rehearsal, believing they were there to help iron out the arrangements so Yes could record the song. 'I kept wondering where Jon Anderson was, and Geoffrey kept wondering where Wakeman was,' Trevor says. 'I kept saying to Chris, "I'd better write this down so Jon can learn it," and Chris kept going, "Uhhhhh... Welllll... I don't... know...." '

Within three weeks, Squire popped the question, which caught the two remaining Yes members by surprise. 'The inital shock of Chris suggesting Geoff and Trevor sank into Steve's head faster than it did mine,' Alan White remembers. 'But it worked.'

Initially, the new recruits weren't too

Above: Steve Howe
Opposite: 'Geoff Downes is the best keyboard player Yes have ever had. He *listens*' – Chris Squire

confident. 'I was a bit worried about it,' Horn admits. 'We'd already had a few arguments with Chris over it, and I kept saying, "It'll *never* work. I'm not gonna stand up there instead of Jon Anderson and sing 'Starship Trooper'." But we were tired of being carted all over Europe to promote the Buggles, and what really convinced us was hearing the band play. We wrote "Machine Messiah" at the rehearsal studio in a day. I thought, "What an amazing opportunity to join a band like this." I'd never heard people play that good, and as a record producer, I've heard a *lot* of people play.'

It takes getting used to. *Drama*, the twelfth album, still sounds like Yes, but then again . . .

'Let's call it, "a re-working of the Yes idea,"' Chris Squire suggests. And it is. Sparse, stripped down (though maybe a bit *too* easy at times), it's Yes after an oil change and a 30,000 mile tune-up, moving out of the cosmic seventies and into the eighties. No skinny ties or short-back-and-sides yet, but as Squire says, more 'current'. A test run for the new line-up that improves with each listening.

Despite pre-release comments by various band members that *Drama* is a return to *The Yes Album/Fragile/Close To Edge* feel, it isn't. *Drama* is Yes Noveau – though fragments of, say, 'Tempus Fugit' are almost creepy – a return to the Yes of twelve years before (complete with Hammond C-3 à la Tony Kaye, and pyramidal Beatles/Association/St Andrew's Church Choir harmonies) in a blaze of hotshot English flash that picks up from where 'On The Silent Wings Of Freedom' left off.

'White Car' is vaguely Byzantine, funereal, and at under a minute and a half, far too short, 'but only because time was short,' Chris Squire explains. 'Into The Lens' (first slated for the second Buggles LP) is Yes's epic grandeur brought up to date – angular, turbulent, a potential encore for 1984.

As a test run for a new line-up, however, *Drama* does have its faults: the initially disorientating false starts, false stops, rubber-burning tempo changes, and puzzling lapses into Black Sabbath/

heavy-metal melodrama (the opening section of 'Machine Messiah'), with a vocal dash of Pink Floyd for a chaser (the middle section of 'Does It Really Happen?'). The production, however, is the cleanest in years (Eddie Offord, in fact, briefly returned to the fold to supervise the backing tracks), adding up to the album that's truly contemporary – sidestepping what Geoff Downes calls 'the Wimp Factor' which had, at times, bogged Yes down. It went to number 1 in England, 16 in *Cashbox*, and the U.S. – U.K. tour was a smash.

Obviously, the Yes of late 1980 wasn't the same group who, as Mabel Greer's Toyshop, played 'Midnight Hour' twice at Rachel McMillan College all those years ago. At last count, only Chris Squire remained.

Nobody denies that the changes have often come fast and furious; that the music has often been the result of battling, bruised egos, and a five-way split, and that the band have individually and collectively made their fair share of misjudged moves over the years. Yes appreciate, as much as anyone can, the fact that you can't please all of the people all of the time. But as one of the premier Mystery Bands of the post-Beatles era, they've created a school of music that set the pace for much of what happened in progressive rock during the seventies.

These days, the long haul is behind

Above: Yes and Brian Lane, beating Led Zeppelin out by one show, 6 September 1980
Opposite: Yes 1980: Steve Howe, Alan White, Geoff Downes, Chris Squire, Trevor Horn

them and Yes can afford to breathe easier. Success has brought them all the traditional fringe benefits, and as Michael Tait suggests, 'Where the band was ninety-nine per cent of their lives before, now it's maybe only eighty per cent of their lives. They've got wives, and children, and houses, and schools to worry about.

'Life's gotten a lot more complicated, and they have to spend more time doing personal things because there *is* more to life than just the band. You've got to plan for the future. You've got to get away from it sometimes, otherwise you can go crazy very easily.'

Stuck in the middle of the London rush hour in his Rolls-Royce, Chris Squire isn't going anywhere at the moment. The flash car is one of those fringe benefits. Without the music, Squire is well aware that his flash car wouldn't exist. That music has always been the direct result of the change that's been part of the band's history since 1968, and those changes have all been directly aimed at improving and sustaining that music.

'That's why Bill, Peter, Tony, Steve, Rick, Aian, Patrick, Geoffrey, and Trevor were chosen,' Squire says, patiently inching the big car down Fulham Road. 'They weren't chosen on their social life-styles or because they looked like rock and roll stars, but because of their musicianship and ability.

'But, you see, Yes has always been a real gamble, right from the beginning. It's a bit like taking a chance – throwing a lot of different characters together – and it hasn't gone without its upheavals, believe me. On the other hand, the price we've paid for the music, Yes music, has probably been worth it in the end. At least I hope it has, and that's the only thing I can think of to justify it all at the end of the day – or even in the morning! But has it *definitely* been worth it? Well ... who knows? That's not really for me to say, is it?'

Chris Squire smiles mysteriously as the traffic begins to move in the distance. 'I mean, *you* tell me.'

139

JON ANDERSON

With the Warriors:
5/65 'Don't Make Me Blue'/'You Came Along' – Decca LK 4620 (B – British release) (Note: 'You Came Along' later appeared on the 1974 rock compilation album *Hard Up Heroes* – Decca DPA 3009/10 (B))

As Hans Christian:
3/68 'Never My Love'/'All Of The Time' – Parlophone R 5676 (B)
5/68 '(Autobiography Of A) Mississippi Hobo'/'Sonata Of Love' – Parlophone R 5698 (B)

Solo:
6/76 *Olias Of Sunhillow* – Atlantic SD 18180 (A)/K 50261 (B) Ocean Song/Meeting (Geda): Sound Out The Galleon/Dance Of Ranyart: Olias (To Build The Moorglade)/Qoquaq En Transic: Naon: Transic Tö/Flight Of The Moorglade/Solid Space/Moon Ra: Chords: Song Of Search/To The Runner
8/76 'Flight Of The Moorglade'/'To The Runner' – Atlantic 45-3356 (A – American release)
11/80 *Song Of Seven* – Atlantic SD – 16021 (A)/K 50756 (B) For You For Me/Some Are Born/Don't Forget (Nostalgia)/Heart Of The Matter/Hear It/Everybody Loves You/Take Your Time/Days/Song Of Seven

With Vangelis:
11/79 'I Hear You Now'/'Thunder' – Polydor 2089 (A)/2001 978 (B)
2/80 *Short Stories* – Polydor PD 1 6272 (A)/POLD 5030 (B) Curious Electric/Each And Everyday/Bird Song/I Hear You Now/The Road/Far Away In Baagad/Love Is/One More Time/Thunder/A Play Within A Play

Guest Appearances:
1971 King Crimson: *Lizard* – Atlantic S 8278 (A) / Polydor 2302 059 (B)
1973 Johnny Harris: *All To Bring You Morning* – Warner Bros. K 56186 (B)
1975 Vangelis: *Heaven And Hell* – RCA AFLI 5110 (A) / RCA RS 1025 (B)
1976 Alan White: *Ramshackled* – Atlantic SD 18167 (A) / K 50217 (B)

Bootleg:
1977 *Jon Anderson – The Sky And His Shadow*

CHRIS SQUIRE

With the Syn:
6/67 'Grounded' / 'Created By Clive' – Deram 130 (B)
8/67 'Flowerman' / '24 Hour Technicolour Dream' – Deram 145 (B)

Solo:
11/75 *Fish Out Of Water* – Atlantic SD 18159 (A) / K 50203 (B) Hold Out Your Hand / With You By My Side / Silently Falling / Lucky Seven / Safe (Canon Song)
3/76 'Lucky Seven' / 'Silently Falling' – Atlantic 45-3317 (A)

Guest appearances:
1973 Rick Wakeman: *The Six Wives Of Henry VIII* – A&M SP 4361 (A) / AMLH 64361 (B)
1974 Eddie Harris: *E.H. In The U.K.* – Atlantic 1647 (A) / K 50029 (B)
1977 *Rick Wakeman's Criminal Record* – A&M SP 4660 (A) / AMLK 64660 (B)

TONY KAYE

With the Federals:
1/64 'The Climb' / 'Dance With A Dolly' – Parlophone R 5100 (B)
5/64 'Marlena' / 'Please Believe Me' – Parlophone R 5139 (B)
10/64 'Twilight Time' / 'Lost And Alone' – Parlophone R 5193 (B)
8/65 'A Bucketful Of Love' / 'Leah' – Parlophone R 5320 (B)

With Jimmy Winston And His Reflections (a.k.a. Winston's Fumbs):
3/67 'Sorry She's Mine' / 'It's Not What You Do' – Decca F 12410 (B)

7/67 'Real Crazy Apartment' / 'Snow White' – RCA 1612 (B)

With Badger:
11/71 *One Live Badger* – Atlantic SD 7022 (A) / K 40473 (B) Wheel Of Fortune / Fountain / Wind Of Change / River / Preacher / On The Way Home
4/74 *White Lady* – Epic KE 32831 (A) / 800009 (B) A Dream Of You / Everybody – Nobody / Listen To Me / Don't Pull The Trigger / Just The Way It Goes / White Lady / Be With You / Lord Who Gives Me Life / One More Dream To Hold / The Hole Thing
5/74 'White Lady' / 'Don't Pull The Trigger' – Epic 2326 (B)

With Detective:
4/77 *Detective* – Swan Song SS 8417 (A) / SSK 59405 (B) Recognition / Got Enough Love / Grim Reaper / Nightingale / Detective Man / Ain't None Of Your Business / Deep Down / Wild Hot Summer Nights
6/77 'Recognition' / 'Grim Reaper' – Swan Song SS 8417 (A)
11/77 *It Takes One To Know One* – Swan Song SS 8504 (A) / SSK 59406 (B) Help Me Up / Competition / Are You Talkin' To Me? / Dynamite / Something Beautiful / Warm Love / Betcha Won't Dance / Fever / Tear Jerker
2/78 'Something Beautiful' / 'Dynamite' – Swan Song SS 70117 (A)

With Badfinger:
11/79 *Airwaves* – Elektra 6E-175 (A) / K 52129 (B) Airwaves / Look Out California / Lost Inside Your Love / Love Is Gonna Come At Last / Sympathy / The Winner / The Dreamer / Come Down Hard / Sail Away

Guest appearances:
1971 Bonzo Dog Band: *Let's Make Up And Be Friendly* – United Artists 5584 (A) / 29288 (B)
1972 Flash: *Flash* – Sovereign SMAS 11040 (A) / SVNA 7251 (B)
1974 Eddie Harris: *E.H. In The U.K.* – Atlantic 1647 (A) / K 50029 (B)

BILL BRUFORD

with King Crimson:
3/73 *Larks' Tongues In Aspic* – Atlantic 7263 (A) / Polydor 2302 061 (B) Larks' Tongues In Aspic (Part 1) / Book Of Saturday / Exiles / Easy Money / The Talking Drum / Larks' Tongues In Aspic (Part II)
3/74 *Starless And Bible Black* – Atlantic 7298 (A) / Polydor 20302 067 (B) The Great Deceiver / Lament / We'll Let You Know / The Night Watch / Trio / The Mincer / Starless And Bible Black / Fracture
3/74 'The Night Watch' / 'The Great Deceiver' – Atlantic 3016 (A) / Islands WIP 6189 (B)
9/74 *Red* – Atlantic 18110 (A) / Polydor 2302 066 (B) Red / Fallen Angel / One More Red Nightmare / Providence / Starless
4/75 *USA* – Atlantic 18136 (A) / Polydor 2306 067 (B) Larks' Tongues In Aspic (Part II) / Lament / Exiles / Asbury Park / Easy Money / 21st Century Schizoid Man
(Note: Selections from the above albums can also be found on *The Young Person's Guide To King Crimson* – Polydor 2612 035 (B))

with Genesis:
7/77 *Seconds Out* – Atlantic SD2 9002 (A) / Charisma GE 2001 (B) Squonk / The Carpet Crawl / Robbery, Assault And Battery / Afterglow / Firth Of Fifth / I Know What I Like / The Lamb Lies Down On Broadway / Musical Box / Supper's Ready / Cinema Show / Dance On A Volcano / Los Endos

with UK:
3/78 *UK* – Polydor PD 16146 (A) / 2302 080 (B) In The Dead Of Night / By The Light Of Day / Presto Vivace And Reprise / Thirty Years / Alaska / Time To Kill / Nevermore / Mental Medication
5/78 'In The Dead Of Night' / 'Mental Medication' – Polydor PD 14491 (A) / 2001 783 (B)

Solo:
1/78 *Feels Good To Me* – Polydor PD 16149 (A) / 2302 075 (B) Beelzebub / Back To The Beginning / Seems Like A Lifetime Ago (Parts I & II) / Sample And Hold / Feels Good To Me / Either End Of August / If You Can't Stand The Heat / Springtime In Siberia / Adios A La Pasada (Goodbye To The Past)
1/78 'Feels Good To Me' / 'Beelzebub' – Polydor 2001 759 (B)
4/79 *One Of A Kind* – Polydor PD 16205 (A) / POLD 5020 (B) Hell's Bells / One Of A Kind (Part I) / One Of A Kind (Part II) / Travels With Myself – And Someone Else / Fainting In Coils / Five G The Abingdon Chasp / Forever Until Sunday / Sahara Of Snow (Part I) / Sahara Of Snow (Part II)
1/80 *Gradually Going Tornado* – Polydor PD 1 6261 (A) / 2311 001 (B)
Age Of Information / Gothic 17 / Joe Frazier / Q.E.D. / The Sliding Floor / Palewell Park / Plans For J.D. / Land's End

Guest appearances:
1975 Steve Howe: *Beginnings* – Atlantic SD 18154 (A) / K 50151 (B)
1975 Chris Squire: *Fish Out Of Water* – Atlantic SD 18159 (A) / K 50203 (B)
1975 Roy Harper: *HQ* – Harvest SHSP 4046 (B)
1979 Annette Peacock: *X Dreams* – Tomato TOM 7025 (A) / Aura AUL 702 (B)
1979 Steve Howe: *The Steve Howe Album* – Atlantic SD 19243 (A) / K 50621 (B)

PETER BANKS

With the Syn:
6/67 'Grounded' / 'Created By Clive' – Deram 130 (B)
8/67 'Flowerman' / '24 Hour Technicolour Dream' – Deram 145 (B)

With Flash:
2/72 *Flash* – sovereign SMAS 11040 (A) / SVNA 7251 (B)
Small Beginnings / Morning Haze / Children Of The Universe / Dreams Of Heaven / Time It Takes
3/72 'Small Beginnings' / 'Morning Haze' – Sovereign SOV 105 (B)
2/73 *Flash In The Can* – Sovereign SMAS 11115 (A) / SVNA 7255 (B)
Lifetime / Monday Morning Eyes / Black And White / Stop That Laughing / There No More
10/73 *Out Of Our Hands* – Sovereign SMAS 11218 (A) / SVNA 7260 (B)
Open Sky / None The Wiser (King) / Farewell Number One (Pawn) / Man Of Honour (Knight) / Dead Ahead

(Queen): Bishop / Psycho Sync (Escape): Farewell Number Two: Conclusion / Manhattan Morning (Christmas '72) / Shadows (It's You)

Solo:
10/73 *Two Sides* – Sovereign SMAS 11217 (A) / SVNA 7256 (B)
Vision Of The King / White Horse Vale: On The Hill, Lord Of The Dragon / Knights: Falcon, Bear / Battles / Knights: Reprise / Last Eclipse / Beyond The Loneliest Sea / Stop That / Get Out Of My Fridge

STEVE HOWE

With the Syndicats:
3/64 'Maybellene' / 'True To Me' – Columbia DB 7238 (B)
1/65 'Howlin' With My Baby' / 'What To Do' – Columbia DB 7441 (B)
9/65 'On The Horizon' / 'Crawdaddy Simone' – Columbia DB 7686 (B)

With the In Crowd
4/65 'That's How Strong My Love Is' / 'Things She Says' – Parlophone R5276 (B)
9/65 'Stop, Wait A Minute' / 'You're On Your Own' – Parlophone R5328 (B)
11/65 'Why Must They Criticise?' / 'I Don't Mind' – Parlophone R5364 (B)

With Tomorrow:
5/67 'My White Bicycle' / 'Claramount Lake' – Parlophone R 5597 (B)
9/67 'Revolution' / 'Three Jolly Little Dwarfs' – Parlophone R 5627 (B)
2/68 *Tomorrow* – featuring Keith West – Sire SES 97021 (A) / Harvest SHSM 2010 (B)
My White Bicycle / Colonel Brown / Real Life Permanent Dream / Shy Boy / Revolution / Incredible Journey Of Timothy Chase / Auntie Mary's Dress Shop / Strawberry Fields Forever / Three Jolly Little Dwarfs / Now Your Time Has Come / Hallucinations

Solo:
10/75 *Beginnings* – Atlantic SD 18154 (A) / K 50151 (B)
Doors Of Sleep / Australia / The Nature Of The Sea / Lost Symphony / Beginnings / Will O' The Wisp / Ram / Pleasure Stole The Night / Break Away From It All

12/79 *The Steve Howe Album* – Atlantic SD 19243 (A) / K 50621 (B)
Pennants / Cactus Boogie / All's A Chord / Diary Of A Man Who Vanished / Look Over Your Shoulder / Meadow Rag / The Continental / Surface Tension / Double Rondo / Concerto In D (Second Movement)

Guest appearances:
1971 Lou Reed: *Lou Reed* – RCA LSP 4701 (A) / SF 8281 (B)
1972 Rick Wakeman: *The Six Wives of Henry VIII* – A&M SP 4361 (A) / AMLH 64361 (B)
1973 Johnny Harris: *All To Bring You Morning* – Warner Bros. K 46187 (B)
1976 Alan White: *Ramshackled* – Atlantic SD 18167 (A) / K 50217 (B)

RICK WAKEMAN

With the Strawbs:
10/70 *Just A Collection Of Antiques And Curios* – A&M SP 4288 (A) / AMLS 994 (B)
Martin Luther King's Dream / Antique Suite – Reaper / We Must Cross The River / Antiques And Curios / Hey, It's Been A Long Time / Temperament Of Mind / Fingertips / Song Of A Sad Girl / Where Is This Dream Of Your Youth
3/71 'I'll Carry On Beside You' / 'We'll Meet Again Sometime' – A&M AMS 837 (B)
5/71 *From The Witchwood* – A&M SP 4394 (A) / AMLH 64304 (B)
Glimpse Of Heaven / Witchwood / Thirty Days / Flight / Hangman And The Papist / Sheep / Cannondale / Shepherd Song / In Amongst The Roses / I'll Carry On Beside You

Solo:
1/73 *The Six Wives Of Henry VIII* – A&M SP 4361 (A) / AMLH 64361 (B)
Catherine Of Aragon / Anne Of Cleves / Catherine Howard / Jane Seymour / Anne Boleyn / Catherine Parr
3/73 'Anne' / 'Catherine' – A&M 1430 (A) / AMS 7061 (B)
5/74 *Journey To The Centre Of The Earth* – A&M SP 3621 (A) / AMLH 63621 (B)
The Journey / Recollection / The Battle / The Forest
3/75 *The Myths And Legends Of King Arthur And The Knights Of The Round Table* – A&M SP 4515 (A) / AMLH 64515 (B)
Arthur / Lady Of The Lake / Guinevere / Sir Lancelot And The Black Knight / Merlin The Magician / Sir Galahad / The Last Battle
4/76 *No Earthly Connection* – A&M SP 4583 (A) / AMLK 64583 (B)
Music Reincarnate (The Warning: The Maker: The Spaceman: The Realisation: The Reaper) / The Prisoner / The Lost Cycle
1/77 *White Rock* (Film Soundtrack) – A&M SP 4616 (A) / AMLH 64614 (B)
White Rock / Searching For Gold / The Loser / The Shoot / Lax'x / After The Ball / Montezuma's Revenge / Ice Run
2/77 'After The Ball' / 'White Rock' – A&M 1937 (A)
10/77 *Rick Wakeman's Criminal Record* – A&M SP 4660 (A) / AMLK 64660 (B)
Statue Of Justice / Crime Of Passion / Chamber Of Horrors / Birdman Of Alcatraz / The Breathalyser / Judas Iscariot
11/77 'And Now A Word From Our Sponsor' / 'Birdman Of Alcatraz' – A&M 2010 (A)
4/79 'Birdman Of Alcatraz' / 'Flacons de Neige – A&M AMS 7435 (B)
5/79 *Rhapsodies* – A&M SP 6051 (A) / AMLX 68508 (B)
Pedra da Gavea / Front Line / Bombay Duck / Animal Showdown / Big Ben / Rhapsody In Blue / Wooly Willy Tango / The Pulse / Swan Lager / March Of The Gladiators / Flacons de Neige / The Flasher / The Palais / Stand By / Sea Horses / Half Holiday / Summertime / Credits
5/79 'Animal Showdown' / 'Sea Horses' – A&M AMS 7436 (B)
6/80 'I'm So Straight I'm A Weirdo' / 'Do You Believe In Fairies?' – A&M AMS 7510 (B)

Film soundtrack:
11/75 *Lisztomania* – A&M SP 4526 (A) / AMLH 64546 (B)
11/75 'Love's Dream' / 'Orpheus Song' – A&M AMS 7206 (B)

Selected sessions:
1969 David Bowie: *Space Oddity* – RCA LSP 4813 (A) (B)
1970 The Strawbs: *Dragonfly* – A&M AMLS 970 (B)
1970 Magna Carta: *Seasons* – Vertigo

6360 003 (B)
1970 Brotherhood of Man: *United We Stand* – Deram SML 1066 (B)
1971 *Piano Vibrations* – Polydor 2460 135 (B)
1971 Lou Reed: *Lou Reed* – RCA LSP 4701 (A) / SF 8281 (B)
1971 Cat Stevens: *Teaser And The Firecat* – A&M SP 4313 (A) / Island ILPS 9154 (B)
1971 David Bowie: *Hunky Dory* – RCA LSP 4623 (A) / SF 8244 (B)
1971 T. Rex: *Electric Warrior* – Reprise 6466 (A) / Cube Hi Fly 6 (B)
1971 Elton John: *Madman Across The Water* – MCA 2016 (A) / DJM 20420 (B)
1972 John Williams: *Changes* – Columbia C 31091 (A) / Cube Hi Fly 5 (B)
1972 Al Stewart: *Orange* – CBS 64730 (B)

Bootlegs:
1974 *Unleashing The Tethered One*
1976 *Rick At Hemel Hempstead*

ALAN WHITE

With the Blue Chips:
10/65 'I'm On The Right Side' / 'You're Good To Me' – Pye 7N 15979 (B)
1/66 'Some Kind Of Loving' / 'I Know A Boy' – Pye 7N 17111 (B)
3/66 'Good Loving Never Hurts' / 'Tell Her' – Pye 7N 17155 (B)

With the Gamblers:
5/66 'Dr. Goldfoot' / 'It Seems So Long' – Decca F12399 (B)

With Happy Magazine:
1/68 'Satisfied Street' / 'Do Right Woman, Do Right Man' – Polydor 56233 (B)

With the Plastic Ono Band:
1/70 *Live / Peace In Toronto* – Apple SW 3372 (A) / CORE 2001 (B)
Introduction / Blue Suede Shoes / Money (That's What I Want) / Dizzy Miss Lizzie / Yer Blues / Cold Turkey / Give Peace A Chance / Don't Worry Kyoko (Mummy's Only Looking For Her Hand In The Snow) / John, John (Let's Hope For Peace)

With Denny Laine and Balls:
1/71 'Fight For My Country' / 'Janie Slow Down' – Wizard WIZ 101 (B)

Solo:
4/76 *Ramshackled* – Atlantic SD 18167 (A) / K 50217 (B)
Ooooh Baby / One Way Rag / Avakak / Song Of Innocence / Giddy / Silly Woman / Marching Into A Bottle / Everybody / Darkness

Selected sessions:
1967 Alan Price: *A Price On His Head* – Decca SKL 4907 (B)
1970 Doris Troy: *Doris Troy* – Apple SST 3371 (A) / SAPCOR 13 (B)
1970 Billy Preston: *Encouraging Words* – Apple SST 3370 (A) SAPCOR 14 (B)
1970 George Harrison: *All Things Must Pass* – Apple STCH 639 (A) / Parlophone STCH 639 (B)
1971 Bell and Arc: *Bell and Arc* – Charisma CAS 1033 (B) / Columbia C31142 (A)
1971 John Lennon: *Imagine* – Apple SW 3379 (A) / PAS 10004 (B)
1971 Yoko Ono: *Fly* – Apple SUBB 3386 (A) / SAPTU 101 (B)
1973 Claire Hamill: *October* – Island ILPS 9225 (B)
1975 Steve Howe: *Beginnings* – Atlantic SD 18154 (A) / K 50151 (B)
1977 *Rick Wakeman's Criminal Record* – A&M SP 4660 (A) / AMLK 64660 (B)

PATRICK MORAZ

With Mainhorse:
7/71 *Mainhorse* – Import IMP 1004 (A) / Polydor 2383 049 (B)
Introduction / Passing Years / Such A Beautiful Day / Pale Sky / Basia / More Tea Vicar? / God
(Note: 'More Tea Vicar?' was later included in the 1977 rock compilation album, *Medium Rare* – Polydor 2482 381 (B)

With Refugee:
5/74 *Refugee* – Charisma 6066 (A) / CAS 1087 (B)
Papillon / Someday / Grand Canyon / Ritt Mickley / Credo

Solo:
3/76 *i* – Atlantic SD 18175 (A) / Charisma CDS 4002 (B)
Descent / Incantation – Procession / Dancing Now / Impressions (The Dream) / Like A Child In Disguise / Rise And Fall / Symphony In The Space / Impact / Warmer Hands / The Storm / Cachaça (Baião) / Intermezzo / Indoors / Best Years Of Our Lives
7/77 *Out In The Sun* – Import 1014 (A) / Charisma CDS 4007 (B)
Out In The Sun / Rana Batucada / Nervous Breakdown / Silver Screen / Tentacles / Kabala / Love-Hate-Sun-Rain-You / Time For A Change (Time To Fly: Big Bands Of Ancient Temples: Serenade: Back To Nature)
7/77 'Tentacles' / 'Kabala' – Charisma CB 304 (B)
11/78 *Patrick Moraz* – Charisma CA1-2201 (A) / CDS 4015 (B)
Jungles Of The World (Green Sun: Tribal Call: Communion) / Temples Of Joy (Opening Of The Gates: Overture: The Feast (A Festa) / The Conflict (Chamada – Argument: Opposing Forces: The Battlefield: Dissolution: Victory) / Primitivisation / Keep The Children Alive / Intentions / Realization

With Syrinx:
7/80 *Coexistence* – Carrere CA 641 (French release)
Mind Your Body / Boonoonoonoos / Soundrise / Adagio For A Hostage / Freedom To... / Coexistence (Black Gold: Moments Of Love: Chain Reaction: Peace On The Hills)

Guest appearances:
1975 Steve Howe: *Beginnings* – Atlantic SD 18154 (A) / K 50151 (B)
1975 Chris Squire: *Fish Out Of Water* – Atlantic SD 18159 (A) / K 50203 (B)

GEOFFREY DOWNES AND TREVOR HORN

The Buggles:
10/79 'Video Killed The Radio Star' / 'Kid Dynamo' – Island IS 49114 (A) / WIP 6524 (B)
2/80 *The Age Of Plastic* – Island ILPS 9585 (A) / (B)
Living In The Plastic Age / Video Killed The Radio Star / Kid Dynamo / I Love You (Miss Robot) / Clean Clean / Elstree / Astroboy (And The Proles On Parade) / Johnny On The Monorail
2/80 'Living In The Plastic Age' / 'Living In The Plastic Age' (DJ version) – Island WIT 6540 (B)

3/80 'Clean Clean' / 'Astroboy' – Island IS 49209 (A)

3/80 'Clean Clean' / 'Technipop' – Island WIP 6584 (B)

(Note: In America, 'Clean Clean' was also released as a 12" single, backed with 'Living In The Plastic Age' – Island PRO A859)

YES SINGLES

6/69 'Sweetness' / 'Something's Coming' – Atlantic 584280 (B)

1/70 'Sweetness' / 'Every Little Thing' – Atlantic 45-2709 (A)

6/70 'Sweet Dreams' / 'Dear Father' – Atlantic 2091 004 (B)

7/71 'Your Move' / 'The Clap' – Atlantic 45-2819 (A)

1/72 'Roundabout' / 'Long Distance Runaround' – Atlantic 45-2854 (A)

7/72 'America' / 'Total Mass Retain' – Atlantic 45-2899 (A)

10/72 'And You And I' (Parts I & II) – Atlantic 45-2920 (A)

1/75 'Soon' / 'Sound Chaser' – Atlantic 45-3252 (A)

9/77 'Wonderous Stories' / 'Parallels' – Atlantic K 10999 (B)

9/77 'Wonderous Stories' / 'Awaken' (Part I) – Atlantic 45-3416 (A)

11/77 'Going For The One' / 'Awaken' (Part I) – Atlantic K 11047 (B)

8/78 'Don't Kill The Whale' / 'Abeline' – Atlantic K11184 (B)

8/78 'Don't Kill The Whale' / 'Release, Release' – Atlantic 45-3534 (A)

10/80 'Into The Lens' / 'Does It Really Happen?' – Atlantic 45-3767 (A)

In the States, 'America' / 'Your Move' has been released as part of the Atlantic Oldies Series – OS1 3141 – and 'Roundabout' / 'Long Distance Runaround' has been re-released in this series – OS1 3140. In Britain, 'Wonderous Stories' / 'Parallels' was initially released in a 12" limited edition, pressed in blue vinyl, while 'Going For The One' / 'Awaken' (Part I) was released as a 12" limited edition, pressed in black vinyl.

YES ALBUMS

8/69 **Yes** – Atlantic SD 8234 (A) / K 40034 (B)
Beyond And Before / I See You / Yesterday And Today / Looking Around / Harold Land / Every Little Thing / Sweetness / Survival

7/70 **Time And A Word** – Atlantic SD 8273 (A) / K 40085 (B)
No Opportunity Necessary, No Experience Needed / Then / Everydays / Sweet Dreams / The Prophet / Clear Days / Astral Traveller / Time And A Word

3/71 **The Yes Album** – Atlantic SD 8283 (A) / K 40106 (B)
Yours Is No Disgrace / The Clap / Starship Trooper (Life Seeker: Disillusion: Wurm) / I've Seen All Good People (Your Move: All Good People) / A Venture / Perpetual Change

1/72 **Fragile** – Atlantic SD 7211 (A) / K 50009 (B)
Roundabout / Cans And Brahms / We Have Heaven / South Side Of The Sky / Five Percent For Nothing / Long Distance Runaround / the fish (Schindleria Praematurus) / Mood For A Day / Heart Of The Sunrise

9/72 **Close To The Edge** – Atlantic SD 7244 (A) / K 50012 (B)
Close To The Edge (The Solid Time Of Change: Total Mass Retain: I Get Up I Get Down: Seasons Of Man) / And You And I (Cord Of Life: Eclipse: The Preacher The Teacher: The Apocalypse) / Siberian Khatru

5/73 **Yessongs** – Atlantic SD 3-100 (A) / K 60045 (B)
Opening (Excerpt from Stravinsky's 'Firebird Suite') / Siberian Khatru / Heart Of The Sunrise / Perpetual Change / And You And I / Mood For A Day / Excerpts From 'The Six Wives Of Henry VIII' / Roundabout / Your Move: All Good People / Long Distance Runaround / the fish / Close To The Edge / Yours Is No Disgrace / Starship Trooper

11/73 **Tales From Topographic Oceans** – Atlantic SD 2-908 (A) / K 80001 (B)
The Revealing Science Of God / The Remembering / The Ancient / Ritual

11/74 **Relayer** – Atlantic SD 18122 (A) / K 50096 (B)
The Gates Of Delirium / Sound Chaser / To Be Over

2/75 **Yesterdays** – Atlantic SD 18103 (A) / K 50048 (B)
America / Looking Around / Time And A Word / Sweet Dreams / Then / Survival / Astral Traveller / Dear Father

7/77 **Going For The One** – Atlantic SD 19106 (A) / K 60379 (B)
Going For The One / Turn Of The Century / Parallels / Wonderous Stories / Awaken

9/78 **Tormato** – Atlantic SD 19202 (A) / K 50518 (B)
Future Times: Rejoice / Don't Kill The Whale / Madrigal / Release, Release / Arriving UFO / Circus Of Heaven / Onward / On The Silent Wings Of Freedom

8/80 **Drama** – Atlantic SD 16019 (A) / K 50736 (B)
Machine Messiah / White Car / Does It Really Happen? / Into The Lens / Run Through The Light / Tempus Fugit

11/80 **Yesshows** – Atlantic SD2 9003 (A) / K 60142 (B)
Parallels / Time And A Word / Going For The One / The Gates Of Delirium / Don't Kill The Whale / Ritual (Part I) / Ritual (Part II) / Wondrous Stories

Also:

Yes Solo LP Sampler – Atlantic PR 260 (A)
Special promotional album (not commercially available) containing two selections from each of the five solo albums.

Superstar Radio Network Presents Yes Music: An Evening With Jon Anderson – Atlantic PR 285 (A)
Promotional music/interview album prepared for radio station use only.

BOOTLEGS

1972 **Live At The Rainbow**
1972 **The Amsterdam Concert**
1973 **Yes Indeed**
1974 **Live At Long Beach Arena**
1974 **Stellar Attraction** (Boston)
1975 **U.S. Tour**
1976 **The Affirmary**
1976 **Sorcerer's Apprentice** (Hollywood Bowl)
1976 **Mark's LP**
1977 **Live In London**
1977 **Live In Glasgow**
72/77 **Yes In Your Own Home**
1977 **Yesshows '77** (Long Beach)
1978 **In The Round** (Los Angeles)

INDEX

Page numbers in italics refer to illustrations.

Action, The, 21
All Stars, 74
Allen, Chris, *17*, 18
Anderson, Jon, *7*, 11-14, *28*, *35*, *50*, *58*, *79*, *82*, *90*, *113*, *118*, *126*, *132*; birth, 11; early life, 11-13; with the Warriors, *12*, 13; in Munich, *13*; on German club circuit, 13; works as lorry driver, 13; joins The Party, 14; as Hans Christian, *18*, 20; meets Squire, 20; at La Chasse, 20; meets Bruford, 23; love songs, 34; marriage, 37; composition, 38; lyrics, 34, 51, 118; and classical music, 67; clashes with Squire, 85-7; *Olias Of Sunhillow*, 107; leaves Yes, 126-8, 129-30
Anderson, Tony, 13
Atlantic Records, 32, 34-5, 36-7, 39, 47

Bailey, Clive, 19, 21, 25
Baker, Roy Thomas, 128
Banks, Peter, *17*, 18, 19, 21, 25, 26-7, *30*; birth, 27; early life, *24*, *25*; solos, 35-6; leaves Yes, 40-1
Barrie, Jack, 20
Beatles, The, 13, 15
Bittersweet, 25
Blaise's, 28
Blue Chips, 71-2
Bodast, 44
Bruford, Bill, 21-3, *29*, *36*, *53*, *61*, *71*; early life, *19*, 21-2; meets Anderson, 23; leaves Yes for Leeds University, 29; returns to Yes, 30; in Switzerland, *34*; begins to write music, 66-7; leaves Yes, 69-70; joins with Wakeman and Wetton, 114
Buggles, The, *133*, 133-6
Burrell, Boz, 30

Carson, Phil, 39, 49
Cavern, The, 13
Chapman, Brian, 13
Charles, Tina, 132, 133
Christian, Hans (*pseudonym of Anderson*), *18*, 20
Church Hill cottage, 45-6
Clay, Paul, 34-5
Close To The Edge, 68-9, *70*, *78*
Colton, Tony, 38
Craddock, Kenny, 72
Cronk, Chas, 57

Danny Rogers Orchestra, 24
Dean, Roger, 62, 116, 120
Dowd, Tom, 50
Downes, Geoff, 132-3, *133*, *137*; joins Yes, 136-7
Drama, *84*, 137-8
Driscoll, Kevin, 43

English Rock Ensemble, 113-14
Ertegun, Ahmet, 34-5, 39, *68*, *74*, 84
Ertegun, Neshui, 49, 84

Federals, The, *20-1*, 24
'fish, the', 38, *60*, 62
Flynn, Roy, 28, 29, 30, 31, 36, 39; rift with Yes, 47
Foster, David, 13, 38
Fragile, 61-2, 64-5, *77*
Fury, Billy, 72

Gamblers, The, 72
Gee, John, 23
Going For The One, 116-21
Greenberg, Jerry, *68*, 74
Griffin, 72-4
Gun, The, 20, 62
Gurvitz, Adrian, 20
Gurvitz, Paul, 20

Hakanarssen, Gunnar, 18
Happy Magazine, 72
Harris, Johnny, 106
Hemmings, David, 48, 89
Horn, Trevor, 131-2, *135*; joins Yes, 136-7
Howe, Steve, *8*, 41-5, *45*, *50*, *79*, *82*, *86*, *89*, *101*, *103*, *109*, *116*, *128*, *136*; birth, 42; early life, 42-3, *43*; joins Syndicats, 43; joins Yes, 44-5; *Beginnings*, 106
Hynde, Chrissie, 133

In Crowd, 43-4

Jackman, Andrew, 15, *16*, *17*, 18, 106

Kaye, Tony, *20-1*, *22*, 23-5, *36*, *40*, *51*; at Camden Festival, *31*; Hammond work, 38; rift with Yes, 54-5; dropped from Yes, 60-1
King Crimson, 46, 69

La Chasse, 19-20
Ladd, Tom, 43
Lane, Brian, 47-8, 51-2, *68*, *74*, 114
Les Cruches, 20
Lowenstein, Prince, 32

Mabel Greer's Toyshop, 19, 21, 23
Mainhorse, 101
Margaret, Princess, 32
Marquee, 5, 18, 27, 31, 35
Marshall, Alan, 72
Melton, Johnny, 43
Moraz, Patrick, *83*, *96*, 99-103, *100*, *105*, *106*, *111*, *114*; early life, 99-100; meets Yes, 100-1; university degree, 100; composes film scores, 101; joins Yes, 102; splits from Yes, 108-11

Nardelli, Steve, *17*, 18
Neat Change, 25

Offord, Eddie, 49-50, 61, 66, *70*, 76, 96, 106, 118-19, 138
Orbison, Roy, 24
O'Riley, Tony, 29

Painter, John, 18
Papathanassiou, Vangelis, *95*, 96-9, 127, *132*
Paper Blitz, 22
Party, The, 14
Plastic Ono Band, 73

Reflections, The, *22*, 24
Refugee, 91, 101-2
Relayer, *83*, 103-4
Rich, Buddy, 35
Roberts, John, 26
Rose, Barry, 15

Selfs, The, 18
Sellers, Peter, 32
Simms, Dave, 57
Small Faces, 24
Speakeasy, 27, 28, 31
Squire, Chris, *6*, 14-21, *16*, *17*, *37*, *52*, 60, *69*, *79*, *88*, *94*, *101*, *112*, *122*; birth, 15; early life, *15*, 15-18; first public appearance, 18; with the Syn, 18; at Boosey and Hawkes music shop, 18; acid incident, 19; meets Anderson, 20; at Camden Festival, *27*; in Switzerland, *34*; clashes with Anderson, 85-7; *Fish Out Of Water*, 106; his triple-necked bass, *119*; at Madison Square Garden, *129*, 130
Stage shows, 7, 94, 124
Star Combo, 24
Stratton-Smith, Tony, 28
Strawbs, The, *56*, 58, 59
Syn, The, *17*, 18, 27
Syndicats, The, 43

Tait, Michael, 29, 30, 47, *91*
Tales From Topographic Oceans, 80-1, 87-92; at Rainbow, 87
Time and a Word, 37-9
Timperley, John, 118-19
Tomorrow, 44, *45*
Topographic balloon, 86
Tormato, 120, 122-4

Wakeman, Rick, *9*, 55-61, *56*, *57*, *68*, *79*, *83*, *115*; birth, 55; early life, 55-7; at Royal College of Music, 57; marriage, 58; leaves Strawbs, 59; joins Yes, 60; *Journey To The Centre Of The Earth*, 93-4; criticizes *Topographic*, 94-5; leaves Yes, 95-6, 130; heart attack, 111-12; *Myths And Legends Of King Arthur*, 112-13; *No Earthly Connection*, 113; joins with Bruford and Wetton, 114; *Criminal Record*, 119; *Rhapsodies*, 125; in Switzerland, *127*, 130; rejoins Yes, 114-16; leaves again, 127-30
Wallace, Ian, 13, 30
Warriors, The, *12*, 13
Warwick, Dionne, 132
West, Keith, *45*
Wetton, John, 114
White Rock, 114
White, Alan, *7*, *8*, 70-5, *79*, *98*, *102*, *106*, *121*; birth, 70; early life, 71-2, *72* joins Yes, 74; *Ramshackled*, 107; in Nashville, *124*; in New York, *134*
Winston, Jimmy, *22*, 24
Winston's Fumbs, *22*, 24

Yellow Passion Loaf, 24
Yes, *41*, *107*, *138*, *139*; albums, *see individual albums*; formation, 20-6 debut, 26; at Blaises, 28; at Albert Hall, 30; at Marquee, 31, 35; uses orchestra, 37, 39; on Swiss television, *39*; arguments over policy, 41; rift with Roy Flynn, 47; on Top Of The Pops, 51, *54*; P.A. system, 52; first American tour, 52-3; second American tour, 64; third American tour, 64-6; gold albums, *74*; disagreements, 85-7; *Topographic* American tour, 94-5; feature film, 107; at J.F.K. Stadium, *110*; at Madison Square Garden, *121*
Yes (Yes's first album), 32-5
Yes Album, The, 49-52
Yes In The Round, 124
Yesshows, 125
Yessongs, 76, 107 (film)
Yesterdays, 106
Yoganda, Paramhansa, 87

145